Hear the words 'debt collection' and your mind turns to a host of unsavoury characters: loan sharks, repossession men or thugs who show up seizing (or smashing) personal property in the name of an even greater-maligned figure, the creditor. Yet credit and debt collection are central economic and affective elements of modern economies and consumer-driven social life. In this unique and trenchant study, Joe Deville explains how the debt collection industry emerged, how it is evolving, and how it is ever more dependent on both data analytics and emotional labour, the two supplementing and amplifying one another far beyond the rational management of risk on which lending historically has depended. Deville illuminates the quotidian work of debt collection agencies and their tools—telephone scripts, collection letters—as well as the intra- and intercorporate and personal relations that make debt collection an affective as well as a political (and profitable) enterprise. The book is nothing less than a theoretically astute reflection on the character of obligation, the making of markets and the character of affect in the entanglements of debt today.

Bill Maurer, *Dean of the School of Social Sciences and Professor of Anthropology, University of California, Irvine*

Debt, it turns out, is not the only thing that is intimate and impersonal, cumulative and disintegrative, charged and discharged. By following out the ways that affect routes though the bodies of debtors and the modulating assemblages of debt collectors, Joe Deville offers a vivid account of consumer default that pulses with everyday intensities and calculative capturings. Immensely readable and deftly argued, Deville displays an astonishing agility for moving among the moods and modes of histories, case-studies, technologies, and theories at precisely the right moment, revealing what folds and unfolds at the fraught materialities of the economic and the affective.

Gregory J. Seigworth, *Professor of Communication Studies, Millersville University*

Lived Economies of Default is a striking achievement, essential reading for students and researchers in the social studies of finance, economic sociology and cultural economy. Not only does Deville provide the first book-length analysis of consumer debt collection in the UK for over forty years, he also charts a new course for the study of the materialities, affects and intimacies of contemporary market lives.

Paul Langley, *Reader in Economic Geography, Durham University*

An incisive and timely analysis of the business of contemporary debt collection, in which repayment is not forced through bodily incarceration or the seizing of assets as in times past but, rather, coaxed through carefully calibrated psychological campaigns and the seizing of affects. Techniques and tools of escalating urgency work to ratchet up defaulters' shame, anxiety, and dread and turn them into responsible borrowers. *Lived Economies of Default* is an empirically fascinating, ethnographically rich, theoretically sophisticated account of consumer-credit capitalism and its discontents.

Natasha Dow Schüll, *Associate Professor, Massachusetts Institute of Technology*

T0298587

Lived Economies of Default

Consumer credit borrowing – using credit cards, store cards and personal loans – is an important and routine part of many of our lives. But what happens when these everyday forms of borrowing go 'bad', when people start to default on their loans and when they cannot, or will not, repay? It is this poorly understood, controversial, but central part of both the consumer credit industry and the lived experiences of an increasing number of people that this book explores.

Drawing on research from the interior of the debt collections industry, as well as debtors' own accounts and historical research into technologies of lending and collection, this book examines precisely how this ever more sophisticated, globally-connected market functions. It focuses on the highly intimate techniques used to try and recoup defaulting debts from borrowers, as well as on the collection industry's relationship with lenders. Joe Deville follows a journey of default, from debtors' borrowing practices, to the intrusion of collections technologies into their homes and everyday lives, to the collections organisation, to attempts by debtors to seek outside help. In the process he shows that to understand this particular market, we need to understand the central role played within it by emotion and affect.

By opening up for scrutiny an area of the economy which is often hidden from view, this book makes a major contribution to understanding both the relationship between emotion and calculation in markets and the role of consumer credit in our societies and economies. This book will be of interest to students, teachers and researchers in a range of fields, including sociology, anthropology, cultural studies, economics and social psychology.

Joe Deville is a researcher at Goldsmiths, University of London, based jointly at the Centre for the Study of Invention and Social Process and the Political Economy Research Centre. He is also the co-founder of the Charisma research network and an editor of *Journal of Cultural Economy*.

Culture, Economy and the Social

A new series from CRESC – the ESRC Centre for Research on Socio-cultural Change

Editors

Professor Tony Bennett, Social and Cultural Theory, University of Western Sydney; Professor Penny Harvey, Anthropology, Manchester University; Professor Kevin Hetherington, Geography, Open University

Editorial Advisory Board

Andrew Barry, University of Oxford; Michel Callon, Ecole des Mines de Paris; Dipesh Chakrabarty, The University of Chicago; Mike Crang, University of Durham; Tim Dant, Lancaster University; Jean-Louis Fabiani, Ecoles de Hautes Etudes en Sciences Sociales; Antoine Hennion, Paris Institute of Technology; Eric Hirsch, Brunel University; John Law, The Open University; Randy Martin, New York University; Timothy Mitchell, New York University; Rolland Munro, Keele University; Andrew Pickering, University of Exeter; Mary Poovey, New York University; Hugh Willmott, University of Cardiff; Sharon Zukin, Brooklyn College City University New York/Graduate School, City University of New York

The *Culture, Economy and the Social* series is committed to innovative contemporary, comparative and historical work on the relations between social, cultural and economic change. It publishes empirically-based research that is theoretically informed, that critically examines the ways in which social, cultural and economic change is framed and made visible, and that is attentive to perspectives that tend to be ignored or side-lined by grand theorising or epochal accounts of social change. The series addresses the diverse manifestations of contemporary capitalism, and considers the various ways in which the 'social', 'the cultural' and 'the economic' are apprehended as tangible sites of value and practice. It is explicitly comparative, publishing books that work across disciplinary perspectives, cross-culturally, or across different historical periods.

The series is actively engaged in the analysis of the different theoretical traditions that have contributed to the development of the 'cultural turn' with a view to clarifying where these approaches converge and where they diverge on a particular issue. It is equally concerned to explore the new critical agendas emerging from current critiques of the cultural turn: those associated with the descriptive turn for example. Our commitment to interdisciplinarity thus aims at enriching theoretical and methodological discussion, building awareness of the common ground that has emerged in the past decade, and thinking through what is at stake in those approaches that resist integration to a common analytical model.

Series titles include:

The Media and Social Theory (2008)
Edited by David Hesmondhalgh and Jason Toynbee

Culture, Class, Distinction (2009)
Tony Bennett, Mike Savage, Elizabeth Bortolaia Silva, Alan Warde, Modesto Gayo-Cal and David Wright

Material Powers (2010)
Edited by Tony Bennett and Patrick Joyce

The Social after Gabriel Tarde: Debates and Assessments (2010)
Edited by Matei Candea

Cultural Analysis and Bourdieu's Legacy (2010)
Edited by Elizabeth Silva and Alan Ward

Milk, Modernity and the Making of the Human (2010)
Richie Nimmo

Creative Labour: Media Work in Three Cultural Industries (2010)
Edited by David Hesmondhalgh and Sarah Baker

Migrating Music (2011)
Edited by Jason Toynbee and Byron Dueck

Sport and the Transformation of Modern Europe: States, media and markets 1950–2010 (2011)
Edited by Alan Tomlinson, Christopher Young and Richard Holt

Inventive Methods: The Happening of the Social (2012)
Edited by Celia Lury and Nina Wakeford

Understanding Sport: A Socio-Cultural Analysis (2012)
John Horne, Alan Tomlinson, Garry Whannel and Kath Woodward

Shanghai Expo: An International Forum on the Future of Cities (2012)
Edited by Tim Winter

Diasporas and Diplomacy: Cosmopolitan Contact Zones at the BBC World Service (1932–2012) (2012)
Edited by Marie Gillespie and Alban Webb

Making Culture, Changing Society (2013)
Tony Bennett

Interdisciplinarity: Reconfigurations of the Social and Natural Sciences (2013)
Edited by Andrew Barry and Georgina Born

Objects and Materials: A Routledge Companion (2013)
Edited by Penny Harvey, Eleanor Conlin Casella, Gillian Evans, Hannah Knox, Christine McLean, Elizabeth B. Silva, Nicholas Thoburn and Kath Woodward

Accumulation: The Material Politics of Plastic (2013)
Edited by Gay Hawkins, Jennifer Gabrys and Mike Michael

Lived Economies of Default

Consumer credit, debt collection and the capture of affect

Joe Deville

Routledge
Taylor & Francis Group

LONDON AND NEW YORK

Centre for Research on
Socio-Cultural Change

E·S·R·C
ECONOMIC
& SOCIAL
RESEARCH
COUNCIL

First published 2015 by Routledge

2 Park Square, Milton Park, Abingdon, Oxfordshire OX14 4RN
52 Vanderbilt Avenue, New York, NY 10017

Routledge is an imprint of the Taylor & Francis Group, an informa business

First issued in paperback 2019

British Library Cataloguing-in-Publication Data
A catalogue record for this book is available from the British Library

Library of Congress Cataloging in Publication Data
Deville, Joe.
Lived economies of default : consumer credit, debt collection and the
capture of affect / by Joe Deville.
  pages cm
  1. Consumer credit–Great Britain. 2. Collecting of accounts–Great
  Britain. 3. Collection agencies–Great Britain. 4. Consumer credit.
  5. Collecting of accounts. 6. Collection agencies. I. Title.
  HG3756.G7D48 2015
  332.7'50941–dc23   2014033839

ISBN: 978-0-415-62250-9 (hbk)
ISBN: 978-0-367-86722-5 (pbk)

Typeset in Times New Roman
by Wearset Ltd, Boldon, Tyne and Wear

Contents

Illustrations

Figures

Table

Preface

There are many ways that a text can be read and I would not presume to impose on the reader a set way to approach this one. That said, there are certain threads that some readers may be more interested in following than others. Perhaps it is useful then for two of the thicker strands to be pulled out here.

One way this book can be read is as an account of the social and material relations and practices surrounding the work of collecting unsecured consumer credit debts from defaulting debtors. In this respect it contributes to a topic that has been much neglected by academics. As far as I am aware, the last full-length sociological book to tackle it is Paul Rock's *Making People Pay*.[1] That book, to which the present one owes much, was published in 1973. That it has taken over 40 years for a book to come out that looks at comparable present day practices is an omission that I hope the pages of what follows will begin to rectify.

In addressing this absence the book opens up for a more public view the contemporary practices of an industry that is both controversial and continues to be poorly understood. In doing so, it attempts to always keep in view that debt collection depends on and feeds off people's lives. Given that so many are currently struggling in much the same way as some of those who were kind enough to give me access to their experiences of default, this account provides a snapshot of a set of contemporary lived conditions that is depressingly familiar. At the same time, the very absence of research into the practical work of debt collection has left much of its longer history untold. Telling this aspect of the story of the collections industry is what I try to do in the fourth chapter in particular, which focuses most of all on the histories of the United Kingdom and the United States. Those with an interest in the history of consumer credit might also want to look at the first chapter, part of which tells another neglected story: that of the birth of the credit card.

A second way the book can be read is as an attempt to stage an encounter between parallel but largely disconnected fields of research. One of these is an approach to economic sociology that draws much from the diverse sets of methods and approaches that have been developed within science and technology studies (STS). Researchers working within this field have become interested in the diverse ways that markets are put together, while observing the role played within them by both people and material things. Often this has involved a focus on the role played by particular 'devices'. Put simply, these are the cogs and wheels that drive the engines of markets, the objects and technologies involved that help to make them function. What makes this approach so important is that it has shown social scientists how essential it is to pay close attention to the ways in which the often quite mundane 'stuff' of markets can have significant effects. This includes shaping the ability of people to make assessments about how to proceed in a given economic situation; how to calculate, in other words.

However, perhaps because of its very enthusiasm for showing how much the material stuff of life matters to economic life, this research has often tended to provide a rather thin account of the role played by the everyday encounters between markets and people. The book thus puts it into dialogue with a largely separate field of research that, while also attentive to the material dimensions of life, has devoted far more attention to working through the precise ways in which people, their bodies, and the technologies and practices that surround them, come to be interrelated. This is a diverse set of work, with an equally diverse intellectual heritage, that can be drawn together under the category of 'affect theory'. The power of affect theory has been to provide a way of attending to and describing some of the most intimate aspects of life. In some cases, this has included focusing on what happens when these encounter markets, although its objects of study have been widespread. The areas where it has sometimes arguably fallen short are precisely those where a STS-influenced economic sociology has excelled: providing an account of where the mundane devices and practices of markets come to matter and in what ways. I have found the encounter between these two fields productive; I hope you do too. But please, read this book in any way that you find helpful.

Note

1 Janet Ford's *The Indebted Society: Credit and Default in the 1980s* (1988) is another important reference point. Its focus is, however, largely on defaults and collections practices associated with secured credit default, in particular in relation to mortgage borrowing in the UK. Other (broadly) sociological books that have addressed some similar issues as part of a wider argument include Dawn Burton's *Credit and Consumer Society* (2008), Hillel Blacks' *Buy Now, Pay Later* (1961), Arlie Hochschild's *The Managed Heart* (1983), Jeanne Lazarus' *L'épreuve de l'argent: Banques, Banquiers, Clients* (2013b) [Monetary Tests: Banks, Bankers, and Customers] and Sullivan et al.'s *As We Forgive Our Debtors: Bankruptcy and Consumer Credit in America* (1999). A handful of journal articles have also emerged over the years looking at particular issues associated with the industry. These include an important ethnography of a collections agency, conducted by Jay Bass (1983), which documents some of the strategy behind US collections letters in the early 1980s, as well as how collections companies organised themselves, aspects of both of which remain unchanged. Genevieve LeBaron and Adrienne Roberts (LeBaron and Roberts 2012; Roberts 2014a; 2014b) have recently explored the consequences of the rise of the debt purchase industry in the US, as well as the association between the industry and the return of imprisonment for the non-payment of defaulting debt. Winifred Poster (2013) highlights the increasing use of outsourcing in collections work, while demonstrating that this is an

industry concerned with understanding and exploiting an encounter that is emotional and affective. José Ossandón (2014) also touches the use of behavioural data in debt collections work in Chilean consumer credit provision, which has some resonances with the techniques examined in Chapter 4. Roland Hill's (1994) study is noteworthy, partly for being unusual in bringing aspects of a Granovetterian economic sociology to bear on the relationship between collectors and defaulters, while exploring how the relationship between the two parties comes to be characterised by the 'depersonalisation' of the debtor in the eyes of the collector. Anat Rafaeli and Robert Sutton (Rafaeli and Sutton 1991; Sutton 1991), while in some respects echoing this analysis, have additionally looked at the particular strategies used by the debt collector and the ways they can be encouraged to follow particular emotional 'norms' (e.g. irritation) in their interactions with debtors. This interaction has also been studied from a psychological point of view, with Faison Gibson and Mark Fichman (2006) outlining how it can be characterised by the management of (negative) affect (see Chapter 4).

Acknowledgements

This book has taken shape over the course of many years during my time at the hugely inspirational sociology department at Goldsmiths, University of London. Particular thanks go to Paul Filmer, Celia Lury and Alberto Toscano, who acted as model advisors and mentors and whose encouragement, support and guidance were central to the development of major aspects of the research. Many thanks also to Franck Cochoy and Mike Michael for their detailed comments on the thesis that the book partially draws on. I am also grateful to the editors of the CRESC book series – Tony Bennett, Penny Harvey and Kevin Hetherington – for their suggestions and encouragement and to Michael Guggenheim for his various forms of support including, above all, so generously allowing me the space to write this book while being part of the 'Organising Disaster' project.

Further thanks are also due to all those who participated in this research. Thanks to both StepChange and the Money Advice Trust for their assistance. I am particularly grateful to Jim Fearnley, Meg Van Rooyen and Frances Walker. Thanks to those borrowers who were willing to let me into their lives and homes and were so giving with their time. Thanks also to those individuals and companies working in and around the consumer collections industry, who were open enough to let me into their world. Although they must remain anonymous, I remain grateful for their trust and willingness to allow a more complicated story of consumer collections to emerge than is often told.

For their financial support I would like to gratefully acknowledge the Economic and Social Research Council (award number PTA-031-2006-00457). I would also like to thank David Stark, Daniel Beunza and the Center on Organizational Innovation at Columbia University for being so welcoming over the course of my stay in New York. It was a time that marked a turning point in my research.

My deep thanks go out to all those who have commented on drafts of chapters at various stages in their development including Brian Alleyne, Andrew Barry, Vikki Bell, Rebecca Coleman, Aurora Fredriksen, Claire Garbett, Jennifer Gabrys, Gay Hawkins, Polly Haste, Paul Langley, Bill Maurer, Andrew Leyshon, Daniel Lopes, Noortje Marres, Donncha Marron, Liz McFall, Liz Moor, José Ossandón, Martha Poon, Martin Savransky, Greg Seigworth, Katy Shaw and Zsuzsanna Vargha. The book has without doubt been improved immensely as a result. I am especially grateful to Paul Langley, Bill Maurer, Greg Seigworth and Natasha Dow Schüll for providing their kind endorsements. Additionally, I would like to thank current and former members of the Goldsmiths sociology department for their support and encouragement including (in addition to those already mentioned elsewhere) Les Back, Zuzana Hrdličková, David Oswell, Marsha Rosengarten, Bev Skeggs, Nina Wakeford, Bridget Ward, as well as, from other departments, Rebecca Cassidy, Mira Vogel and Martin Williams.

I am also thankful to all those who have posed range of stimulating questions at workshops, events and the spaces in-between. I can't list you all by name but for discussions and questions that got me thinking thanks to Martin Giraudeau, Ann Kelly, and Andrea Whittle. Thanks also to Tomás Ariztía, Christian Borch, Franck Cochoy, Ann-Christina Lange, Turo-Kimmo Lehtonen, Anna Mann, Annemarie Mol and Pascale Trompette for inviting me to come and present my work at various events and for hosting such rich, insightful discussions. For invaluable assistance with the design of the book cover many thanks to Alex Wilkie, Catriona Gray and everyone else who offered their feedback.

Many others including friends, friends of friends and members of my family, have supported me in various ways at different points over the course this project, all of whom I still owe much to. These include Simon Brasse, Allan Day, Alice Deville, Yael Gerson, Nadia Iqbal, Mark Ratcliff (and all at Murmur) and Jonathan Robbins. Thanks also to Colin and Belinda Day, Gil Eyal, Jeanne Lazarus, Megan Horvath, Cesar Rodriguez, and Lou Rispoli and Danyal Lawson for an assortment of generous, helpful acts.

Every effort has been made to contact the copyright holders for their permission to reprint the images that feature in this book. The publishers would be grateful to hear from any copyright holder who is not here acknowledged and we will undertake to rectify any errors or omissions in future editions of this book.

My biggest thanks of all go to Aurora and to my parents, Tim and Lucy Deville.

Abbreviations

ACA	American Collectors Association / ACA International
ANT	Actor-Network Theory
APR	Annual Percentage Rate
BOS	Bank of Scotland
CAC	California Collectors Association
CBGS	Credit Bureau of Greater Syracuse
CCCS	Consumer Credit Counselling Service
CCJ	County Court Judgement
CCR	Credit Collections & Risk
CFPB	Consumer Financial Protection Bureau
CSA	Credit Services Association
DCA	(Contingency) Debt Collection Agency
EU	European Union
FCA	Financial Conduct Authority
FENCA	Federation of European National Collection Agencies
FICO	Fair Isaac Credit Organization
HBOS	Halifax Bank of Scotland
IBM	International Business Machines
ME	Myalgic Encephalopathy
OFT	Office of Fair Trading
SMS	Short Messaging Service, i.e. Text Message
STS	Science and Technology Studies
TCF	Treating Customers Fairly
UK	United Kingdom
US	United States of America

Introduction
Lived economies of default

We have become all too used to default. Ever since the first global recession of the twenty-first century broke towards the end of its first decade, the issue of credit default has not been far from the lips of media commentators, politicians and, sometimes, academics and the public.

This is perhaps surprising. Within the credit industry, default is a largely technical term, used to refer to the moment at which a borrower is deemed to have broken the conditions of their credit agreement by not repaying a debt according to its agreed schedule. Now, however, the term has come to stand for a crucial part of contemporary social and economic life that seems to in some way have become 'broken'.

The reason for the movement into the mainstream of talk about default can, of course, be found in those moments in and around 2007 when the credit-driven origins of the ongoing economic turmoil became publicly visible. Amidst the range of factors that set in motion what was to become a global economic crisis, it was the rapidly increasing volume of defaults on sub-prime mortgages in the United States (US) that achieved particular public prominence. As many of us came to learn, these mortgages were deeply wrapped up in the global financial system. Complex financial products had been built on the promise that they would generate a financial return. When this promise turned out to be empty, a destructive chain of events was set in motion that saw the threat of default spread from individual borrowers' mortgage products to major financial institutions, to the central banks of what had previously seemed to be financially secure, well established capitalist economies. Default was the spectre that haunted the global economy; in many ways, it still is. The response, as we now well know, has often been for governments to pour money into the ailing financial system, while subjecting much of their populations to extended periods of so-called 'austerity'.

The varied after-effects of these threatened and actual defaults – including welfare cuts, growing unemployment (and underemployment), higher costs of living, the devaluation of savings and pension portfolios and the difficulty of obtaining affordable credit – have, in many parts of the world, been compounded by a related but distinct tale of default: that of consumer credit default. This is the book's object. More precisely, it provides an account of the wide ranging set of practices, technologies and lived experiences that come, for a variety of reasons, to be associated and 'attached', to consumer credit default. These come into play when a borrower is unable, or perhaps unwilling, to continue to make payments on particular types of loan: loans that are intended to be relatively short term and that are often not tied to a particular piece of property. The most familiar of these are those associated with credit card borrowing, unsecured personal loans and forms of hire purchase (rent-to-own as it is sometimes known in the US).

A large part of the book's interest is in the calculative challenges facing borrowers and defaulters. It follows the changing calculative challenges that they confront, whether associated with moments of borrowing, or the ongoing management of debt, or being confronted by debt collectors. At the same time, it looks in at the debtor from the perspective of the collector, to try and examine in more depth the attempts that are being made by collections organisations to shape and influence debtors' calculative practices. By exploring this encounter between debtor and debt collector, the book opens up a domain of social and economic life that not only is often seen to be highly controversial, but also is yet to be adequately understood.

The empirical focus of the book is mainly on the United Kingdom (UK). However, given that the credit and collections industry is global, with its expertise flowing increasingly easily across national boundaries, there are important lessons for, and parallels to, how consumer credit default is now being managed and experienced in many other countries. I will draw out some of these connections where relevant.

In doing so, the book employs a diverse assembly of material. This includes interviews with borrowers, defaulters, collectors, industry analysts and spokespersons, most of which were conducted in 2008 and 2009, but some of which took place as recently as 2014.[1] In 2009 I was also able to spend some time at three large, industry-leading debt collection agencies in the UK (which I will refer to as Alpha, Beta and Delta) and to observe their operations, including listening in to collections calls and speaking to staff in a range of different positions. The book thus captures experiences and collections practices from a quite particular slice of life in default in the immediate aftermath of the global economic crisis, although many of the specific sets of practices and experiences that it documents have changed little in recent years. I will highlight both points of continuity and difference as the book progresses. This field research has also been supplemented by documentary and archival research, in particular drawing on material from both UK and US industry publications, as well as visits to major industry conferences in the UK, events that I have attended throughout the research process. This methodological diversity is in part a product of my desire to track consumer credit collection and default across the varied terrains in which it operates, as well as, more pragmatically, a product of the considerable challenges that confront researchers attempting to enter to an often quite deliberately closed-off domain. Partly these barriers are an effect of the controversies that tend to surround the practices of debt collection, as I will highlight further on.

As well as shedding more light on an under-examined area of social and economic life, the book makes a proposition: that economic sociology could benefit from more careful, more precise attention to the role played by both things and people in markets. In brief, the proposition is that there is room to bring into closer dialogue understandings of markets drawing influence from science and technology studies (STS) – which I refer to as the 'economisation' programme – with an attention to 'affective' modes of social action and economic calculation.

I will come on to outline this problematic in more detail shortly. However first it is worth reflecting on some of the terms through which the 'issue' of consumer credit default, and in particular debt collection, can come to be articulated in public. This is partly because I want to draw attention to some important political questions that such public articulations may obscure. Additionally, given that the majority of this book focuses on consumer credit practices, technologies and experiences that are largely hidden from public view, it is important to connect some of the public and private manifestations of this issue together.

A controversial object

The object that I am going to pursue in this book is one that has, in different ways and at different historical moments, been articulated as controversial.[2] Such controversies have tended to turn around the question of how far we, in our various societies, are prepared to allow a creditor to go in their attempts to reclaim what they are owed.[3]

On the eve of one of my visits to a collections agency in 2009, one way this question played out was in the airing of a documentary entitled 'Undercover Debt Collector' that was aired on a major UK television channel, as part of the *Dispatches* series (Channel 4 2009).[4] The documentary took as its subject what it referred to as 'one of Britain's least loved but fastest growing industries'. Partly an exposé, it drew on footage filmed by a reporter working undercover at Marlin, a mid-sized British debt collection agency. It split its attention largely between revelations about the inner workings of the industry and the consequences, for debtors, of being subject to debt collection practices. This dual focus allowed the programme to tell a story of interconnected controversies: the controversies that surround the practices of debt collection and those that surround its effects. Its account both opens up some of the issues that are at stake when studying consumer credit default while also pointing towards certain modes of analysis that the book hopes to avoid.

The documentary focuses on the actions of one particular collections agent, alongside whom the Dispatches reporter had worked undercover. The former is not only shown to be making offensive gestures while on the phone to debtors, but also appears to break a number of regulatory guidelines relating to the misleading use of legal threats against callers. The industry-focused controversy is broken up by a domestic focus, with two couples providing emotional accounts of their experiences of being subject to the actions of debt collectors, including both Marlin and Halifax (the collections operations of the latter are also the subject of Chapter 5). The Halifax case enables the programme to narrate the controversial nature of everyday collections technologies and, in particular, telephone-mediated collections work. Against repeated intercut footage zooming in on a ringing phone, the audience learn about the 'careful couple who always paid their way and hated being in debt' who were subject to '762' phone calls from Halifax, as well as the insensitivity of one collector who reminded a debtor about her economic responsibilities while her husband was in hospital with a terminal illness. The Marlin case meanwhile, serves as a vehicle for further exploring the controversial nature of the external collector: a couple who 'had been carefully budgeting to be able to meet monthly instalments on some credit cards' are hit 'out of the blue' by an old debt that Marlin had purchased. The result, we are told, is 'six months of hell'.

The documentary establishes a series of binaries: debtor as victim, collector as predator; debtor as economically prudent, collector as economically ruthless. It is clear why the documentary makers enact these distinctions: researching debt default and collections is an affecting experience. Speaking to defaulting debtors is to be a witness to the sense of confusion, distress and anger that can accompany the experience of default. As we will see, the prompts of the collector are intrusive and can feel overwhelming as they come to be wrapped up in some of the most intimate aspects of domestic life.[5] It would also be hard when listening to certain skilled operators speak to debtors not to be shocked by the apparently dispassionate, calculating modes of address that are being deployed against debtors, as well as the use of threats towards legal actions that may in fact be very far off.[6] As a site for the operations of a market, these interactions are deeply ambiguous, strategically managed sites, in which, for defaulters, market transparency seems often absent and market detachment can seem impossible.[7]

When looking for a simple way to tell the story of default and collections, the construction of quick binaries offers a compelling narrative structure. However, while there may be important insights we can draw from such oppositions, we may want to hesitate before rushing in and adopting them wholesale. They are each what Isabelle Stengers calls a 'slope', which pulls us towards what we already know. If venturing onto such slopes, we should at least introduce some resistance to slow down our travels, in order, as she writes (in a quite different empirical context) 'to make interesting the moment when the various ingredients of an ecology of practices come into play' (2003, p. 180).[8]

What, then, of the point of view of the collector? A few months before the Dispatches documentary, Kurt Obermaier, the executive director of the industry's trade body, wrote an article in *The Times*, which attempted to address the 'mixed messages' that he felt were surrounding collections practices. His response was largely to sidestep such criticisms by shifting the terrain of the debate onto the challenges the debt collections industry was facing as a result of the economic downturn (Obermaier 2009). A more direct retort, but one equally interested in reframing the issue of credit default, was a petition lodged with the government towards the end of the same year by *Credit Collections & Risk*, a British debt collections industry trade journal. It included the following assertions and demands:

- We [,] the undersigned [,] petition the Prime Minister to make a public statement of support for the Collections and Enforcement industry, acknowledging that it is made up of *some of the most professional and ethical companies in the whole of [the] UK economy.*
- *If consumers do not pay* then – just like good drivers having to pay for bad drivers through higher insurance premiums – *everyone will suffer in higher interest rates* and charges.
- [...] all *consumers should also understand that they have a morale [sic] duty to pay back* what they owe. Consumers must understand that the morally right thing to do is to pay what is owed, in the time-frame agreed or in the quickest time that is reasonably possible.
- *The collections industry demands and deserves genuine fairness of its own* and that does not mean the biased consumer-focused fairness so beloved of the local and national media and the government, but real fairness. Only this true fairness will allow the Collections and Enforcement industry to play an important role in the fledgling economic recovery.

(The Prime Minister's Office 2010; emphasis added)

Whereas 'Undercover Debt Collector' tells its account of the controversies of debt collection through small case studies, the petition tries to provide the 'big picture'. On the success of consumer collections, it argues, rests the interest rates that are being charged to 'everyone' at the point of lending. Consumer collections, therefore, is an activity that contributes to a (unrecognised) common good. Meanwhile, it is not debt collection, but consumers that have a moral deficit, failing to fully understand their 'moral duty' to repay. The 'true fairness' that this petitioner seeks is one that recognises the bigger economic and moral picture.[9]

Here, then, we see a new a set of binaries being set up. These oppose the ethical collections industry (as a whole) and the morally deficient consumer (also, as a whole) and the 'real' fairness provided by seeing the bigger picture, as compared to the narrow 'consumer-focused' approach adopted by both the national media and the government. This is undoubtedly a less affecting, less human story than that provided by looking either into the homes and lives of the defaulter or the unfair and potentially illegal practices of individual collections agents. But it too offers a powerful account. In attempting to counter the sensationalist power of mediatised narratives, it seeks recourse to the power and authority of situating cases in their wider socio-economic 'context'. The message is that whilst highlighting individual cases may be a compelling way of narrating and sensationalising the relationship between collector and collected, it is neither a sufficiently representative nor dispassionate mode of analysis. The attempt is to relocate the terms of the debate into a discussion of what counts as an 'objective' analysis of the politics of the collections industry.

This book seeks a route not simply around, but through the binaries provided by the debt collections industry and forms of mass media reportage, while aiming to neither dismiss the importance of individual cases, nor to dissolve such cases within wider socio-economic forces in the belief that this operation, in and of itself, produces objectivity. This is the pursuit of forms of explanation that privilege neither 'actor' nor 'system', an approach that has become a hallmark of work within both science and technology studies (STS) and the related actor-network theory (ANT) project (see, for instance: Latour 2005, p. 169). But it is also an effect of a commitment to a mode of attention characterised by care.[10] This means cultivating an awareness of the significance of nuance. Attending to the nuances of what we encounter is crucial if we are to develop an in-depth understanding of how *exactly* the various objects, practices, discourses and technologies being examined operate and what their effects are. This is an approach that has been foregrounded by the sociologist Les Back. For Back, sociology is a listening art, one set against an approach which is

> defined by its focus, often intrusively, on uncovering scandalous revelations, thick on occlusive detail but containing truths that have a short time span. [...] [S]ociology should cast itself against the forms of *intrusive empiricism* and *moral cannibalism* widespread in the mass media. [...] The challenge for sociology, like that of the alchemist, is to develop critique that captures life's light and heat. [...] My concern [...] is [...] how the development of a sociological imagination also necessitates the art of discernment or a capacity to shift through piles of information.
>
> (Back 2007, pp. 20–21; original emphasis)

This is a call for a sociology that treads lightly on its subject matter, avoiding sensation for sensation's sake. This is not a retreat into dispassionate, rootless forms of (social) scientific witnessing that Donna Haraway (1997), for instance, so vividly writes against. Instead, it is a case *for* tracing the political dimensions of life, in all its subtle variation. I translate this in this book into an attention to how a range of actors themselves both articulate the problematics of debt and debt default and attempt to solve them. This does not mean ignoring television exposés and public petitions, but seeing them as very much part of the 'piles of information' that comprise the object being pursued (see also Barry 2001).

The empirical can, however, not be the sole guarantee of a social scientific argument. As the book progresses it will thus introduce a number of conceptual resources to help to sort through and make sense of the diverse assembly of information that will be presented. There are some currents that flow more or less consistently throughout the text, three of which it might be helpful to introduce here.

Devices

Devices are what John Law and Evelyn Ruppert have called 'patterned teleological arrangements' (Law and Ruppert 2013, p. 229). That is to say, these are things, potentially composite things (hence: arrangements), that are designed to stimulate forms of engagement along particular lines, according to particular patterns. Especially amongst researchers working in STS, the device has formed an important part of the vocabulary that is brought to the attempt to describe how materiality matters in social settings, even when the material object in question appears to be quite ordinary. This has meant charting how these devices operate to mediate and format a range of encounters and situations.

Within this research, devices are often discussed in relation to specific objects and self-contained technologies. When it comes to the role played by devices within markets, this includes an attention to how they shape/pattern the decision-making capacities of individuals and organisations – that is to say, their assessments and judgements as to how to proceed in a given situation. This has included looking at objects as mundane as shopping carts (Cochoy 2009), credit scores (Poon 2007; 2009), financial equations (MacKenzie 2007; 2009), trading screens (Beunza and Stark 2004) and particular visualisations used in sales demonstrations (Vargha 2011). This book quite consciously adds to this list – it spends time looking at the role of some quite mundane credit devices: the credit card and the collections letter.

At the same time we may want to at least think about whether to broaden our understanding of devices beyond specific things (see Moor 2012). This would mean developing a broader perspective than some of the strongly object-centred approaches that have characterised much of the work within, or influenced by, STS. Perhaps a particular set of ideas can, in the right circumstances, act as a device for assembling certain market encounters – how to conduct and standardise a process of market research, for instance (Ariztia 2013). Or a set of expertise will – how a bank interview is devised to 'test' the characteristics of a good banking customer, perhaps (Lazarus 2013b). We may also wish to consider the way certain situations allow people to act as devices. There may be a tension in doing so – devices have tended to be thought about as closed, bounded entities; this does not seem to map very cleanly onto the messiness of human life and human experience (see McFall 2014, p. 24). At the same time, we have to recognise that not only are people perfectly capable of being encouraged and/or compelled into performing themselves according to quite specific criteria but also their practices are routinely aided and part-determined by all kinds of technological and social apparatuses. In this sense, in certain settings, it can become hard to draw a clear line around where the human begins and the material ends.

Take the contemporary debt collections worker as an example. Sitting in a call centre, she or he will perhaps be sitting in front of a sheet of paper with a range of pre-prepared prompts that can be turned to if necessary. Calls are recorded for processes of ongoing monitoring and appraisal (see p. 114). The calls themselves are largely controlled by technology, an autodialler – that provides collectors with a mix of both inbound and outbound calls, without them having to find and dial different numbers, or wait for a telephone to ring (this is because calls will only be put through to collectors if the automatically-made outgoing call is answered). The collections worker will also be working with a piece of account management software that, as soon as a call comes through, provides an instant view of the recent history of the account in question. And, almost certainly, she or he will have been subjected to forms of training that aim both to standardise the approach taken by collectors at that particular organisation and to make sure they comply with the relevant regulatory requirements. If, as I will claim, the collections worker becomes a device, then devices should certainly be considered hybrid entities.

Economisation

The devices described in previous paragraphs each aim to stimulate a market-oriented form of engagement; they can be described, in other words, as 'market devices'.[11] They are all concerned with eliciting and formatting the processes and practices involved in making markets operate. The diverse body of scholarship interested in tracing and following this specific type of device can be gathered under a loose umbrella term: an approach to economic life interested in the study of processes of 'economisation'; the 'economisation programme', in short.[12] As the term emphasises, the aim in this approach is not to take for granted the way things (behaviours, organisations, institutions, objects[13]) are 'economic', but to see their *becoming economic* as a very particular accomplishment. This is a body of research which draws particularly heavily on the writing of French sociologist and STS scholar Michel Callon, writing often pursued in collaboration with others.[14]

One of the most important things that the economisation programme has achieved, partly through an attention to the role of devices, is to show just how much that which happens in markets is affected by their social and material infrastructures.[15] Perhaps most significantly, it has demonstrated some of the ways in which people come to make judgements and decisions about how to proceed within market settings *according to the logic of those settings*. This marks a contribution to a question that has been central to both economics and economic sociology as well as, increasingly, to economic psychology: how people *calculate* in markets (or 'qualculate' – but I will come onto this in the first chapter). As the studies of the economisation programme have variously shown, the devices and infrastructures of markets do not simply sit in the background in order to clear the way for the kinds of disembodied, rational, maximising economic calculation that are taken for granted by the large majority of economic theory. Rather, they play a dynamic and active role in shaping both the conditions for and practices of calculation. This book will provide further evidence of this, with respect to the calculative practices surrounding lending and borrowing.

A related contribution of this approach has been to provide a richer account than is found either in economics or much economic sociology of the ways in which products come to act *as* products in markets. The proposition made by the economisation programme is that products are not stable entities, but are subject to ongoing processes through which their 'qualities' are qualified and requalified. It is this ongoing act of requalification – which we might also want to think of as a kind of redefinition – that sets the framework for subsequent calculative work, for 'evaluations and judgements' (Callon *et al.* 2002, 199).

This unceasing process of qualification is highly mediated: market devices combine with the work of what Callon *et al.* call 'professionals of qualification' (marketers, designers, and so forth) and a range of other market-oriented infrastructures to establish the terrain for particular market encounters (ibid.). How shopping carts allow people to move around the supermarket (Cochoy 2008), how a door-to-door insurance agent is shaped so as to fit into the daily lives of customers (McFall 2011), how a financial equation affects the flows of global finance (MacKenzie 2006): each of these involves the conduct of markets being shaped by unique combinations of people and things in the composition and recomposition of unique market 'assemblages'.[16]

The approach has also sought to account for the processes of movement involved in this ongoing work of market recomposition. One way these movements have been described as 'struggles of market attachment'.[17] This is a way of talking about markets that I will return to throughout this book. Describing markets in terms of movements of attachment – and detachment – is intended to draw attention to how the social and material assembly of market exchange involves multiple and ongoing processes of association and dissociation between actors in these markets. On the one hand, products within markets need to become attached to buyers. Products and, once they are bought, 'goods', need to be made to matter to the buyer – they need to fit tightly into their worlds, into the conduct of their everyday life. This is equally the case for spaces of consumption as for the spaces of high finance. Attachment devices relevant to the former might include marketing work and product design; to the latter, this might include specific analytical technologies. On the other, products have to be detached, or 'disentangled' from the range of associations that might threaten the stability of the transaction. In an ideal typical transaction, buyer and seller must end the exchange 'quits'. That means that the object being purchased should be sufficiently detached from things that might disrupt the successful conduct of the market – sufficiently alienated and qualified, to put it another way – so that it is able to pass securely from one party to the other without there being any unwanted ties left between them. For instance, once a shopper exits a supermarket she or he would be unlikely to want the supermarket to come and reclaim part of the shopping because of some kind of continuing ownership over these products. That this is extremely unlikely is in part the achievement of a range of well established devices (including both legal and socio-technical) designed to prevent this kind of thing from happening.

I suggested earlier that we might not want to impose a limit on what kinds of entities might compose devices – that these could, for instance, be made of assemblies of ideas, people and things. We may want to be similarly open about what devices actually do. Market devices, as I have outlined, are designed to elicit forms of engagement according to the logics of market settings. However, this is just one 'mode' of engagement that such devices may prompt. Noortje Marres has explored the potential for devices to become involved in what she calls the 'co-articulation' of different logics, different domains, different 'modalities of action' (2012, pp. 62–63; see also Callon 2009). She looks for instance at the role of devices used by people in their everyday lives to keep track of their carbon emissions. Such devices, she writes,

> are explicitly attributed [by their users] the capacity to evaluate action along multiple axes, from ethics to consumption to innovation […] they enable the organization of spaces of multivalent action, in which a routine act like making tea is at once a technical, economic and ethical act.
>
> (Marres 2012, p. 70)

We should not be too quick, therefore, to assume that what seem to be 'market devices' are just concerned with the making of markets. They may well prompt engagement, prompt 'participation' (the latter being Marres' particular interest) in potentially diverse registers. One register may indeed be the economic. But it is perfectly likely that there are other forms of engagement that are solicited. We will see this in action later in the book (especially Chapters 2 and 4), in the collector's attempts to transform the routines and relations of everyday domestic life into a way of generating calculative engagement. The collections device, then, can be simultaneously concerned with the formatting of a debtor's life in markets and in his or her home.

Affect

However fruitful the insights are that have been produced by the study of processes of economisation, this book will suggest that there are areas where it has exhibited some blind spots. One of these concerns the terrain upon and through which markets operate. As has been observed, much of this work seems to be concerned with the technical and organisational dimensions of market-making, with a consequence that the role played by the more intimate and everyday spaces of social and economic life has tended to be underemphasised (see Cochoy 2008; Deville 2014; Langley 2008b; McFall forthcoming). Perhaps this echoes the more general tendency within economic sociology to focus on firms and corporations rather than more intimate aspects of the economy (see Zelizer 2005, p. 44). It is also likely a vestige of the field's heritage in STS and ANT: on the one hand, in both the ambition has been to provide a counterweight to the privileging within sociology and related disciplines of the role played by *people* in composing social action of all kinds (see Latour 1993); on the other, both have found looking at the technological a particularly rich and fruitful way to make this argument.

This question need not, however, be reduced to a debate about how much emphasis to give to the role of materiality in constructing social life. What this would miss is the quite self-evident but often underappreciated fact that people are clearly material too. Social life is embodied life. And the bodies that make up that life matter greatly, including to the life of markets. With this in mind, this book puts the study of economisation into dialogue with the loose body of social theory and research that has been assembled around the concept of 'affect'. This work has sought to trace the consequential role played by bodies in mediating relations between people, and between people, things, and a range of other non-humans.

Attention to affect has been stimulated in particular by the philosophy of Giles Deleuze (see Deleuze 1988b; Deleuze and Guattari 1987). It is an approach very much interested in the messy and interstitial relationships between bodies and worlds, the 'intimate impacts', Kathleen Stewart calls them, of a range of forces in circulation (2007, p. 40). From the perspective of affect theory, the skin is a porous surface, through which a range of social processes pass, and to which relations sometimes become attached. As Gregory Seigworth and Melissa Gregg write, '[a]ffect is found in those intensities that pass body to body [...], in those resonances that circulate about, between, and sometimes stick to bodies and worlds, and in the very passages or variations between these intensities and resonances themselves' (Seigworth and Gregg 2010, p. 1).

This concern with the in-betweenness of life, with resonances, with intensities, marks the quite specific domain that has interested affect theorists. It is the domain in which entities and bodies meet one another and, in the process, become something potentially quite different. Ben Anderson suggests that one way to think of affect is 'as a bodily capacity emergent from encounters' (2014, p. 4). This specific formulation gestures towards aspects that are central to much affect theory. The attention to 'capacity' emphasises that working with affect provides a way of describing the *manner* in which particular lives come to be lived, or *are rendered possible to be lived*. Capacity, then is a particular mode of engagement that is elicited and/or becomes formatted in a given situation and setting. This, in turn, is a product of the 'encounter'. At the centre of affect theory is the relation: things, capacities, possibilities are not inherent or given, but are made and constantly remade in the interconnections, in the *encounters*, between entities of all sorts. Affect 'is not located within us but it happens to and across us', as Rebecca Coleman puts it (2009, p. 163). And finally, considering bodily capacity as 'emergent', indicates an attention to the way in which entities reach out to and become tangled up with one another in ever-changing combinations.

This last aspect of affect theory is worth unpacking a little, for the reason that accounting for social life in terms of movements of emergence does at least two important things for this book. First, it emphasises that things never, quite, stay the same, but are always 'becoming' something different. As I suggest in the next chapter, this can be understood as a renewing of what was previous, with something other and different also being rendered present – even if, as is often the case, this difference is very slight indeed.[18] Second, it connects to a long-standing interest in STS in the role of the 'affordance', a term originally introduced by the psychologist James Gibson (1977). Within STS, this terminology has been particularly used to describe the way in which objects and environments offer themselves up for the conduct of some form of human action. A hammer, a bed, a bouncy castle: each offer an affordance for a particular kind of action. In STS-terms each might be considered to possess its own form of material agency. From the perspective of affect theory, part of this material agency might also be considered as being constituted through processes of emergence.[19]

Trying to hold together an interest in both devices and affect would then point towards how particular objects and processes push and pull us in one direction or another, while also sensitising our attention to what happens in the space of encounter between a device and a body. Take, for instance, the debt collections letter, a device that will appear at a number of times over the course of this book. If, when it drops on the doormat, the debtor recognises it as such, why might s/he be *drawn towards* opening this particular device more than another? If, after having read it and put it down somewhere in the house, why is it that some of the letter's contents continue to nag at the debtor, intruding unwanted into their thoughts, potentially at inopportune moments? Affect provides one way to begin to provide answers to such questions, without assuming that the only answer is to turn to psychology. For affect theory is also social theory. It does not assume bodily capacities, but sees them as outcomes of very specific, very contingent arrangements of social (and material) processes.

In the social life of consumer credit default, one particularly important set of processes is arranged around what I call, after Brian Massumi (2002, p. 35), the 'capture' of affect. Moments of affective capture are those in which the diverse and often unnoticed relations that are constantly composing and recomposing the affective are pulled into the more readily accessible domain of perception (although affect is never fully captured; there is always something that escapes). Emotions, which have been the object of much affect theory, are one expression of this process of capture, 'the most intense expression', Massumi suggests (ibid.). However, there are other possible expressions. As we will see, forms of economic calculation may too emerge through the capture of affect.

Lawrence Grossberg, while supportive of the turn to affect within some of the social sciences, has argued that too often affect has come to serve as something of a 'magical' term. We need to work harder, he suggests, to specify both what he calls the 'modalities and apparatuses of affect' and how affect might be distinct from (and, I would suggest, interacts with) other 'non-semantic effects' (Grossberg 2010, p. 314; see also Probyn 2010, p. 74). In other words, identifying the existence and production of affect, or naming things as affective, is not, in itself, 'good enough'.

This is a challenge to which those using the intellectual resources of affect theory need to respond. This book's attempt to do so is by bringing some of STS' empiricism to affect. In so doing it is by no means alone, however. Writers including Christian Borch, Celia Lury, Natasha Dow Schüll and Nigel Thrift have all drawn on a similar intellectual architecture in order to explore with some precision how affective processes can become the subject of sometimes highly strategic socio-materially derived practices of management and capture (Borch 2007; Lury 2004, 2009; Schüll 2012; Thrift 2005, 2007).[20] Further, a handful of researchers aligned with the economisation programme have undertaken work that is in many ways closely related. Franck Cochoy (2007, 2011) has called for a more concerted study of both material 'devices' and human 'dispositions', directing attention to how markets can become oriented towards a range of embodied human states, ranging from habit, to curiosity, to weariness, to temptation. Liz McFall, meanwhile, drawing on Gabriel Tarde's social theory, has argued for the value of attending to the central role of 'sentiment' in markets; the 'trick' of markets, she writes, 'is all in the orchestration of technique and sentiment; in the way sentiment is put into relation with products and the way relations are transformed into sentiment for products' (McFall 2014, p. 7; see also Latour and Lépinay 2009).

These writers have begun to contribute towards an empirically rich analysis of how what I call affect, and what some others might call disposition or sentiment, plays a crucial role in shaping the conduct of markets. Leaving aside quibbles around terminology, what such work is starting to reveal are the ways in which economies come into being by passing through some of the most intimate dimensions of human experience. Economies feel and are felt. They breathe and hope and suffer. *Economies live.*

Outline of the book

The book follows a path undertaken by many debtors: from borrowing to default. The first chapter explores how a device-oriented perspective might help us understand why people's consumer credit borrowing practices become unmanageable. It focuses in particular on the archetypal consumer credit device: the credit card. This mundane monetary object, it is argued, has long posed particular calculative challenges for borrowers. Drawing on both historical evidence and contemporary accounts from defaulting borrowers, the chapter examines how borrowers' attachments to consumer credit products come about, arguing that it is in part because of the ability of these products to *ease* life, without – at least for a period – overly disrupting it. It also seeks to provide a contribution to how we might understand the role played in social life by monetary objects of all kinds. To help describe some of these processes, I also introduce the work of the philosopher Alfred North Whitehead and the role played by what he calls 'lures for feeling'.

If many of the devices assembled around borrowing are concerned with the easing of life, then those that come into play when an overdue debt needs to be repaid are (to a large extent) about disruption. This is the focus of Chapter 2, in which we encounter the technologies of the debt collection industry for the first time, in the process finding the presence of affect particularly hard to ignore. Moving into the domestic spaces of defaulting debtors, this chapter begins to examine precisely how the attachments between defaulting borrowers and creditors are maintained and re-established through debt collection technologies. Drawing on a Deleuzian vocabulary, this is described in terms of twin movements of 'enfolding' and 'unfolding'. It explores how mundane, socio-material technologies of debt collection become folded into the everyday lives of defaulters, before unfolding into their interactions with others, including the debt collector itself. It is this double movement that provides the conditions for the capture of affect and its transformation into both emotion and economic calculation. In the process, I propose that to understand practices of market attachment, more attention is needed to how they intersect with, and exploit, some of the other attachments that people live with and confront.

The next three chapters shift away from the everyday and domestic spaces of consumer credit borrowing and default and to the perhaps more unfamiliar world of the debt collections industry. As they variously demonstrate, this is a domain of the market where familiar market norms do not seem to apply and where conventional market terminology can strain. It is a world where 'customers' are delivered to the industry already bound by 'obligations', where the aim of the 'producer' is often to amplify the calculative challenges of its 'products' rather than to simplify them, and where the language of threat tends to dominate over the language of entreaty.

Chapter 3 outlines how the collections industry first 'discovered' and then began to work out how best to 'capture' affect. It begins by moving far back in time, to examine the historical antecedents of contemporary collections practices and to see what they reveal about logics that may, or may not, have carried over into the present. What we find is a long-standing concern with the body of the debtor, whether through its enslavement, torture or imprisonment. However, following the abolition of debtors' prisons, collectors in the twentieth century were confronted by a problem: how to convince debtors to repay without seemingly being able to threaten the debtor as an embodied subject. At this point, the empirical focus narrows down to the US, for it is here that this problem was explored earlier and with more intensity than anywhere else. The solution, I show, took time to emerge. It initially involved drawing on the promise of a new academic discipline – psychology. This 'intellectual technology', as I call it, helped collectors reframe their work and expertise as being concerned with emotion and how to manage it. As the century progressed, this interest became sidelined by the promise of more practical technologies, in one of which can be found the roots of some of the most sophisticated contemporary collections practices: the conduct of experiments with unwitting populations of debtors.

Chapter 4 explores the sometimes strange world of consumer collections in part through the eyes of collections call centre workers, arguing that they too can be seen as a 'market devices', of central importance to the contemporary collections industry. The chapter's analysis begins with a single collections conversation. It uses this to explore the analytical challenges of assessing a mode of interaction that, on the face of it, seems to bear only partial relationship to the highly emotionally charged landscape of default described by debtors. It concludes that, in tracing the variable modes of market attachment enacted by the collections industry, it is necessary to see linguistic interaction as only one of multiple, co-present, not necessarily successful 'modes of ordering'. The chapter proceeds to trace the central problem of 'market attachment' that the collections industry is still presented with. The challenge for the debt collector is not to attach borrowers to their credit products, as legally they already are. Instead, the challenge is to reattach *value* to the product. In order to analyse this problematic, the chapter argues for the productivity of placing into dialogue the analysis of the capture of affect with

Franck Cochoy's analysis of practices of 'captation'. In so doing, we learn more about the role of experimentation in the industry by examining the increasing deployment of experimental, econometric modes of analysis to both predict and respond to the actions of debtors. These kinds of technologies draw on the emergent, anxious states of debtors, which offer themselves up to the collector as potent affordances for processes and practices of 'affective captation'.

Chapter 5 pursues these issues further by focusing on creditors' own internal collections processes, while also opening up for view another central collections technology: the collections letter. In so doing, a key area it explores is the performative enactment of a separation between practices of 'lending' and 'collections', which will be key to understanding key aspects of the particular politics of consumer credit default. By dramatising a collections trajectory and examining the historical role of 'trading styles' in the UK collections industry, the chapter argues that this distinction itself comes to play a role in the creditor's attempt to reactivate the attachments a debtor has to their debt. More particularly, I argue that the collector exploits the generative potential of 'passing out' a debt and convincing debtors that their accounts have left the safety of the lender and moved into the more threatening world of the collector. In a reflexive move, what are more conventionally seen as the 'overflows' of market making – the tendency for moral issues to be differentially articulated in different domains of market practice – are turned into a market opportunity.

Finally, in the conclusion, I bring together some of the arguments and empirical insights that have emerged over the course of the book, including reflecting on some of the work that bringing affect to markets might do. Part of this work, I suggest, is to open up the relational politics of default. This is the precise way in which the connections between the various entities that compose both consumer credit and the issue of consumer credit default become formatted and intermingled. It also focuses attention on the faint 'lines of flight' that might be detected around market settings, that which escapes market capture and captation. In the case of consumer credit default this is not just about debtors seeking market detachment – although I document some of their attempts to do so – it is also about attending to the possibility that, in the social and material forces that cluster around markets, there might be contained the potential for different, novel orderings of the relations between people, things, and economies.

Notes

1 In 2008, 20 heavily indebted and defaulting debtors were interviewed, with the assistance of two credit advice services: National Debtline and Consumer Credit Counselling Service (CCCS; now called StepChange). These each put me in touch with eight of their clients. Four were recruited via personal contacts, 12 interviews were conducted in the interviewee's home, with five phone interviews, and three in an alternate location suggested by the participant (either for practical or privacy reasons). Twelve lived in London, with the remainder spread across both England and Wales. There was a fairly even spread of ages, ranging from 25 to 65, of which 11 were male and nine female. Seventeen had either defaulted on their consumer credit debts or renegotiated their debts with creditors. At their peak, most respondents had had unsecured debts of between

£10,000 and £20,000, excluding student loans; for some, this figure rose as high as £43,000. Few had a household income over £30,000, while for many this was under £15,000 a year (including benefits). This placed all respondents in the bottom 60 per cent of household income as measured by the Office for National Statistics in a comparable period (2008–2009), with many in the bottom 20 per cent (Office for National Statistics 2010). This is unsurprising. Again, to compare, in 2008, only just over one in 10 of CCCS's clients had an annual household income over £30,000; for the majority this figure was under £20,000 (CCCS 2009, p. 10). This snapshot of UK consumer credit perhaps then captures a flavour of experiences and situations that were likely being shared by many at the time. Given the sensitivities involved in gaining access, my fieldwork in the three debt collection companies was brief – two days in two of the agencies, one in the third, all undertaken in 2009 – but this was enough to gain an insight into key aspects of their internal operations. It involved long days sitting alongside and talking to collectors or listening to recorded calls accessed via a calls database, observing quality control and complaints departments, departments that deal with financial hardship cases (where these existed), as well as undertaking interviews with directors and other staff in these businesses. As well as the various forms of documentary research this book presents and the interviews conducted during my visits, this field research has been supplemented by interviews with a regulator, a credit reference agencies consultant and an analyst, a director of a commercial debt management company, a debt collections industry trainer, a retired collections company director, and a collections industry spokesperson. The last two interviews were conducted in 2013 and 2014 respectively, the rest in 2009. Throughout, all names are pseudonyms.

2   In following a controversial object, the book locates itself in relation to a body of work for which the study of how controversies and public issues are made, resolved, and shaped has been a rich and productive intellectual endeavour. See, for example, Brante (1993); Callon (1986b; 1986a); Collins (1981); Engelhardt and Caplan (1987); Latour (1987); Marres (2007; 2012); Meyer (2009); Mol (2002, pp. 88–116); Pinch and Bijker (1984).

3   This question is in turn connected to a yet broader one: just how tenable is it to continue to assume that consumer debts have to be repaid at all? How this question is debated by debtors themselves will be a theme in the book's conclusion (see also Cooper (forthcoming) and Graeber (2011)).

4   During the same year, well known newspaper journalists including Polly Toynbee (2008) and Johann Hari (2009) also authored articles focusing on the practices of the debt collections industry, an industry that Hari, drawing on the *Dispatches* documentary, branded 'cruel and out of control'. The *Sunday Times* ran a highly critical piece of investigative journalism centring on the in-house collection procedures at Lloyds, a well-known retail bank (Insight 2009), exposing the role of incentives for collections works and potentially misleading practices (for instance, claiming to be calling from a solicitor's firm). Since then, newspaper stories about the industry, often pursued along similar lines, have appeared in the press with an almost predictable regularity, although the focus has increasingly shifted to the intersection between debt collection practices and those of a new controversial consumer credit object: the payday loan industry. Public interest in the workings of the collections industry has also been confirmed by the ongoing success of a daytime reality television show looking at the work of high court enforcement officers. Entitled *The Sheriffs are Coming*, the show recently completed its third series, having first aired in 2012.

5   See Chapter 2.

6   See Chapter 4.

7   See Chapters 2 and 5.

8   Stengers is writing about the slope created/assumed by twentieth-century physics.

9   To the magazine's disappointment, no such fulsome public endorsement was forthcoming from the government – instead it issued an ostensibly bland statement: 'The

Government recognises that the debt collection industry provides an important function to both the business and consumer sectors, where debts are being pursued in accordance with the OFT guidance' (The Prime Minister's Office 2010).

10 I am also here thinking alongside that work within feminist ethics and STS that has looked towards care as potentially productive way of attending to the contingencies of relationality (see Harbers *et al.* 2002; Held 1993; Held 2006; Mol 2008; Noddings 1984).

11 For good introductions to the concept, see Muniesa *et al.* (2007) and McFall (2009a).

12 The precise term 'economisation programme' is not used by Çalışkan and Callon (2009; 2010) in their two key papers on the subject; however, their repeated invocation of the study of processes of economisation as a 'research programme' points quite clearly in this direction. An alternate terminological umbrella is 'new new economic sociology', which emphasises a distinction with the more culturalist 'new economic sociology' (see McFall 2009a; McFall and Ossandón 2014).

13 See Çalışkan and Callon (2009, p. 370).

14 Callon's most influential texts have been his two contributions (1998b; 1998a) to the *The Laws of the Markets* collection, which he also edited. Many of his other single and co-authored papers will be drawn on over the course of this book.

15 I am also thinking in particular here of Bill Maurer's (2012a; 2012b) work on the importance of attending to various forms of socio-material market infrastructure (see also Susan Leigh Star (1999)).

16 This is a term with a specific heritage, associated most of all with the philosophy of Gilles Deleuze. It draws attention to the movements of gathering and dispersal involved in the entry of more or less coherent entities in the world, the uneven distribution of agency within such entities, the distribution of agency between humans and non-humans (including things, beings and assorted concepts, discourses and forms of language) and processes of emergence and affordance (see Anderson and McFarlane 2011; Fredriksen and Sullivan 2014; Phillips 2006). Within the strand of economic sociology I draw on here, talk about assemblages has been complemented by the use, in English, of *agencements*, the parallel term in French (see Callon 2007; McFall 2009b). This is to a large degree because of the desire to emphasise not just the work of gathering involved in processes of assembling, but also what might be termed the emergent agency of such assemblages/*agencements*; this includes highlighting the fact that devices themselves are *agencements*. Principally in order to keep the book as readable as possible, and given I use the term only infrequently, I prefer the English translation: assemblage.

17 See Callon (1998b); Callon *et al.* (2002); Callon and Muniesa (2005); Lazarus (2013b); McFall (2009a); Muniesa (2009); Muniesa *et al.* (2007).

18 I have bracketed here a discussion of Deleuze's concept of the virtual and concomitant processes of actualisation. This is very much in the background of my thinking, but to avoid unnecessary philosophical detours, I prefer not to actualise this here (any more than I already have, that is!).

19 In both cases, we would have to include a range of other forces, including the discursive and conceptual, as well as the various pasts and potential futures imbricated in a given situation. The examples are deliberately simplified.

20 This in turn can be seen as sitting in dialogue with a related set of scholarship interested in how affect operates within markets, although this has often focused on debates surrounding the production and measurement of value in light of the apparent rise of affective and immaterial labour (see Arvidsson 2005; Clough *et al.* 2007; Dowling *et al.* 2007; Dowling 2012; Lazzarato 1996; Negri 1999; Zwick and Denegri Knott 2009).

1 'A curious and sort of subconscious temptation'

The lure of consumer credit

I think I shouldn't be allowed around these things.

Interview with Angela, 2009

What drives people to borrow? More precisely, what drives so many to borrow so constantly, so heavily, that their debt becomes unmanageable? These are the kinds of question that you learn to expect fairly soon after you declare an interest in consumer credit. They can be posed in a range of different ways, as readily by those who have had difficulties with their own borrowing as those that have not. And they demand an answer.

In the years before the rise of the sub-prime credit crisis similar questions were already being asked in public in the UK. In particular, 2004 was a year when certain British newspaper editors decided this question was a matter of broad public interest. 'CREDIT "KILLS" A FAMILY MAN', screamed the cover of the *Daily Mail* in early March – the story addressed the case of a borrower who had committed suicide, perhaps as a result of high levels of borrowing and being chased by multiple debt collectors (Poulter and Wilkes 2004). Six days later it followed up with another splash, concerning a potentially looming 'CREDIT CARD MELTDOWN' – this time, the story was the dangers to the national economy of the rising levels of personal debt, as well as the ongoing effects on families (Poulter 2004). The next week the *Daily Express* weighed in: 'CREDIT CARD MADNESS', it shouted, with its front page highlighting the fact that UK citizens were accruing an apparently huge proportion of Europe's total amount of credit card debt (Vickers 2004).[1]

In these mass-circulation publications with tabloid, right-leaning sensibilities, an issue that might more conventionally be seen as a macroeconomic fact (the economy's increasing reliance on consumer credit spending) becomes variously recast in lurid front page spreads. Blame for the apparent problem of excessive consumer credit borrowing was on the one hand levelled at business practices (the 'greedy' banks (Poulter and Wilkes 2004)) and, on the other, consumer culture ('a "spend now, pay later" culture' (Poulter 2004)). At the same time, the apparently cognitively deficient borrower is also held at least partially to blame, with articles such as the above also proclaiming the irrationality ('madness') of such high levels of consumer credit spending (often articulated in terms of a reckless 'addiction' to consumer spending).

However sensationalist these headlines and their accompanying stories may be, these three 'figures' as we might call them – that is, consumer culture, a cognitively deficient borrower, and the practices of the credit industry – in many ways find their parallel in causal arguments that are mobilised in academic and policy debates that too have sought to examine the causes of high levels of consumer-credit borrowing, even if with a little more care.

Of the three, it is the attention to the role of consumer culture that comes closest to a sociological response. While for much of the twentieth century consumer credit simply was not subject to much sociological attention as an analytical object in its own right, as Dawn Burton (2008, p. 31) has argued, one reason for this is the near monopoly that economic theories and models had over research into consumer credit) this situation began to change in the mid- to late-1990s. Important field-defining work was undertaken by writers including Lendol Calder (1999), Robert Manning (2000) and George Ritzer (1995).[2] Although their arguments do not always map cleanly onto one another, this work outlined the significant role played in the expansion and adoption of consumer credit by major cultural and economic shifts engendered by and connected to the rise of forms of mass consumption. It also succeeded in resituating consumer credit within a diverse set of historical trajectories, showing the necessity of attending to the slow but steady institutionalisation and normalisation of consumer credit in, most notably, American society. Finally, amongst a range of other themes, this work also shed light on the crucial role played by the aggressive expansion and marketing of consumer credit, in which consumers were increasingly encouraged to use their newly acquired borrowing instruments, in particular their credit cards, to fund their everyday consumer needs.

An emerging body of more recent work continues to explore these currents, while adding layers of nuance. In what can be seen as a broadly post-Foucauldian analysis, connections have been drawn between the expansion of consumer credit and the rise of new models of economic personhood. In these, the responsible consumer credit borrower is revealed as an entrepreneurial and idealised figure, imagined to be able to manage successfully and benefit from the risks entailed in everyday borrowing practices (see Langley 2008a, 2008b, 2014; Marron 2009, 2012). Attention has also been directed to the relationship between consumer credit borrowing and what has become known as 'financialisation': that is the increasing dependence of social and economic relations of all kinds on the ups and downs of the global financial markets (Langley 2008b; Martin 2002; Montgomerie 2006, 2007, 2009). On the one hand, new financial instruments (asset-backed securities, for instance) can be seen to have played a direct causal role in the growth of, and national economic dependence on, consumer credit borrowing. On the other, as debtors' lives become intertwined with the flows of finance, they become ever more filled with uncertainties and insecurities. Further research has looked at how the consumer credit market, and some of its specific social and material agents, can be seen to have affected other social and economic domains. Most notably, this has involved drawing direct causal connections between the rise of the credit rating as a measure of individual economic competence and, via its spread into global markets as debt became repackaged, the global economic crisis that erupted into public in 2007 (see Poon 2009; Rona-Tas and Hiss 2010).

If we turn towards more policy-oriented writing, or the specifics of government policy itself, we can observe a far narrower, more restricted focus on the analysis of the causes for and effects of what is seen as a problematic reliance on consumer credit products. A recurrent concept in these accounts is 'over-indebtedness'. As Donncha Marron (2012) has documented, over-indebtedness in the UK has been largely represented within governmental discourse as a problem of self-government. That is to say, people's problems with their borrowing are largely assumed to stem from either individual calculative failures or failures to manage themselves properly as ideally entrepreneurial subjects. In other words, what we have here is the summoning up of the figure of the cognitively deficient debtor. A major part of the problem is held to be debtors' financial management skills, to which the response, overwhelmingly, is to recommend more and better financial education for debtors. Similar tendencies can be found in North American and European contexts (Arthur 2012; Lazarus 2013a; forthcoming (a); forthcoming (b)). A particularly striking example from the US is the institutionalisation of compulsory credit counselling and financial education courses for those applying for bankruptcy, introduced as part of the Bush-era bankruptcy reforms (Lawless *et al.* 2008; U.S. Code 2012, §§ 109, 727, 1328).

The same apparently faulty individual decision-maker that is the target of these pedagogical interventions is also the target of a related attempt to improve the conditions of consumer credit borrowing: the provision of more and better information. This is often framed around ideals of informational transparency (more or less explicit in which is the assumption that this will, in turn, lead to more efficient markets).[3] This can be seeing as addressing the third figure in our account – the practices of the credit industry. This is a causal explanation focused on the role of the commercial organisation. For instance, writing about the 'incomprehensible fine print' that can accompany credit applications, the newly established Consumer Financial Protection Bureau (CFPB) in the US makes transparency central to its ambition: 'Companies shouldn't compete by figuring out how to fool you best', they write, '[t]ransparency means that markets really work for consumers' (CFPB 2013b). Very similar language features in both recent EU-wide legislation on consumer credit agreements[4] and a sequence of government-sponsored reviews of the UK consumer credit market (see Marron 2012).[5]

From a conventional sociological point of view, the problem with the turn to either education or transparency as the solution to problems of excessive borrowing is that it obscures the underlying structural factors that drive credit borrowing in the first place, and indeed the way in which the individualisation of responsibility in this way can serve particular political agendas. At the same time, in this focus on the capacity of these quite specific tools to influence market-oriented decision-making there are echoes of the device-oriented approaches that were outlined in the book's introduction. The 'economisation' programme, which brings this focus into the domain of economic relations, highlights the role that quite specific devices can play in shaping and directing the calculative endeavours of users, albeit in some quite different terms.

A device-oriented perspective therefore needs to be clear about whether and how it can provide a distinct contribution to these debates. With this in mind, I will put devices to the test in this chapter and, in the process, propose some other intellectual resources that may required. In particular, I introduce the work of the philosopher Alfred North Whitehead and the role played by what he calls 'lures for feeling'. This approach will allow room for understanding ways of being and relating to one another – ontologies – which a device-centred perspective has been less successful in following.

The early history of the credit card

Pinning down exactly what we mean when we talk about consumer credit is by no means straightforward (see Calder 1999, p. 5). Technical definitions tend to variously stress:

- the particular temporality of consumer credit – it is usually intended to be relatively short term;
- its constituency – the 'public';
- the basis for the guarantee of the loan – tending to be 'unsecured' and thus not tied to a particular asset (the contrast is usually with mortgage lending, in which debt is secured on property);
- particular credit products – here often including personal loans, credit cards, and forms of hire purchase;
- and, finally, its object – consumer goods and services.[6] It is perhaps these that have occupied social scientific attention more than the others.

However, if we look at the kinds of credit products that are included under the consumer credit umbrella – personal loans, credit card products, and forms of hire purchase – we see that these do not necessarily map cleanly onto some of the criteria I have just outlined. The repayment schedules for consumer credit products can be eminently long term – with credit card products the borrower can vary what they will repay each month and of course even if a single debt is repaid, a user may use and return to the same credit card over the course of many years. Hire purchase loans, meanwhile, are usually 'secured' on the products they are used to buy, often high value consumer goods – cars or expensive household equipment for instance. These remain as assets that can be reclaimed if repayments are not maintained. And consumer credit may well be used to fund expenses that are quite far from the kinds of pleasure-oriented, conspicuous consumption with which it is often associated. It is perfectly possible to obtain consumer credit loans to pay off other loans, or to withdraw cash on a credit card (at high rates of interest) to meet rental or mortgage repayments for instance, or to simply use forms of consumer credit to put food on the table for your family. Unsecured credit can also be converted into secured credit: releasing equity from a property to pay off some unsecured debts for instance.

Consumer credit is therefore clearly a heterogeneous entity. And what it is and to what other debts and entities it can become connected depends very much on the places and times where it is inserted alongside its users. As we will see in later chapters, this is worth keeping in mind given the particularly stretched temporalities that can accompany the routine experience of consumer credit default. That said, there is one form of consumer credit that has become the main analytical placeholder, in both academic and popular writing, for the shifts in the distribution of personal debt that has taken place in many economies over the past 100 years or so: credit card enabled borrowing. It is this object that has taken pride of place in the titles and front-cover imagery of some of the most important social scientific books on consumer credit.[7]

This focus is understandable. In the UK, for instance, although in recent years other types of consumer credit make up almost two thirds of the annual outstanding debt,[8] when you look at monthly figures for gross lending – which includes lending which is then repaid in full on a monthly basis – credit card debt makes up almost three quarters of the amount lent out.[9] This kind of information is not publicly available in the US, although, similar to the UK, non-revolving forms of consumer credit make up around two thirds of outstanding debt.[10] However, given that of the approximately two thirds of American families use credit cards and just over half of these report usually paying off their balances in full each month (Bricker *et al.* 2012, p. 67), it is clear that transactional credit card borrowing permeates millions of people's everyday routines.

Despite this, however, little serious analytical attention has been paid to this mundane monetary object *itself*.[11] The credit card tends to stand as the *symbol* for consumer credit and, in occupying this symbolic, referential position, its specific capacities come to be glossed over. The credit card, in these instances, becomes simply the carrier of credit relations, the transmitter of much broader, more significant socio-economic forces. 'The idea is to keep people at the business of consumption', writes George Ritzer, and that

> [t]his is nowhere clearer than in the case of credit cards, which *lure people into consumption* by easy credit and then entice them into still further consumption by offers of 'payment holidays,' new cards, and increased credit limits.

He continues:

> The beauty of all this, at least from the point of view of those who profit from the existing system, is that people are kept in the workplace and on the job by the need to pay the minimum monthly payments on their credit card accounts and, more generally, to support their consumption habits.
>
> (Ritzer 2005, p. 26 emphasis added; see also Ritzer 1995)

Ritzer's argument follows a trajectory that is common in (broadly) sociological writing on consumer credit, in which the 'devices' of consumer credit tend to figure as largely bit part actors in a drama whose central characters are the forces involved in putting these objects in front of borrowers in the first place.[12] It is these forces that are held responsible for the 'lure' of credit. Another more recent example is provided by Maurizzio Lazzarato, whose approach in this specific respect, if not necessarily either his conclusions or the theoretical apparatus that is brought to bear, mirrors Ritzer's. Lazzarato moves the terrain away from consumption and towards neoliberalism, where debt, of whatever type, becomes 'the most general power relation through which the neoliberal power bloc institutes its class struggle' (2012, p. 89; this claim is explored further in the book's conclusion). When his attention turns specifically to consumer credit, we find the often unnoticed credit card transformed into a powerful apparatus of de-individualisation, with its user functioning 'like a cogwheel, a "human" element that conforms to the "non-human" elements of the sociotechnical machine constituted by the banking network' (2012, p. 148). While this is not a total denial by Lazzarato of the agency of the borrower (the other component of this 'machinic' subjugation is that which is 'social', where the borrower performs as decision maker and calculative agent), again the intimate and quite specific formatting of the encounter between borrower and credit technology fades from view.

What happens, then, when we look a little more closely at what this apparently mundane, everyday consumer device actually does? For, while the credit *product* may shift repayment forward to another moment in time, the credit *card* does something else entirely. It, and the organisational and material network into which it is inserted, provide the basis for credit as something that can become associated with routine transactions. For Jean Baudrillard, this process was defined by what he called 'the resolution of tensions' within a particular consumer-oriented setting (1998 [1970], p. 29). Credit cards, from this perspective, are part of the systemic lubrication that enables and encourages the effortless passage of the consumer through consumer spaces. But this kind of *easing* does not just happen. It has to be socially and materially arranged around quite specific devices and specific infrastructures. As we shall see, and as Bill Maurer (2012a; 2012b) makes abundantly clear, the precise way in which payment and credit infrastructures are arranged can matter a great deal.

In this respect, the history of the rise of the credit card in the US is instructive, making it possible to track a crucial instance of what Daniel Lopes (2013) has identified as the ongoing 'metamorphoses of credit'.[13] Before this US invention was exported around the world, the qualities we take for granted today were less stable and much more open to question. What we find is that the issuers of early credit cards were far more concerned with the specifics of users' encounters with these devices than whether or not a particular borrower would prove to be a good investment.

The problem for lenders was that, in order to have a successful credit card product, you needed a large number of customers with cards in order to make it worthwhile for merchants to accept a particular bank's card and house its accompanying infrastructure. The US solution was simple but highly effective: issuers realised they could simply *post* these new, lightweight, plastic cards to borrowers. Starting in the late 1950s, but in particular in a period from 1966 to 1970, in what the president of Bank of America, Rudolph Peterson, called 'the great credit-card race', around 100 million plastic credit cards were mailed, unsolicited, to potential users (Nichols 1967; see also Guseva 2008, pp. 11–15; Nocera 1994, p. 54; O'Neil 1970; Stearns 2011, p. 33).[14]

One report, drawing on an American Bankers Association survey, suggests that, at least in the earlier years, only around half of these new credit card offerings were accompanied by credit checks (Furness 1968, p. 65). Some events in the period became infamous. In Chicago in 1967, for example, a series of competing regional banks mailed five million cards to the city's residents, with some families in the more attractive suburbs claiming to have received up to 15 cards, including – if reports are to be believed – toddlers and convicted criminals (Jordan 1967; Nocera 1994, p. 54).

The practice of sending out unsolicited cards in this way was not, however, just about market share. This was made clear in an experiment that was presented to a 1968 government hearing on the practice by a spokesperson from the American Bankers Association. In the experiment in question, New York-based Marine Midland Bank sent 33,357 promotional credit card application forms to potential users. They received responses from only 221, or 0.7 per cent. However, when cards were sent directly to 731 recipients, 19 per cent were actively using them within 60 to 90 days (Bailey 1968, p. 24). The spokesperson expanded on this theme:

> At the time of the receipt of the application [the recipient] may not have any use for it, and at that point doesn't think he [*sic*] wants to have a card. However, if he has a card in his pocket, he knows his credit has been established … I am sure he will welcome the opportunity to use it when the time comes.
>
> (Bailey 1968, p. 27)

Having arrived, as another witness put it, 'like a gift from heaven' (Jackson 1968, p. 32), physically present, ready to be used as and when required, with no application needed and no need to assess at the moment of receipt whether or not it would be needed in future, the card was not just slightly more attractive to borrowers, it was significantly so. Indeed, the data from this experiment was proffered as unashamed evidence of the very need for the practice of unsolicited credit card mailings. It was seen as an essential strategy for banks seeking to challenge the competition. However, at the hearing this effect was also seized upon by critics, who provided numerous case studies of individuals who, by virtue of having received an unsolicited card, had been encouraged into borrowing at levels they would not, it was asserted, have entered into otherwise. For both sides, however, we can see that the credit card is understood to be a device at the centre of struggles of particular kinds of attachments: those directed towards stimulating and shaping relationships between people, things and markets – market attachments in other words.[15]

Something similar is captured in a *Life* magazine article from 1970 on 'the great plastic rush' (O'Neil 1970, p. 55). The piece imagines a typical conversion of a person (here, presumed to be male even though women were also targeted) from a 'sorehead', actively annoyed by and resistant to the solicitations of the creditor, to a borrower:

> The average man, his senses dulled by an endless reception of junk mail, simply chucks his card into a desk or cupboard or dresser drawer if he is among those who are not instantly galvanized by their bank's sudden new interest in their well-being. He may eventually betray reactions characteristic of the sorehead group: when the bank send him a follow-up statement … he may poke holes in it or punch it full of staples and send it back to confuse the bank's computer. But as long as the card stays in his dresser he is subject, though he is not aware of it, to a curious and sort of subconscious temptation. Bank records indicate he will eventually dig it out and give it a try and will thereafter tend to use it again … and again …
>
> (O'Neil 1970, p. 50)

As we saw earlier, Ritzer understood credit card products as deeply connected to the amplification of the 'lure' of consumption. But, in his focus on the product and not the card he, like many other writers, misses the role of the device *doing the work* of attaching consumer to product. The credit card, once delivered into the homes of borrowers, comes to play an active if understated role in their everyday lives. It retains an important capacity: to exert a small but significant effect on the user to whom it has been directed, what the author above describes as a *curious and sort of subconscious temptation*. This might be a pull on the memory, jogged by event or circumstance; it might be its sheer physical presence, as a forgotten card is later stumbled upon; it might be a very constant and nagging attraction which is resisted only so long. Whichever trajectory it takes from drawer to hand (or not), what this apt turn of phrase points towards is that consumer credit devices, like all things, should be considered as processual, emergent entities operating in and through the affective dimensions of life. Seen in these terms, it is not just credit, consumption, or underlying social structure that act to lure and to attract, but also the cards themselves (of course in interaction with a range of other forces).

What exactly is meant here by 'the affective' and references to the 'processual' will be explained further as the chapter and indeed the book progress. However, I want first to bring this story of the agential role of the credit card a little more up-to-date. To do so I will begin with some of the voices of debtors who have recently struggled to manage these and other consumer credit devices.

Shifts in the modes of calculation

A research participant that I met, who I'll call Peter, offered a response to my question about payment media that, on the face of things, turned the course of our conversation to a different topic entirely:

JOE: does it ... bring it home to you more, what you're spending, when you're spending with cash?
PETER: yes, because, again, what we do now, rather than take a big basket round and fill it up, we now take one of the smallest trolleys round and fill it up, which is half the size. Last time we went shopping we didn't even do that. I had two of the hand baskets and the wife had one. So once they were full, that was it. And instead of our bill being the average what it used to be, [£]150, I think it was about [£]70. You know, sometimes the size of the basket you take a round straightaway will limit you to what you can carry, so rather than have one of those big deep, you know, trolleys, you get one of those half sized ones, which [means that] again, you're gonna reduce what you can put in there, which in turn is going to reduce what you spend. So of course when you go down to having hand baskets it reduces it even further, so once they're full, that's it.

Peter shifts the conversation away from my interest, monetary devices, towards a different consumer device: the shopping cart. Having had to cut up all his credit cards and now rely on cash as part of his attempt to deal with his debts, he and his wife had changed how they were manoeuvring around the supermarket. Specifically, they were trying to shop with as small a shopping cart as possible.

This account offers up a serendipitous point of connection to some research undertaken by Franck Cochoy that has focused on this very issue: on the agential effects of the shopping cart and how this material devices can act to shift trajectories of calculation or – as he puts it to emphasise the often inevitable bleed between quantitative and qualitative forms of assessment – 'qualculation' (see Cochoy 2002; 2008).[16] This research has revealed how, despite intervening *after* the shopper 'chooses' a particular good from a supermarket shelf, this device can transform the object of calculative attention, shifting it from a budgetary constraint into a volumetric one (2008, p. 21), creating what Cochoy refers to as 'a short moment of abundance and a pause in calculation' before the user reaches the till (2008, p. 20; drawing also on Pia Pozzato 2001). It is not that calculation ultimately stops, but that the *mode* of calculation is shifted away from a quantitative judgement and towards a judgement that is *spatial*. This account builds on the broader interest within the economisation programme, which sees economic calculation as a property of neither the individual (for example, the maximising self-interest of the rational economic actor) nor the social (for example, as embedded in social relations), but as 'equipped' in and through quite particular settings and devices.[17]

What I want to propose is that credit cards too, themselves, equip and enact shifts in modes of calculation. However, these modes are less spatial than temporal, and interact in a quite different way with embodied practice. Some of this can begin to be detected in the following extract of my conversation with Julie:

> you almost don't think about it, you just hand your card over, it almost becomes your debit card, because you know in the back of your mind you don't have this money available, but there is no other way you can afford to pay for it. But then again you don't see it [...]. What you should do is say, well I can't afford it so we are going to have to cut back on something, like the shopping or something like that, but [...] you don't.

The presence of the credit card is indeed 'easing' Julie's passage through her purchases. Having it ready and available renders far smoother the immediate experience of passing through a particular transactional space. Like all credit, this is in part because of its ability to shift the repayment of value into the future, forestalling the potentially painful financial sacrifice for the economic good in hand until the day comes when, it is to be hoped, payment is easier. This is a common theme in discussions about debt of all kinds: 'you know this kind of feeling flying around that one day you will have to deal with it, but that's not yet so it's alright', a respondent called Ruth told me. Or there's Danielle's reflection on the multiple forms of borrowing she undertook as a student:

> I was thinking well this is just a student period, I'm allowed to have all these student loans and spend as much money as I want and have a really good time, be really hedonistic and then I'll get a good job after I've got my degree and so I'll pay it off.

But there is a further dynamic in play here – which is about how it *feels* to spend on credit cards – this is something quite distinct. The presence of the ostensibly insignificant credit card device, coupled with the forms of temporal 'stretching' that credit products of all kind enable, combine to peculiar effect. Momentarily, the senses are fooled: it feels like there is only a dyadic market attachment in play here: between object of purchase and purchaser. For Julie this appears to connect to the visibility of what is being spent and the interrelated processes of cognitive engagement and embodied practice, the latter of which seems to become near automated: '*you almost don't think about it*' ... '*you don't see it*' ... '*you just hand your card over*'. The result is that the credit card (almost) *becomes* (to pre-empt some of the terms I will discuss further below), not a borrowing device at all. This is a theme that is expanded on by Richard:

> you just pay everything on credit cards, and you don't even know how much money you've got in your account, you know, that's kind of the situation I was getting myself into. I can leave my credit card behind the bar and I never have to actually go to a cash point, bring out money, you

know, I don't physically see how much I've got in the account. So it just gets too easy.

This shift in calculation can be partly explained as an outcome of the lack of 'transparency' of information available to the borrower who used consumer credit which, as we've seen, is the favoured territory for policy interventions in this arena. However there is more to it than that. In this example, it is the very fact that the card can just be left behind the bar that also matters. It means none of the labour, including calculative labour, involved in obtaining and managing cash. The device gets on and deals with the more uncomfortable business of payment in the background, leaving life to be continued in the foreground. This can mean that using a credit card can quite readily seem not like borrowing at all:

ANGELA: I don't know why I did it, it felt really bad at the time, [...] but, I think I did see it as borrowing money, [...] when you spend money on a credit card it doesn't really feel like it, I mean, everyone always says that, spending money on Visa cards, you know, you should just have cash, because then you can see it ...

* * *

GARY: you see it's funny, you use the term borrowing and you don't think of it like that [...] Do you know what I mean? [...] borrowing to me is, [...] these friends of mine that have lent me say 200 [pounds] [...] I call that borrowing. And yet with that lot I don't call it that. Although obviously that is what it is.
JOE: [...] what do you think the difference is?
GARY: I don't know. Because you're, it's almost like you're charging it. [...] but it's funny [...] you've used the word borrow a couple of times [...] and [...], you don't see it as that [...] I don't know, because you [...] slap something on the counter [...] and then they give you a bill.

These are two examples of where there is clear disjuncture between what a user perceives credit card borrowing 'to be' and what it is to experience it *in the moment of transaction*. Gary's account also brings to mind Viviana Zelizer's (1994) analysis of the meanings attached to different monies, the way they can be differentially 'earmarked' by users, depending on the particular social ties they mediate, as he draws a clear distinction between money borrowed from friends and the borrowing effected by the credit card.[18] I will return to Zelizer's work shortly. But it is the intimate affair of living through these moments that I want to focus on for now. These moments can be emotionally charged ('it felt really bad'), with the potential to experience a tension between what either others or another internal voice realise to be 'true' about credit card debt ('I think I did see it as borrowing money'; 'obviously that is what it is') and the fact that, in practice, it can feel quite different. These are also moments characterised by a distinct, quite underdetermined embodied practice. For Angela, as for Richard, the contrast to cash is explicit – cash, at the very least, asks more of a user's visual awareness ('then you can see it'). In Gary's case, like Julie, the experience involves little in the way of cognitive processing: the card is just something to be 'slapped' upon the counter.

Aspects of this particular form of embodied transactional encounter have been investigated by behavioural psychologists, although their studies don't always seek to differentiate the specific effects of electronic payment cards in general from credit cards in particular.[19] A recent qualitative study, for instance, elicited responses that echo those above. Using focus group data, it explored the very question of whether there might be differential emotional, material and calculative effects of using cash as opposed to payment cards. Here are just a few of the accounts respondents provided:

> Because it's real money you actually feel like you are spending real money, so you sometimes get that little bit of guilt.

> You can see the pile of notes diminishing whereas you can't when you use electronic money, you can't physically see that.

> I feel like I'm parting with something if I hand over cash.

> It's just more tangible than when I hand over a card and I just get a small piece of paper back.

> It just disappears so fast electronically, you never actually have the money physically – there's more accountability with physical money – I remember where I have spent a note.
>
> (Kahn 2011, pp. 77–79)[20]

Inviting participants to contrast the experience of using cash to using payment cards (and hence not, it should be noted, credit cards) brings out a series of implied oppositions: real versus unreal, visible versus invisible, tangible versus intangible, material versus immaterial. The author and moderator, Jashim Kahn, argues that such characteristics need to be understood in terms of what he calls 'embodied cognition', a concept he connects to the psychologist and philosopher William James.[21] As Kahn puts it, 'the characteristics of the physical entity used would produce unique cognitions and emotions via touch, sight, counting and smell. These would differ within and across the payment mode types' (Kahn 2011, p. 35).

The agential effects of different modes of payment have also been the subject of experimental research. Recent work by Priya Raghubir and Joydeep Srivastava (2008) has replicated an early influential study (Feinberg 1986), which seemed to show that the mere presence of the ability to pay by credit card (as indicated by a logo – in the control this is absent) increases the amounts participants are willing to pay for an imaginary meal, a phenomenon which is sometimes referred to as 'the credit card effect'. Perhaps more relevant here, because it gets closer to the role played by the active handling and use of payment mechanisms, are studies which have compared the use of cash to other payment forms. This has shown that people are more willing to spend using electronic cards used in Laundromats and for photocopying than they are when they use cash (Soman 2003) and that people who use gaming chips in games of poker gambled significantly more than if they used cash (Lapuz and Griffiths 2010).

Experiential differences between different payment mechanisms have also been explicitly targeted by card issuers themselves, as they have sought to change the way they and their devices are inserted into the transactional moment. In a set of early and ultimately unsuccessful attempts to introduce users to 'Mondex', a form of electronic cash, a series of trials focused on demonstrating the supposed temporal and spatial 'inefficiencies' and cumbersome qualities of cash as compared to Mondex's new payment devices (Stalder 2001). A similar tactic was used in 2008 in campaigns run by Maestro – a debit card – and Barclaycard OnePulse – a type of cashless payment device incorporating a public transport swipecard. In both campaigns, cash figures as a weighty, cumbersome thing, taking up both unnecessary space and time: this might be communicated by drawing attention to the problem of 'having to fiddle for change' (Maestro 2007), or, as highlighted to visitors of a dedicated website set up by Barclays, by 'Danny Chiba', a fictional professor who welcomes guests to the equally fictional 'Institute for Future Living'. 'Chiba', who addresses his audience from an apparently space-age setting, all glass and white, airy clean lines, warns his online visitors of the 'dangers' of their cash falling or, more accurately flying out of control, in an animation in which an unwitting individual trying to do nothing more ordinary than buy a coffee experiences the misfortune (and apparent embarrassment) of seeing her cash spray across the café in a wide arc when she opens her (apparently spring-loaded!) purse.[22] In the Maestro campaign, such material encumbrances are in turn connected to embodied experiences of delay in a different realm – public transport – in their 'Coins: Expect Delays' campaign (Figure 1.1b). In each, the intention is clear: to attempt to introduce into the calculative space of the transaction an assessment of the merits of not only its *object*, but also its *mode*.

Of course, looking at the moment of transaction offers only a partial view on the calculative spaces surrounding the use consumer credit. Consumer credit sits in dynamic relation to a range of other processes, market attachments and, indeed, other consumer credit devices. When it comes to credit card borrowing, the principal device meant to restore some of the calculative apparatus that is absent at the point of transaction is the credit card statement (there are others: annual statements, receipts; borrowers could also keep track of their spending themselves). On a monthly basis, these re-present the user with a retrospective record of their credit-card mediated consumption practices. It is the decontextualised, linearly formatted, echo of these past moments in the present through which the user is supposed to assess their past actions and their relationship to the credit product as a whole. It is also these credit statements that have been the object of policy interventions designed to improve the borrower's calculative apparatus – to enable successful market 'detachment'; most prominently this includes the summary box, which I mentioned earlier, but may also include key

a

b

Figures 1.1a and *1.1b* Maestro campaign, 2008.[23]

product features, information on whom customers should contact should they have a dispute with their creditor, an indicative amount of interest that would be paid on the following month if only the minimum payment was made, as well as a 'health warning', detailing the consequences of making only minimum payments. As with many other such financial detachment devices, the aim is to enable the user to somehow manage and contain the inherent uncertainty and opacity of the unknowable future (a theme I will return to in the next chapter).

Clearly, however, this often cannot be achieved. This was the case with Angela:

JOE: What about credit statements [...] looking back a bit further, when you were using the credit cards [...] how would you interact with those?

ANGELA: I hate them, boring, just not really look at them at all. I hate them, oh god just thinking about it now just horrible.

JOE: Sorry.

ANGELA: No, no, no it's alright ... just thinking of the evil horrible people that put them together that would care enough to like ... it's so awful of me, what's wrong with me I feel really bad, but I don't know ... [...] it's good that you know what you spent your money on I suppose and how much they're charging you and all of that. *I think I shouldn't be allowed around these things* [emphasis added]. I think I need ... [trails off, upset]

This exchange represents the point in the interview at which Angela becomes most visibly upset – the emotive trigger seemingly her own sense of failure at having been unable to interact with consumer credit devices as she feels she should have. Angela appears to be grappling for some form of calculative prosthesis, some solution to her self-perceived inability to act as she feels she should: as a rationally calculating *homo economicus*, that venerated figure of liberal governance (Foucault 2008). While recognising this as an ideal figure, one able to interact with these devices – and in particular credit statements – as they (the issuers, or, as she puts it, 'the awful horrible people') suggest they *should* be interacted with, her own response is to feel overwhelmed by the inability of statements to prompt her to perform as such. Her conclusion is simple: for whatever reason, forms of consumer credit are 'things' with too much agency for her.

What I wish readers to take away from this assortment of material is that it seems extremely likely that, in our movements through a range of payment spaces, different transactional devices are routinely eliciting different responses in quite distinct ways. This is important for our understanding of monetary objects of all kinds, given that money is so often thought of as something that is itself utterly devoid of causal impact. Usually, money is assumed to be consequential only for its ability to deliver value from one party to another. This is territory that has been thoroughly investigated by Viviana Zelizer, whose work I mentioned earlier. Zelizer draws on a long-standing anthropological interest in how people come to understand monetary objects through the circulation of beliefs and values. However, she and I differ in terms of our empirical attention.

The differences Zelizer identifies are understood to be related to the projection onto money, by social groups, of 'meaning' (the title of her most influential book on the topic makes this explicit: *The Social Meaning of Money* (1997)). Meaning is understood in a way that has become conventional within social science – as something generated and differentiated in and through people and their cultural forms; the meanings produced are assumed to become projected onto and attached to, objects of many kinds.

Science and technology studies has shown, however, that objects achieve their ability to disturb and shape patterns of human behaviour, their agency in other words, not simply through the projection of qualities onto them. Bringing these insights into the study of monies would help disrupt the separation of monetary 'objects' from their associated 'meaning' by focusing attention on the agential role of both particular monetary media and the wider range of human and non-human actors with which these media become entangled. This would, in turn, offer a response to the so-called 'bifurcation of nature' (see Whitehead 2004 [1920]) into discrete realms comprising, on the one side, humans and their understandings of the world and, on the other, pretty much everything else. This bifurcation has become associated with the long endeavour of modern knowledge (see Latour 1993; Stengers 2011). However, as Bruno Latour argues: '[o]perations like thinking, abstracting, building pictures, are not *above* other practical operations like setting up instruments, arraying devices, laying rods, but are *in between* them' (Latour 1988, p. 35; original emphasis). The meaning of money therefore not only happens in and through the device it is also *formatted* by the device. The device and its capacities contribute towards making up the *quality* of transactional, calculative settings, their 'manner' of assembly, including to what other entities they become connected.

It is certainly true that in many situations, the materiality of the monetary object may *not* obviously 'mean' much – it may not matter – for the very reason that powerful, performative socio-technical assemblies exist to render their material properties of little relevance to everyday users. For example, the physical properties of banknotes will often appear to be inconsequential for the average user. There is some inconvenience of having to visit ATMs to obtain them; they may be lost or damaged; they may render a wallet or purse a little bulky. These are, however, likely to be experienced as relatively minor nuisances and are ameliorated by the contemporary reliance on a wide range of monetary storage and transaction devices, ranging from electronic payment cards to digitally accessible bank accounts. However, I have argued that, in the case of specific forms of consumer credit borrowing, the material properties of monetary media certainly can matter. Monetary objects *always* retain the capacity, under certain conditions, to become directly implicated in causal effects that are generated co-constitutively with their users. This can even extend to cash: in informal or grey economies its physical properties may matter greatly, with the potential for issues to arise concerning its secure storage or its depreciation if it cannot be successfully transformed into an appreciating asset. How, exactly, a particular monetary medium comes into presence is an outcome of range of interconnecting relations, operating in and between a diverse range of registers. These can be human, material, conceptual, or pertain to entities that sit at the crossings of each.

In the examples that I have presented, we have seen monetary objects become attached to the functions they perform, including to whether they transfer value instantly (cash), quickly (debit card), or from the future to the present (credit card). They have become attached to the tactilities associated with different devices, or to the everyday practicalities of either being forced to match a physical and material process – counting out money – to a calculative process, in the case of cash, or not, in the case of payment cards. They become attached to different everyday habits and routine practices that form part of the embodied experience of moving through spaces of consumption: using cash can simply feel more calculative than using cards; handing over a credit card and not subjecting the act to much in the way of cognitive interrogation, on the other hand, can feel near-automatic. Finally, those mediums in which the transfer of value is not instantaneous also become attached to devices – bank or credit statements – that aim to 'restore' some of the calculative apparatus that may be absent at the point of purchase. As we've seen there is absolutely no guarantee that this attempt is successful. This is because, despite attempts to render consumer credit, and the consumer credit statement 'transparent', it cannot escape its dependency on the incalculable, on life's irreducible uncertainty (Knight 1921). In particular, for those users who do not have the financial means to make full payment or, as many do, make only the minimum payment, the future is going to become yet more opaque. The lending organisation of course has a range of devices at its disposal to disentangle or 'detach' as yet unknown future actions that could jeopardise the stability of the consumer credit-user interaction, including contractual obligations, credit referencing agencies, arbitration services, and late payment fees. However, from the user's point of view, it is perhaps only by cutting up his or her credit cards that the future, as represented in the credit card statement, becomes quantitatively calculable.

To really understand the dynamics of these devices and the 'curious sort of subconscious forms of temptation' that credit cards offer, we may, however, require further intellectual resources. I began this chapter by suggesting that a device-oriented approach might have its limits. The material that I've highlighted here points towards some of these. We've seen repeatedly that when it comes to the way these devices are wrapped up in the everyday of borrowers they come into intimate intersection with embodied lives, with feelings, emotions, with forms of action that seem pre-cognitive and at the limits of empirical observation. As outlined in the book's introduction, these are dimensions that much of the work on devices has struggled to grasp. Therefore, and to 'think with' some of the propositions provided to us by the philosopher Alfred North Whitehead, I want to suggest that we consider credit cards, and indeed many of the credit devices that this book will explore, as *lures for feeling*.[24] Introducing Whitehead's particular processual account of life and associated conceptual apparatus will be crucial in opening up questions to which the rest of this book will continue to respond: that is, how to account not only for the interactions between people and things, but also the *manner* of these interactions.

Lures for feeling

In the English language, the roots of the term 'lure' can be traced back to the four-teenth century, where we find it being used to refer to the lures used in falconry. As distant from the concerns of this book as this etymological association is, the prac-tice of assembling and training birds to use these devices is particularly helpful in exploring what lures are and what they do. Take the following mid nineteenth century work on the topic (whose title page makes plain its colonial ambition: to expand Victorian British empire into the skies: 'dominion over fowls of the air'!).

> The *lure* may be made in several ways, any of which will answer the purpose. For instance, take a heavy piece of wood, and cut it into somewhat the form of a horseshoe, which may weigh about 1½lb. At the two ends fasten the wings of a pigeon, as that will probably be the bird to which you will first 'enter' [i.e. introduce] your young hawks. Through the sides bore holes, and pass strings through them, by which, when the lure is in use, food can be attached. Red cloth may or may not, as you please, be nailed onto a portion of the sides. In the centre of the curve, at the outside, fix a ring; and to this ring fasten the strap of a shot-belt by its swivel. [...]
>
> The nestlings standing on the lid, eagerly attentive to your whistle [...], gently place the lure, well covered with beef, in the midst of the hungry creatures. Encourage them to peck at it – constantly, however, supplying them with the choicest pieces from the hand. On the next occasion swing the lure round your head as you approach, taking care, however, not to alarm them; they will soon place this movement in their list of signs which denote a full meal.
>
> (Freeman and Salvin 1859, p. 60; original emphasis)

The purpose of a lure in falconry is not to act as edible bait, but rather to be a device that will attract the bird's attention and then encourage them to return to the falconer's glove (hence the feeding at this stage of 'choice pieces' of meat by hand). However in order to be able to do so, a quite complex set of relations need to be first established between non-humans, people and things. The device, as is described here, has to be shaped and decorated for the specific task in hand. On the part of the birds, in their journey to adulthood, the lure is to be a familiar companion, with the intention being that eventually, and of course only when swung in a certain way and in certain settings, their attraction to the lure becomes near automatic. In order for that to happen, the trainer has to engage in a long process of bringing the relations between bird, lure, and human ever closer. These relations are not projections onto objects and things, but – and here the specific terminology of falconry is apt – *enter* these respective beings, what could also be considered a process of 'enfolding' (a term that will become par-ticularly relevant in the next chapter).

But there is a fourth actor here: food – or, sometimes, its promise. To draw the birds to the lure, it has, initially, to be covered in food. This is then gradually withdrawn over time, so that ultimately the only possible reward that will come from the falconer is that which is in the hand that holds the lure. Although it is eventually withdrawn, the lure has to *become something akin* to the meat. This is not ultimately a case of physically transferring properties (smells, tastes, etc.) from food to lure. What needs to change are the relationships that surround bird, lure and food. The bird and the lure and the food need to come to matter to one another in new, subtly different ways than was previously the case. For this to happen, each of the parties has to be adapted (even the trainer: the glove, the particular set of calls, holding or not holding food, body language, etc.) to fit the other, with these adaptations occurring through connected moments of experience. In the process, on every successive occasion, each becomes something slightly, but significantly, different.

This is a process that could be described in Pavlovian terms, as an example of human-animal conditioning. However, this is an analytical framework that would reduce the focus to transformations that occur across a very narrow set of registers, involving animals being seen to be transformed by their repeated encounter with (responses to) objects (stimuli) formatted according to human aims and non-human drives. What this would obscure are the far more extensive set of relationally constituted transformations that are being put into play. It is worth here drawing a connection to Gilles Deleuze and Felix Guattari's famous image of the relational coming together of always mutually adapting wasp and orchid (or their less well known example of the snapdragon and bumblebee) in which 'the two becomings interlink and form relays in a circulation of intensities' (Deleuze and Guattari 1987, p. 10). Here both entities become together and become entangled in and amongst one another. Deleuze and Guattari imagine this occurring over evolutionary time. In the case of the encounter between lure and bird, however, we can see these changes in single lives, through processes in which both have to be made to become relevant, made to matter, to each other.[25] As Nigel Thrift puts it, '[n]early all action is reaction to joint action, to being-as-a pair, to the digestion of the intricacies of talk, body language, even an ambient sense of the situation to hand' (2007, p. 7). This situation does not, therefore, involve humans simply putting lures in front of birds in order to illicit a desired set of increasingly automated responses but rather the creation and constant mutual readjustment of at least six interrelated pairs: bird-food, bird-lure, bird-human, lure-human, lure-food, and human-food. Both the changes in things, and their achievement of apparent fixity, are constituted through activities that are mutual, relational and processual, through attachments that can bind as much as they can loosen.

The way I have described these mutual dependencies is designed to highlight the interest in ontological character of things, practices and processes that I am pursuing in this book (see Marres 2009b, 2012; Woolgar and Lezaun 2013). This sees combinations of relations as constantly generating new entities and ways of being and living with one another, a style of analysis and empirical attention that questions the apparent closure and autonomy of things. Being attentive to processes of ontological (re)composition is not to claim privileged access to a 'better' understanding of world, but rather, as Steve Woolgar and Javier Lezaun put it, to aim 'to interfere with the assumption of a singular, ordered world, and to do so by re-specifying hefty meta-physical questions in mundane settings and in relation to apparently stabilized objects' (Woolgar and Lezaun 2013, p. 323).

What, then, might this kind of processual, relational, ontologically sensitive analysis of the lure and, ultimately, the lure of certain credit devices look like? One of Alfred North Whitehead's creations can help here – itself a new form of 'joint action', a new 'being-as-a-pair', to echo Thrift – and that is his joining of 'lure' to 'feeling': *lure for feeling*. To understand the relationships that this conjoined pair implies, we have to delve a little into Whitehead's own ontology.

For Whitehead, in a move that foreshadowed and has influenced the work of influential figures in contemporary social theory (e.g. Latour 1996; Deleuze 2001; Stengers 2011) as well as the style of analysis I just outlined, the entities and processes that make up the world, both apparently inert and organic, needed to be radically reconsidered. Put simply, 'reality' is not an entity onto which humans project their understanding and analysis, but rather something that is continually reinventing itself through, and with, an extraordinary wide range of entities. Rather than the world being populated with disconnected sets of entities, things of all sorts are constantly 'experiencing' (in a much broader sense than is usually understood) mutual interaction and 'becoming with' and into one-another (for an excellent and far fuller exploration of this, which I draw on in part here, see Halewood 2011). To use another of Whitehead's terms, entities are engaging in a constant process of 'prehension' – that is, grasping for one another (this can also be compared to movements of 'unfolding' and 'enfolding', as will be explored in the next chapter). Thus, while I am interested in the place of human experience in the composition of consumer credit, including the role of emotion and affect, the book's empirical scope is broader, informed less by phenomenology than an attempt to attend to generic forms of relational, prehending experience.

It is this diverse and relational approach that informs Whitehead's understanding of the 'lure for feeling'. Lures are elements in experience that exert a push and/or pull towards to some form of novel engagement with the world. Whitehead, perhaps because he is a philosopher, is particularly interested in the role 'theory' can play in such processes. Theories are, Whitehead asserts, prehensions and can thus act as lures. To illustrate what he means by both theory and the pull of a lure for feeling he uses the example of an audience watching Hamlet's 'To be, or not to be … ' soliloquy. The power of the speech, he asserts, cannot be understood in representational terms – that is, whether or not the existential question raised by Hamlet corresponds to an underlying truth (or not). Rather 'at some point in the reading, judgement is eclipsed by aesthetic delight. The speech, for the theatre audience, is purely theoretical, a mere lure for feeling' (Whitehead 1978, p. 185).

As should be clear from this example, Whitehead, as so often, adopts a non-conventional terminology. A 'theory' does not have to stem from high philosophy, but can be any intervention that exerts a draw on an entity or set of entities towards novelty – in this example, the theory is the soliloquy, the entity being lured is a theatre audience and one of the things which emerges as novel is the experience of aesthetic delight. The lure is not *in its own right* a powerful causal force (it is, as he says, after all a 'mere' lure for feeling) but rather allows entities to alter their manner of interaction with one another and thus for these entities to become *differently*.

By invoking *Hamlet* Whitehead shifts the territory of theory from philosophy to theatre. However we can push him into territory that is yet more mundane. Even a credit card can be understood as 'theoretical' in a Whiteheadian sense: at the precise moment at which it comes to matter to a user enough for him or her to reach out towards it, for its capacity to provide access to the possibility of funds in the present that otherwise might not be available until a future moment, it exerts a lure towards a novel set of possibilities. It provides, in Whitehead's terms, an otherwise unrealisable mode of engagement with the world. It provides access, in other words, to novel experience.

In this context, the following account of the role of lure for feelings seems apt: 'the primary function of theories is as a lure for feeling, thereby providing *immediacy of enjoyment and purpose*' (1978, p. 184; emphasis added). The point is not that consumer credit operates through enjoyment conceived in terms of the pull of unfettered, hedonistic consumption (see Daniel Miller's (1998) critique of such work within consumption studies). It is rather that, for the borrower, the use of consumer credit offers an *ease* to the pressures of the present. In the process, a new pair is born: the human-borrower. In the formation of this pair, the aim, the 'purpose', of consumer credit begins to become realised.

Economic encounters thus often work not through force but through lures. If there is 'grasping' happening in the consumer credit market, it is, to draw on Liz McFall's terms, 'not a high pressure choke-hold, but to engage, to gear, in the manner of establishing a connection that makes the exchange move forward' (McFall 2014, p. 90). This process of mutual grasping and the achievement of connection (Deleuze might say folding) does not necessarily mean that things are constantly changing. Rather novelty (the fact that things will never quite be as they once were – they may, however, be very similar) needs to be understood as intimately connected to dynamics of both repetition (of what was into what will now be).[26] As Whitehead puts it – and again, it should be noted that experience here is not something that he intends to be understood as limited to human, or even organic subjectivity: '*experience* involves a becoming, that becoming means *something becomes*, and that *what becomes* involves *repetition* transformed into *novel immediacy*' (Whitehead 1978, pp. 136–137; original emphasis).[27] To really get at what Whitehead is driving at you have to go with his emphasis: experience always results in something becoming; exactly what this something is, its particular quality, results from both a renewing of what was previous, with something other and different also being rendered present.

It is in this context that Whitehead invokes the idea of 'feeling' as speaking to these kinds of ongoing, dynamic processes of becoming/prehension/interrelatedness. As Halewood writes:

For Whitehead, that which is prehended is not inert matter, instead, prehensions are the *feeling* of another entity. Again, Whitehead has chosen a surprising term to explain his conceptual construction. The term 'feeling' would seem to invoke a whole host of humanly subjectivist notions; emotions, irrationality and so on. In one sense this is exactly what Whitehead is attempting to do. He is trying to shock us out of our scientistic, materialist complacency by insisting on the quality of experience which inhabits all experiences.

(Halewood 2011, p. 31; original emphasis)

All sorts of things are thus feeling and experiencing – as long as we hold onto Whitehead's quite particular understanding of both of those terms. As Halewood later puts it, '[it] is not to anthropomorphize to state that coal experiences warmness, or diamonds adamantineness, or charcoal flakiness, though it is to stretch language and thought beyond its normal bounds' (2011, p. 98). With specific reference to the concept of feeling, this has the effect of broadening our understanding of its role in social life.

While Whitehead's notion of feeling, like with his understanding of experience, is not humanist, echoes from this legacy may be important. Some parallels at this point may be drawn to Raymond Williams' more classical cultural theory and his attention to the social role of feeling. A 'structure of feeling', for Williams, is used to denote 'a particular quality of social experience' – a quality that is hard to detect by an individual given its position 'at the very edge of semantic availability', that is transmitted through everyday life, that is emergent and ever changing, and that is shaped according to the conditions at a particular historical juncture (Williams 1977, pp. 131–134). It is this aspect of Williams' work that has been taken up and developed by a number of more contemporary theorists of affect (e.g. Anderson 2012; Berlant 2011; Grossberg 2010). Feeling, from Williams' perspective, as something transmitted through and from human lived experience, is a crucial part of the glue that ties the small scale and personal to the larger and distributed scene of social life. Williams' work is important in making a strong case for the role of feeling, in a more conventional sense, in shaping the conditions of everyday life. It is important not to lose sight of this – as we will see in the following chapters, understanding the felt, emotional experience of everyday human life is crucial to understanding the lived economies of consumer credit default. However, it will also be important to appreciate the degree to which Whitehead radically extends the canvas upon which feeling can be experienced: feeling may well be transmitted through the everyday; it is certainly emergent, ever-changing, and historically contingent – but it is and can be all of these things among a collection of entities that *should by no means be limited to the human* (or the organic, or the sentient, etc.).

This, then, brings us back to the credit card which we can now more confidently identify, following Whitehead, as a 'lure for feeling'. The 'curious and sort of subconscious temptation' it offers can now be better understood as a reaching out, a prehension, a grasping of consumer credit device to consumer credit user. Just because it is shoved in a drawer somewhere, does not mean that these prehensions do not happen – it exerts a weak but significant force, which retains the potential to strengthen if the person that shoved it in somewhere *feels* ... the curiosity, the necessity, the desperation, the temptation, the obligation ... to open the drawer, pull it out, and start to use it to borrow. The sorehead, to return to the terms above, is in many ways the same. But something has happened: the sorehead, in a flash of 'novel immediacy', *has become a borrower*. And when this happens, what does the credit card become? And what does it feel, in a Whiteheadian sense? We can speak for it: it has become a working credit card. And it feels: *used*.

Conclusion

Writing from a behavioural economics perspective, Oren Bar-Gill describes the credit card as a 'complex, multi-attribute product': it is 'a bundle of different products and services', he writes, continuing, '[t]he credit card bundles together transacting and borrowing services. It also implements intertemporal bundling, where borrowing now is bundled with borrowing later' (2006, pp. 48–49).[28] This helps to point towards the fact that consumer credit products of all kinds combine a variable mesh of borrowing services, potentially including present borrowing, the possibility of future borrowing and – to extend Bar-Gill's description a little – the easy management of potentially large past debts, as long as minimum payments are made on time.

Complementing these 'attributes' – which we might also think of as 'properties' or 'qualities' – are a range of devices specifically designed to operate in and through the everyday lives of borrowers. This chapter has focused on the most high profile of consumer credit's borrowing devices – the credit card – as well as briefly highlighting the role of its indispensible Other: the credit statement. As I will come on to argue (see Chapter 5), the latter should in fact be understood as having as much to do with collecting debt as extending credit.

However, neither quality nor device are stable, given entities. When forms of consumer credit extend out the moment of exchange, they offer affordances for multiple and highly variable relations and attachments. These include the future actions of borrowers themselves, which are an intimate part of the bundle of features that compose consumer credit. This is exemplified in the charging of interest, with the level at which it is set being (in theory at least) the result of a calculation that attempts to pre-empt the distributed consequences of potential future actions by all the borrowers associated with that product. But, as we'll see much more in what follows, it also includes potential unintended attachments: to other household members, to specific points of domestic architecture – the letter box, the phone, folders and storage boxes, to name but a few – to particular emotional states, to particular spaces, futurities, pasts, spaces of anticipation, feelings of shame and regret, to ill health, to job loss, to a lack of calculative know-how/desire, or to a sheer over-optimistic assessment of future earnings prospects. These relations, these 'feelings' – in an expanded Whiteheadian sense – and many more besides, can all come to compose consumer credit under certain circumstances.

This is the work that is done by thinking with the lure of devices, with their processual reaching outs, with their mutually formatted entanglement with other entities. It can help bring a richness to accounts of the role played by devices in social and economic settings. It also brings the distinctiveness of a device-sensitive account of market operations as compared to policy-oriented accounts into sharper view, with the former attending to a broader set of actors (both human and non-human) and being far more open to the possibility of their inter-penetration. Considering credit cards, and indeed many consumer credit devices, as potential lures for feeling is not meant to enact a wholesale redistribution of the causal relationships that prompt people to borrow. It would not only be empirically untenable, but also an analytical absurdity to deny a range of inter-secting forces or, to stay with the more dynamic scheme I have proposed, lures. Poverty, money management skills, attitudes to credit, attitudes to consumption, the cost of credit, its convenience and availability, how it is marketed and pre-sented, regulatory and consumer protection frameworks: each of these, and many more besides, have the potential to become tangled up in experience. Each may shape and be shaped by the range of the other objects, devices and statements about the world that make up everyday life. Each in turn becomes bound up in sets of causal trajectories that, in varying ways – at different historical junctures, in different places, in different lived contexts, with different forces, and always in dynamic relation with one another – contribute towards shaping the vast, complex and expanding global landscape of consumer credit that continues to unfold around us. What the focus on the lure of the device does, however, is shift attention to an under appreciated aspect of the *quality* of consumer credit borrowing: *how* it occurs, through which types of encounter, through which enti-ties, and with which aspects of lived experience.

As we'll see in the next chapter, when it comes not to borrowing but instead to default, this perspective may be particularly valuable in helping us to under-stand the lived character of default – and, more specifically, in answering the question: how are we to understand market attachment when detachment, even if desired, appears extremely difficult? Answering this question will also bring a Whiteheadian attention to questions of feeling into closer proximity with ques-tions of affect. For, when it comes to borrowing, affect can be a rather subtle force; when it comes to default, it becomes harder to miss.

Notes

1 The story drew on survey results that seemed to show that, of the total amount spent on credit cards in the EU, UK citizens were accruing 75 per cent. A more reliable comparative analysis is presented in Chapter 3, Figure 3.1.
2 See also: Caplovitz (1968; 1974), Klein (1999). Rock (1973), Sullivan *et al.* (1999; 2000).
3 For more on transparency as a regulatory ideal, see, for example: Brown and Michael (2002); Muniesa *et al.* (2008).

4 See European Parliament & Council of the European Union (2008, pp. 67–69).
5 This includes reviews conducted under both Labour and Conservative-Liberal Democrat administrations. For instance, in the early 2000s, the then Department of Trade and Industry published 'Fair, clear and competitive', a review which dedicated a whole chapter to the problem of 'Establishing a Transparent Market' (Department of Trade and Industry 2003, pp. 29–42). Or there is the more recent review that focuses specifically on the relationship between consumer credit and personal insolvency, which, as the Ministerial foreword suggests, on the one hand aims to enable 'all consumers to be empowered to make better choices for themselves', while on the other 'working with the industry to address consumer concerns about lack of control and transparency' (Department for Business Innovation & Skills 2011, p. 3).
6 Drawing variously on Black *et al.* (2009), Law and Smullen (2008) and Moles and Terry (2005).
7 This is in part of course a function of the role in publishing of picture editors, photo libraries and so forth. Examples include: Ritzer's *Expressing America: A critique of the global credit card society* (1995), Manning's *Credit card nation* (2000), or the imagery on the covers of Burton's *Credit and consumer society* (2008), Langley's *The everyday life of global finance* (2008b), and Marron's *Consumer credit in the United States* (2009).
8 September 2011–August 2013: Monthly average: 64.8 per cent (Bank of England 2013b, author's calculations).
9 September 2011–August 2013: Average percentage: 74.8 per cent (Bank of England 2013b, author's calculations).
10 September 2011–August 2013: Average percentage: 71.2 per cent (securitised assets excluded, drawing on G.19. dataset from the Federal Reserve Bank of the United States (2013a; 2013b, author's calculations).
11 On the neglect of money as an object of social scientific research in its own right, see, amongst others, Carruthers and Ariovich (2010), Dodd (1994), Gilbert (2005), Hart (2000), Ingham (2004), Maurer (2006), Zelizer (1994).
12 Notable exceptions include: Langley (2008b), Leyshon and Thrift (1999) and Poon (2007; 2009).
13 Here and in the historical analysis that follows I draw in part on some earlier work of mine, on the history and material significance of the plastic credit card as a transactional monetary object (Deville 2013b).
14 The practice was repeated in the UK. As Ian Martin documents, the first British mass market credit card, the Barclaycard, not only used technology licensed from Bank of America (see Chapter 4), but also quite deliberately adopted its marketing tactics: in 1966 1.25 million credit cards were sent, unsolicited, to customers and associates that branch managers had 'recommended might be suitable for the card' (Martin 2010, p. 189). Martin notes that initially 'there were not enough envelopes available in the country for the mailshot, and when even more envelopes were imported from Germany, the mail service in Northampton was overwhelmed by the volume of post' (Martin 2010, pp. 189–190). The 'race' was somewhat less frantic, however, with credit cards being initially largely spread via Barclay's own customer base (Worthington 2001, p. 487).
15 See Callon (1998b); Callon *et al.* (2002); Callon and Muniesa (2005); McFall (2009a); Muniesa *et al.* (2007); Muniesa (2009).
16 I will not use the term 'qualculation' to describe each such instance of qualitative/quantitative practice, but will rather draw on this language when a discussion of the assessment of quality becomes particularly pertinent.
17 As comprehensively summarised by Çalışkan and Callon (2009; 2010).
18 Themes also explored by Ariel Wilkis (2013) in a book that examines how differentiated monies become tied to credit and debt relations.

19 Sociologists have tended to be sceptical of such research, given it often comes with significant disciplinary baggage. At worst, behavioural psychology can involve a denial of the formative and dynamic role of social life and a reduction of human action to innate behavioural traits. However, what I am collecting in this chapter are traces of the ways monetary objects disturb the passage of life. I am happy to be open as to the methods and approaches that might detect such traces; arguments about the exact causal mechanisms that are in play can be put aside for another day.

20 Some punctuation added for clarity.

21 I mainly mention this in the spirit of interdisciplinary diplomacy – James' pragmatism has been a touchstone amongst major currents within social theory (e.g. Latour 2010; Stengers 2011) and the analysis of affect (e.g. Brennan 2004; Connolly 2002; Massumi 2002).

22 It was not possible to reproduce these visuals, for copyright reasons.

23 Figures 1.1a and 1.1b: writer's own photographs, London Victoria station, May 2008.

24 A process of inevitable 'experimentation and putting to the test', as described by Isabelle Stengers (2011, p. 253).

25 I am thinking here of doctoral research recently completed at Goldsmiths by Martin Savransky on the question of relevance in social theory, in particular in relation to the philosophy of Alfred North Whitehead. This is related to the question of what makes creations 'count' (see Savransky 2012). This approximates to Isabelle Stengers' interrogation of how entities come to 'matter' (see Stengers 2005).

26 This is a sketch that is, as I say, simplified. I have reduced this to an understanding of process grounded in changes over time, however it should properly understood to be occurring across a range of modalities, including both time and space (that are themselves also continually being (re)constituted through such processes).

27 I have tried to avoid delving into too much Whiteheadian theory. However, it is worth being absolutely clear that Whitehead, in a move that appears on the face of it to fly in the face of much philosophy and social theory, extends the potential for subjectivity, and indeed 'society', to all entities.

28 As Franck Cochoy (2012) has noted, many products that seem cohesive might in fact be thought of as 'bundles' along these lines or, to bring this closer to the language of recent debates within economic sociology, 'assemblages' or 'agencements' (see Callon 2005; Lury 2009; McFall 2009b).

2 In the fold of default

Living with market attachments

> We understand nothing about impasses of the political without having an account of the production of the present.
>
> (Berlant 2011, p. 4)

This chapter explores the increasingly uncomfortable everyday life of default.[1] It analyses encounters between defaulting credit borrowers and the organisations designed to collect the outstanding debt, which we can group under a terminological umbrella: debt collectors.[2] In later chapters we will look at their organisational work. However, if we move to into these organisations too hastily there is a danger of misunderstanding the character of the domain that is the object of so much of their endeavour.

As the last chapter showed, the lending devices of consumer credit work in part by acting as 'lures for feeling', by easing the passage of borrowers into otherwise unrealisable modes of engagement with the world. The price paid for grasping these lures is partly financial, in the shape of the gradual application of interest to a loan. However, there is also an ontological price: the transformation of a person into a borrower. The borrower is a hybrid figure, an amalgam of a particular individual and a particular socio-economic technology. For many, this hybrid life may be uneventful: repayments proceed without incident and the borrower may ultimately succeed in uncoupling this aspect of their hybrid existence as a loan is paid off. For some, however, things take a different turn: the set of connections, of attachments, that were set into motion the moment a credit card was used, or a loan was taken out, becomes harder to coexist with. Repayment amounts start to exceed disposable income, penalty charges start to accrue, and payments start to be missed. If this continues, a new ontological shift occurs as the borrower becomes a defaulter. The result is to begin to confront a different set of lures, designed not to encourage borrowing but repayment. Oriented in particular around two technologies of mass contact – the letter and the telephone call (although these are increasingly being supplemented by electronic means: emails and text messages, for example) – they are also not formatted to ease life but to render it uncomfortable.

Thinking with the lure helps in attending to the emergent and processual character of the relationships between entities. When it comes to describing how these relations operate in and through the intimate and bodily domains of human experience, this can be complemented by an account of the role played by what we can call the 'affective'. From this point forwards in the book, affect will be a central analytical category. As we will see in the next chapter, the importance of successfully harnessing the potential of affect has long been a concern of the collections industry (even if it does not refer to its interest in these terms). In this chapter I introduce why this might be the case, while putting affect into dialogue with some of the conceptual and methodological apparatus developed by the economisation programme and related work within science and technology studies. This includes examining the role played by devices of consumer credit collection, while being concerned with how aspects of a life in default come to form an association with one another, how they come to matter to each other and in what way.[3] This means exploring empirically how the modes of implication of debtors' involvements in the consumer credit market become charged, via the mutual grasping of debtors and technologies of debt collection in the shared space of the life of default.

Exploring the lived character of default, as it is mutually constituted with and through range of material devices will help provide an answer to the question that I ended the previous chapter with: how are we to understand market attachment when detachment, even if desired, appears extremely difficult? Answering this question will involve bringing some further conceptual resources to bear on the problem. The first is a way of describing a specific movement of attachment. Here I draw on Deleuze's account of the fold as a helpful way of pointing to what is at stake in the attachments surrounding debt default. The second is to put more pressure on the concept of market attachment, as it has been formulated by the economisation programme. What analytical possibilities does it offer? What does it foreclose? How does it relate to alternate understandings of what attachments are and what they do? It is with this second set of questions that I begin.

Markets, attachments, folding

As I argued in the last chapter, forms of consumer credit need to be understood as products that offer affordances for multiple and highly variable connections and attachments, including the future of borrowers themselves. Although the shape of the future is unknown to the borrower at the point of borrowing, as it moves from that which is to come, to that which is lived in the present, and in due course into the past, it becomes an intimate part of the variably enacted bundle or assemblage that is consumer credit.

What this points to is that market attachment – certainly in the case of consumer credit, but actually in the case of many if not all consumer objects – is a distributed process, involving multiple moments, places and practices through which notional 'consumers' (sometimes borrowers, sometimes defaulters) are approached or encouraged to in some way engage with their consumer credit product.[4] The act of attachment is thus not a one-off event, but a process that needs to be continually refreshed.

This processual understanding of market attachment can be detected in writing within the economisation programme, in particular in discussions concerning how attachment sits in dialogue with its indispensible twin: detachment. As Callon *et al.* write, within markets, this double movement is of central importance:

> All attachment is constantly threatened. This mechanism is central in the question under consideration here. Competition between firms occurs precisely around this dialectic of attachment and detachment. Capturing, 'attaching' consumers by 'detaching' them from the networks built by rivals is the mainspring of competition.
>
> (Callon *et al.* 2002, p. 205)

From this perspective, competition is framed as the battle between producers to secure attachments with customers – potentially by detaching them from their rivals. Each producer that has successfully instigated an attachment is, in turn, seen as constantly threatened by the consumer's detachment and subsequent reattachment to a competitor.

Some have detected in this formulation an echo of more normative accounts of market activity. This is certainly the suggestion in Daniel Miller's critique of Callon. He argues that

> Callon writes from the basis of an economists' vision, which has at its heart the assumption that most transactions within the capitalist word are indeed market transactions and that his task is to understand the mechanisms that allow them to work as markets.
>
> (2002, p. 219)

The effect is to ignore how, following Polanyi and Granovetter, so-called 'economic' considerations are bound up and entangled in a far more extensive set of social and cultural forces (p. 227). Part of his suggestion is that what Callon's account misses are the 'upstream' processes that lead consumer and producer to meet in the first place, as well as format their particular mode of engagement.

Perhaps in response to such critiques, there has been a shift in the work of Callon and those he writes with, to take into account a fuller span of the socio-material processes of adjustment between consumer and producer (for example: Çalışkan and Callon 2010; Callon 2005; Callon and Muniesa 2005). As Fabian Muniesa suggests, these might be particularly associated with the work of marketing and branding – as well as the management of any continued attachments between buyer and seller after a sale is complete, whether relating to a continued claim to intellectual property rights over a product, or any social bonds that might shape a buyer's continued engagement with a particular purchase (2009, p. 129).

This process of ongoing adjustment does not, however, pertain only to the things and experiences that are put in front of buyers. In this respect, Liz McFall brings out a parenthetic comment from Callon and Muniesa: 'through objectification, the object becomes a thing, and through singularization, it becomes "a thing whose properties are adjusted to the buyer's world, *if necessary by transforming that world*"' (McFall 2009a, p. 271; McFall's emphasis; citing Callon and Muniesa 2005). Similarly, Muniesa *et al.* write that '[t]he ways in which market devices are tinkered with, adjusted and calibrated affect the ways in which *persons and things* are translated into calculative and calculable beings' (Muniesa *et al.* 2007, p. 5; emphasis added). In both of these quotations there is an implicit call for the analysis of market calibration to retain a symmetrical attention to the role of both objects and people. In other words, those interested in following processes of market attachment should be concerned with the ontologies not just of market settings, but also of the people that populate these settings. This is important for, as we'll see, the degree and mode of mobility of people in and out of markets is by no means a given, but is rather subject to a quite specific ontological politics (see Marres 2009; Mol 2002; Woolgar and Lezaun 2013; Woolgar and Neyland 2013). However, given that the full span of the work of the economisation programme is not even-handed in its attention, the call for symmetry is somewhat rhetorical (see also Cochoy 2008; Entwistle and Slater 2014; Langley 2008b; Moor 2012).[5]

I thus want to make a case for an economic sociology that is sensitive to the social and material formatting not only of market settings but also people's lives. People – how they live, feel and act – matter as much to markets as markets do to people. However much I am drawn to the economisation programme for its ability to account for the consequential effects of potentially quite intimate, quite mundane things, devices and processes in markets, the intimate formatting of life has been bracketed from many of its accounts.[6]

One of the reasons for this – and here there is an echo of Miller's critique, although the object of my discomfort is slightly different to his – is a sometimes overly instrumental account of processes of attachment. A closer attention needs to be paid to how process and devices that are explicitly designed to compose and recompose the connections between market actors – for the sake of simplicity, what I will continue to refer to as 'market attachments' – intersect with and are composed and are recomposed by the range of other attachments that compose life. Following the precise ways in which markets knit into the fabric of everyday life will enabler a thicker account of the production of the present which, as Lauren Berlant calls for, may help open up what she calls 'impasses of the political' (see the citation at the top of this chapter). One such impasse is how to account, analytically, for the relationship between people and markets – as the debate between Callon and Miller demonstrates, this remains an open question, one sitting within a far longer history of disagreement about how the social and the economic are interrelated.

It is to Berlant, and to a number of other writers who draw on currents within feminist and queer theory,[7] to whom I look to try to develop a more nuanced understanding of lived and ambivalent quality of processes of attachment.[8] Building on earlier theoretical work undertaken by Judith Butler (1997), Berlant

(2006; 2011) attends to attachments characterised by what she calls a 'cruel optimism': these can be characterised as oriented around a relationship of desire towards an object ('the good life', for instance, or a particular political project) that ultimately engenders a relationship of harm towards the desiring person. These are attachments that bind a person to a particular condition of life, not just despite the harm involved, but often because of it.[9] In Berlant, as in Butler,[10] attachment is a way to describe not just generic movements of connection and disconnection, but a particular kind of movement, concerned with often only partially conscious desires and drives, with emotion, and with the ways in which bodies are push and pulled in one direction or another. These are, then, attachments that are analysed as they operate through affect.[11]

Attending to attachments that operate through the bodily and the affective is to shift the registers through which to understand the encounters between people and markets. Berlant does some of this work herself in her analysis of a variety of market-influenced settings – including those affected by relations of debt, as well as (amongst others) relations of consumption and labour – and, in the process, succeeds in capturing the visceral, often painful, and differentially distributed bodily attachments that can compose contemporary economies, such as the fatigue and 'slow death' of low income workers' bodies (Berlant 2011, pp. 95–119). Within the economisation programme, these might be accounted for as 'overflows' of the market – drawing on its actor-network theory heritage, the task then becomes to analyse how and whether or not these overflows achieve the status of a political 'object of concern' (see Callon 1998a). While this might be an interesting project in its own right, Berlant is more interested in how exactly bodies are shaped by their intersection with the processes and forms of violence that characterise key aspects of many contemporary economies.

This set of work can also contribute towards an analysis of the precise manner in which bodies become shaped and formatted through processes of market attachment. Sara Ahmed makes the processual character of attachment absolutely clear, which she characterises in terms of movement:

> What moves us, what makes us feel, is also that which holds us in place, or gives us a dwelling place. Hence movement does not cut the body off from the 'where' of its inhabitance, but connects bodies to other bodies: attachment takes place through movement, through being moved by the proximity of others.
>
> (Ahmed 2004, p. 17)

Attachments are constituted and reconstituted in the very instance of movement: in those moments, those situations, when an encounter between a person and another person, or a person and a particular setting, change the relationships that are in play between them. With respect to bodies, Ahmed argues that these movements, these shifts, occur through occasions of felt, bodily intensification. She gives an example:

say I stub my toe on the table. The impression of the table is one of nega-
tion; it leaves its trace on the surface of my skin and I respond with the
appropriate 'ouch' and move away, swearing. It is through such painful
encounters between this body and other objects, including other bodies, that
'surfaces' are felt as 'being there' in the first place.

(p. 24)

Pain, the feeling at issue here, is thus a vector of intensification, which has the
effect of bringing body boundaries, bodily 'surfaces', into the domain of human
experience. In the example she gives, this occurs as a dynamic relation between
a body part – a toe – and a particular object – a table. This painful intensification
leads, in turn, to a reconfiguration of body to world, 'the reorientation of the
bodily relation to that which gets attributed as the cause of the pain' (ibid.).
Human feelings, as something that might be assumed to be personal and
'internal' and private, are, Ahmed suggests, always relational. It is this relational
aspect of life that provides the conditions for processes of connection and disconnection, attachment or, indeed, detachment (although Ahmed doesn't refer
explicitly to the latter). There is a movement away from the table, an immediate
spatial detachment, a redrawing of the boundary between entities, but at the
same time there is a new attachment generated: a memory that will, it might be
hoped, prevent such incidents in the future.

Ahmed's particular interest is in what these process of bodily reconstitution
and attachment reveal about the social interactions between (human) bodies.
However, as her toe-stubbing makes clear, this process can equally occur
between bodies and things. With this in mind, I would like to bring Ahmed's
work and her account of attachment into dialogue with another way of describing how the surfaces of bodies come to be formed and reformed through movement and that is as related to processes of *enfolding* and *unfolding*.[12]

The concept of the fold, as many readers will recognise, is drawn from Gilles
Deleuze (notably: Deleuze 1999, 2001).[13] Deleuze used it as a way of accounting
more dynamically for the relationships between matter and subjectivity and
between that which appears to be internal to things – more formally: interiority –
and that which appears to be external – exteriority.

As with Ahmed's attention to the dynamic and relationally constituted nature of
bodily surfaces, thinking in terms of folds directs attention to the movements associated with processual forms of interaction and attachment. Things – including
markets and the bodies and devices that inhabit them – however stable they appear,
are constantly being folded into other things. A table thus *enfolds* a toe-stubbed
against it (perhaps there is a mark, a trace of DNA, a toe-print, a minute shift in its
position in the room) just as the body enfolds the table, through a wound, a
memory, a modification of its trajectory. In this sense, to return to the terms used in
the last chapter, both entities may well 'feel' and 'experience' in a Whiteheadian
sense. Describing processes of composition, of combination and recombination, in
terms of movements of folding echoes this symmetrical empiricism, while attempting to disrupt the opposition between inside and outside, and to think of the surface

of things – even if apparently smooth, and even, more metaphysically, for things that are immaterial (ideas for instance) – as always existing in dynamic relationship other entities.[14] Attachments, from this perspective, would then be forms of connectivity that are being continually remade through this process. These in turn are also part of the continual remaking of what Ahmed calls surfaces or boundaries: the forms of apparent fixity that seem to render entities distinct from one another – a body as compared to a market, for instance.

As is implicit in the relational schema I have outlined so far, when it comes to understanding the specific causal role that bodies can play in particular settings or encounters, it is important to be clear that the body isn't just a sponge that absorbs an outside. This is important for two reasons. The first is that such an account would render the body as far too passive a thing, a trope that has been resisted by much feminist theory, including both Ahmed's work and Butler's (1999; 2004). The body, instead, needs to be seen as playing an active and 'creative' role in shaping the contours of the relationships within which it becomes implicated; as Vikki Bell puts it, 'the embodied *lives*' (Bell 2007, p. 104; original emphasis).[15] Thus, and second, this suggests the need to complement an account of processes of enfolding with one of *unfolding*. Unfolding is a way of describing processes of emergence, or acts of affordance, the way in which one entity reaches out to another, in the process of it becoming grasped and attached (there are echoes here, of course, with Whitehead's description of the lure for feeling, or the 'prehension'). It is this continual process of unfolding and enfolding that contributes into making the relationships, the connections, the attachments and detachments, between things as they are. As will become clear in this chapter, this is particularly helpful in enabling an account of how, precisely, defaulting bodies come to matter for the debt collector and, concomitantly, for the co-emergence of both bodily *and* calculative attention.

Helped by Ahmed, Berlant and Deleuze we now have access to a richer account of how and where attachments might come about. The image of the fold provides a way of describing the movements and processes that generate overlapping relations of attachment and detachment. It also points to the way in which processes of attachment and detachment are distributed not only across time, but across a range of different registers, with it being not only possible but likely that attachment in one register may be complemented by a detachment in another. And, echoing Ahmed's attention to the continual recomposition of bodily boundaries, it provides a way of accounting for how markets and people may, in one movement, interlock with each other or, with another, reach out to one another. From this perspective, Berlant's analysis of how markets come to matter to the embodied lives of their human participants can be understood as bearing witness to some of the consequences of the bodily enfoldings and unfoldings that surround the intersections of people and markets.

With this revised account of attachment now in place, we can begin the exploration of the particular human-market encounters that are the concern of this study. I will start with some of the processes of enfolding that characterise life in default. This will be followed by an examination of movements of unfolding.

Enfolding the market: living in anticipation

As will be explored in more detail in the next chapter, the embrace of consumer credit by the UK started in earnest in the 1980s; in recent years, British households may even have relied on credit to supplement their income to a greater extent even than their counterparts in the US (see p. 82), a country that has historically been the trailblazer for new consumer credit technologies and innovations. When it comes to consumer credit default, some comparisons with the US are also instructive. Figure 2.1 shows the recent write-off rates on consumer credit and mortgage loans in both the US and the UK. Based on data reported to central banks by lenders, these rates show the amount that a lender writes-off the value of a loan – that is, it removes it as an asset from its balance sheet – during the period, as compared to the total amount of lending that remains outstanding. If a company reports a write off rate of 10 per cent, this would therefore mean that it had deemed a tenth of its credit-based assets (which is what promises to pay by borrowers effectively are) uncollectable in the time-frame in question.

This chart is worth paying close attention to. Firstly, as a more general point of interest, it highlights the very different role played by defaults on mortgages in the two countries. Unsurprisingly, given the well-known problems experienced in the US mortgage market, part of which ended up playing a central role in the unfolding of the crisis that hit the global financial system in 2008, we can see how US mortgage default rates rose to unprecedented levels from around 2008 to 2012. However, in the UK, this was not repeated; there are many likely reasons for this – one is certainly the fact that the UK has seen nowhere near the same level of sub-prime mortgage lending as the US.

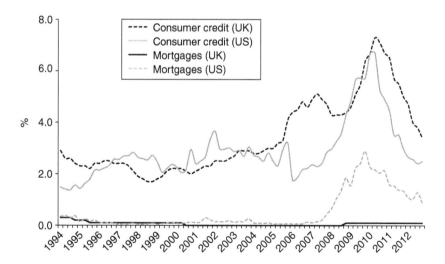

Figure 2.1 Write-off rates on consumer credit and mortgage products, UK and US, 1994–2012[16] (sources: Bank of England (2013a), Federal Reserve Bank of the United States (2014)).

This leads to the second point: that in the UK, the story of credit default is one that centres resolutely on unsecured lending – although, as the chart shows the recession also led to huge rates of default in the US; given much of the public focus in the US has been on mortgage defaults and home foreclosures, this is part of the story of the crisis that remains to be fully explored. In the UK, however, these defaults started to build as early as 2001 and accelerated rapidly from around 2005. This reflects a long-term increase in the amount of defaulting consumer credit debts in the UK, one that began to become normalised well before the first stirrings of the crisis (see also Bank of England 2010, p. 10). The UK, then, is a country that has a particularly long history of consumer credit default; the global financial crisis may have exacerbated its effects, but it appears to be in many ways an issue with its own partially unique trajectory.

Third, in both countries we can observe that default rates have fallen recently, from a peak in around 2010 (excluding UK mortgage lending that is). This is potentially a combination of two factors: the first we can be more confident about: it is well known that since the crisis hit, lenders have become far more risk-averse; put simply, they have been far more cautious about who to lend to. Lending to more reliable borrowers would indeed bring the default rate down. But there is an intriguing second possibility: and that is that lenders have got better at collecting debt. The quantitative data to substantiate this claim is lacking. However, as we will see in this chapter and those that follow (in particular Chapters 4 and 5), evidence from elsewhere suggests that this may well be the case.

The fourth observation is broader: that, behind these figures, these shifting patterns of borrowing and failed repayment, lie the stories of hundreds of thousands of people each of whom has had to live the life of default. In the UK, large numbers of debtors have been living this life for almost a decade now. In what follows, we will begin to hear a few of their accounts.

Stay a while in the life of default

Let's say you build up a debt, maybe on a credit or store card, maybe because you took out a personal loan, and you find that you're unable or unwilling to repay. Not only do you find yourself on a road towards a technical default, you find aspects of your daily home life undergoing a shift. Imagine that your telephone, perhaps also your mobile phone, formerly more or less benign carriers of conversation, become imbued with a new, unpredictable power. Each ring brings with it the possibility that the caller will ask you uncomfortable questions about the status of your debt, your income, about how and when you might repay, as well as to inform you of the consequences you might face if you don't. Imagine also that the front door, actually always quite a porous thing, becomes the passage point for sequences of collections letters that slip through the letter box to accumulate below, in a messy mix of other reminders, bills and assorted mail.

Let's also say that, like many borrowers struggling with their debts, you owe money to around half a dozen creditors (see p. 117). You took out a personal loan to consolidate a number of credit card debts. This briefly cleared the balance on these accounts, giving you some relief from the monthly pressure of having to work out how to distribute limited funds between them. But the balances slowly crept up as you found you weren't able to live quite as frugally as you thought you could, compounded by a sequence of unexpected one-off costs that forced your hand. You are now unable to meet the repayments from either the loan or the cards. You also have catalogue debts. These allowed you to put off payment for important household items like kitchen equipment or clothes, which not only seemed convenient, but also allowed you to provide for your family as you thought you should.[17]

Now all of these debts are outstanding and those tasked with collecting them are making their presence felt. Each individual collector doesn't know exactly how many other collectors are also trying to reclaim their debts from you, or how much you owe to others, but each can reasonably assume that they're not alone. For them, the pressure is on to get for their organisation what within the collections industry is often referred to as their 'share of wallet'.[18] You, however, only feel the multiplication of prompts and solicitations. Although formally individualised, they intermingle and interact to become an unstable, unpredictable and unpleasant entity that almost inevitably shapes your daily home life.

Many of their prompts come by letter. Many refer to 'legal proceedings', 'intended litigation' and you receiving a possible 'county court judgement'. One talks about a potential court order, which, if granted, would see your employer get sent a letter instructing them to direct part of your earnings toward the creditor.[19] One letter leaves little room for doubt: taking up the full width of the page and surrounded by a thick red box is some text, also in red, informing you that the letter is a NOTICE OF INTENDED LITIGATION.[20] You get used to this pressing tone: URGENT COMMUNICATION DO NOT IGNORE;[21] you MUST contact us URGENTLY;[22] PAYMENT IN FULL is required IMMEDIATELY.[23] Some letters seem kinder at times – but perhaps they are trying to make you feel guilty? 'Let us help you to repay the money that you have spent'.[24] Another lets you know they're in this for the long haul: 'This problem account will not go away or be forgotten – it makes sense to pay now'. Taking all this in over the course of many weeks combines to create a sense of what you recognise as 'stress'.[25] Perhaps your response is to nervously check the mail. Perhaps it is to actively avoid it.

Then there are the telephone calls: these don't lie in wait like the letters; they demand to be heard. In the UK, there are regulations in place designed to ensure that collection companies don't 'harass' debtors by attempting to call them constantly, but you don't know that.[26] It feels like harassment to you. In any case, given that, like many others defaulting debtors, you owe multiple debts, the combination of many collectors each trying to get in contact means that the calls keep coming. The phone mostly rings during the day, but it can be early in the morning or late in the evening. There doesn't seem to be a pattern, although you suspect that if you don't answer they try a few times in a day. Perhaps you turn to minor technological counterstrikes: employing the caller ID function on your

phone to screen out at least some of the calls, or unplugging the phone altogether. Perhaps you will change your phone number. Perhaps, however, for practical reasons, you don't: you need the number for work; you don't know how to;
you are already isolated enough and are worried people won't be able to get hold
of you.

Occasionally, though, someone catches you and you do answer the phone.
Your guard is down. Or you just give in. Or you finally feel ready to sit down
and try to do something about your situation. The conversation goes better
than you expected. The person at the other end seems nice enough. She actually offers to knock almost a third off your debt if you paid it all back today.[27]
But that's not going to happen. Not with the amount of cash you could spare.
And anyway, what would you say to the others? You spend a lot of the call
going through what money you've got coming and what's going out and on
what. She then asks if you could pay £150 a month. That's a lot. You respond
with a figure that you could maybe, just, manage: £50 maybe? She presses you
for a while. Things get a little tense when she says she's going to need at least
£100 to 'stop the action'. You're not quite sure what that means, but you know
that you really can't afford that much. Then after a while she sounds nicer
again. She says: I tell you what, I'll take £50 today and then we'll set up an
arrangement to take £100 a month after that. How does that sound? You pause.
You agree. At least that will be one off your back. You'll just have to find the
money. She did sound nice. You put the phone down, relieved. Half an hour
later the phone rings again. Is it another one? You decide not to answer.

Your stay is over

The risk that any debtor might shift from being a borrower, successfully able to
manage their debts, to a defaulter, unable to meet their repayments, is one that
the consumer credit industry is clearly well prepared for. Its diverse assembly of
workers, strategies, technologies and legal instruments incorporate multiple
means at the creditor's disposal to make sure they are dealing with the 'right'
borrowers in the 'right' way (from their point of view). Many of these are pre-
emptive mechanisms, including the assessment of creditworthiness prior to the
point of borrowing, restricting the range of borrowers that are offered credit, or
who will be granted credit, or increasing the cost of borrowing for less reliable
borrowers, as well as lowering or failing to increase an existing borrower's credit
limits. However, once an account looks like it is moving towards default, it is
the work of the collections industry that comes into view, acting as the principal
safety net that underpins much of this activity. This is an industry that is diverse
in its constituency and in which I include not just companies working externally
to the original creditor on their behalf, but also dedicated internal collections
departments located within creditor organisations (see Chapter 5).

As we saw from the brief visit to a life in default above, the vast majority of
collections work centres on two mundane technologies: the letter and the
telephone. The success of collections work depends on how these technologies

of market attachment are deployed by those working on behalf of the creditor and grasped by debtors; exactly how both are being harnessed to increasingly sophisticated techniques will be explored in due course (Chapters 3 and 4). To remain for now with the 'feeling' of default, as this foray into the intimacies of default begins to suggest, the routine encounter with these two technologies often involves a routine, ongoing experience of 'anxious anticipation'.[28] As described by Vincanne Adams, Michelle Murphy and Adele Clarke, anticipation is an increasingly commonly experienced affective state. It is characterised by a 'predictable uncertainty':

> an excited forward looking subjective condition characterized as much by nervous anxiety as a continual refreshing of yearning, of 'needing to know.' Anticipation is the palpable effect of the speculative future on the present. The anticipatory excitement of the cliff hanger as a narrative mode is as familiar as terror-inducing apocalyptic visions. *As an affective state, anticipation is not just a reaction, but a way of actively orienting oneself temporally.* Anticipation is a regime of being in time, in which one inhabits time out of place as the future.
>
> (Adams *et al.* 2009, p. 247; original emphasis)

Affect is a force that is translated through the body. In this extract it is variously an anxiety, a yearning, a terror, *a palpable effect*. Among the meanings of the Latin verb *palpare* are 'to stroke' and 'to coax'. A stroke calls forth the intimacy of touch, while coaxing, in an echo of Whitehead's 'lure', emphasises a process of establishing relationality: the bringing of a relation out of, or from, something and towards something else. Anticipation is one such feeling, an intimate, multi-dimensional process of simultaneous reaching out and grasping; not a reaction but a relation – in this case, one organising the temporality of the everyday. For defaulting debtors, anxious anticipation means, on the one hand, knowing that they will be subject to ever continuing prompts from the collectors but, on the other, not quite knowing when these will come, or how. This includes one particular, ever present indeterminacy: the potential of domestic intrusion and the expropriation of property by a bailiff, an image cut through with the imagined possibility of violence of some kind.[29] Although this is in fact often a far remoter possibility than debtors imagine (see Chapter 4), the belief that such an intrusion is possible nonetheless can contribute towards heightening an experience of anxiety.

The effects of living this life on the cusp of the future and the past, of safety and insecurity, can become significant as the effects of the devices deployed by debt collectors become enfolded. Angela, for instance, reflected that life in debt 'just feels like … fear. Feels like just a bit of fear. Like fear like someone's out to get you, or somebody can harm you, or you're in danger. I can't really explain it'. She continued later: 'it's made me more of a sad person in some ways', before later adding,

[y]eah it does, it becomes part of your life, part of your personality … it's like you've no option, you're like yeah, I'm in debt, I'm this, I'm that, I'm a woman, I live in London [laughs], I don't know, it's like almost part of who you, what you are.

The processes of being confronted on such a regular basis by the lures of the collector, their attempts to secure her attachment to her debt, accompanied by the sense that something harmful might be about to happen, transform the boundaries between Angela and the debts she is routinely being made to confront. While the legal status of the attachment of Angela to her debt may remain unaffected, an attachment operating at a far more intimate register is in the process of being strengthened. Her debt becomes folded into her – it is now, as she puts it, a *part* of her.

We can find echoes of this process of intimate enfolding and attachment in the following account, from Julie. Her debt is characterised by a particularly variable presence: sometimes felt and actively subject to cognitive work, sometimes sitting more passively in the background of life:

[Y]ou dip into different, … *your thoughts about the debt changes depending on your mood*, what you need to get, what you need to buy, how you are feeling at that time, it's, *it's not a surface level thing*, it's not like or I'm going to ignore it now from now on. It's, it's very, very reliant on how you're feeling at that moment in time. So there's a lot of subconscious, *you sort of think of debt subconsciously all the time*. It's there in the back of your mind all the time, but *you consciously choose to ignore it* at the times when you want to, because there was, there was many a time when I thought to myself look, I'm healthy, I've got two lovely children, I've got a house, I'm, I'm just not going to worry about it, because I'm going to make myself feel ill if I carry on like this. And so I would consciously stop myself from thinking about it.

(Emphasis added)

Julie's account traces a process of enfolding and unfolding through distinct registers, in which everyday life becomes marked by the unpredictable degree to which debt is present. One way she accounts for this is by drawing on the language of psychology, as involving tensions between different levels of consciousness: a conflict between the ever-presence of debt as a subconscious worry and a paradoxically conscious attempt to wish it away. A register through which her attachment to debt becomes detectable is thus cognitive. Debt is a constant liminal presence, but liable to intensify at key moments, to surface into consciousness. Moving her account away from psychology, we can thus see how her mind/body can be rethought of as having enfolded those moments where she is explicitly asked to confront her outstanding debt through, for example, letters, but also that these are constantly unfolding into consciousness, to the extent that her everyday existence is now characterised by a repeated emergence and re-embodiment of her debt. Another register is bodily and psychic dependability: the variable and unpredictable presence of debt poses a threat to health ('I'm going to make myself feel ill if I carry on like this'). We might presume this refers to mental illness, given that elsewhere in the interview she describes her ongoing battles with anxiety and depression. This particularly damaging form of enfolding is one that is common to the life of default, with a large body of research having shown the strong relationship between problematic forms of indebtedness and mental illness.[30] In such instances, then, acts of attempted market attachment get tangled up in the very processes through which individuals are composed as actors, including the extent to which they feel in control of themselves.

While anxious anticipation is one particularly common affective state in the life of default, it builds on and becomes shaped in different ways by many others: guilt about past spending for instance, or a generalised sense of regret about unspecified past purchases,[31] maybe peaking into anger or self-blame.[32] Such feelings can be connected to specific things: an overseas break,[33] or revealed when moving house and having to confront the presence of a plethora of consumer goods that now sit unused in unopened boxes.[34] Living default can also mean the routine experience of embarrassment: a debtor having to borrow money from his own children;[35] the pressure another feels to go on an overseas trip he knows he can't afford but feels he can't turn down;[36] or another, who describes being in a supermarket at the till and, because she has to live on cash, has to start taking products off the conveyor belt because the total amount is more than she expected, feeling the queue building up behind her, eyes watching and judging.[37] Embarrassment can in turn spill over into practices of concealment: a debtor hiding the trouble he's got himself into from his partner, who always seems so good with money.[38]

In the case of consumer credit default, the forms of affective co-presence that characterise all of our lives become particularly intimate parts of debtors' attachments to markets. Attempted attachments designed with the market in mind – market attachments – are constantly intersecting, and becoming entangled with, a range of other attachments, other forms of connectivity. This is then in part about recognising the passionate basis of many economic relations; as Michel Callon suggests, in the heart of markets it is indeed perfectly possible to find feelings, dissatisfaction, and regrets (2009, p. 541; see also Latour and Lépinay 2009; McFall forthcoming). As we will see, the effectiveness of debt collection processes depends on the repetition of encounters between debtor and collector. It is this repetition that generates the ongoing anticipatory states in debtors that can then become involved in the quite specific forms of becoming surrounding the move from a generalised affective state into the more focused, moment of calculative attention sought by the collector. To echo both a Deleuzian vocabulary and Sara Ahmed's terms as sketched previously, these are moments of affective 'intensity' or bodily intensification: 'peaks' in the rhythm of life, where entities and potentialities are pulled together, folded into one another and qualified, with the boundaries between them being redrawn.

Unfolding the life of default: calculation and the capture of affect

One of the debtors I met over the course of my research, whom I will call Eve, exemplified how a diffuse, anticipatory anxiety has the potential to coalesce into a moment of intensive attention. At the point at which we met, Eve was living in social housing in London with her three young girls and was to a large extent, dependent on welfare support. She had built up large debts, having used credit cards at least in part to pay for her day-to-day expenses and to supplement the income she received from low paid irregular work, or to tide her over in periods of unemployment. For Eve, collections letters had become an all too familiar household actor:

> When you come back, oh my god, is [there] any letter waiting for me, any bills? So sometime[s] when I come home, Jenny says to me, mummy is that a bill? … You know, they start worrying at their age you know, mummy is that a bill … every time I come in I was just like, maybe they sensed I'm worried about the bill, so they say, is that a bill? Is that [a] bill?

The rhythm of daily family life in her household was routinely being punctuated by the interruptions effected by the intrusion into the home of collections letters, the most persistent of the various demands for payment she was receiving. Collections letters are devices designed to secure a particular debtor's attachment to his or her debt. However, as is clear from this extract, in Eve's case attachments are being generated that extend to other household members. If these letters are, like the credit cards explored in the last chapter, 'lures for feeling', then these lures are reaching out not only to Eve, but also to her children. Anxious anticipation, the palpable effect of living a life of debt default, is then clearly spreading well beyond the individualised debtor, with Eve's children's persistent questions mirroring her own internal dialogue: are these letters demanding payment of some kind?

For the children, the effect of these intrusions is to set up a point of potential bifurcation in the flow of household relations. If the letter is a bill (of which those relating to consumer credit constitute a major portion), they will have to deal with the unfolding anxiety of their mother, as she is invited by the letter to immediately confront her debt position. If not, then they can expect a moment of relief, with the implications of the outstanding debts being allowed to resume their place in the 'background' of both their lives and Eve's.

As this example begins to show, part of the dynamic of technologies of debt collection is to punctuate the regular rhythm of the household and to construct an intensive 'moment' around which attention is focused (I will return to this). This has the effect of placing the defaulting debtor centre stage as a household actor. For the debtor, the unopened letter is a lure; it reaches out to him or her, with other household actors potentially coming to know that the quality of the soon to be realised emotional landscape of the house depends on its contents and how they are grasped. The debtor, his or her unfolding reactions, those of other household members, all become assembled around the newly arrived letter, which becomes an unavoidable passage point in the construction of the household's immediate future.

The collection letter's ability to act as a 'lure' for relations in this way echoes the potential agential effects of the credit card, as explored in the previous chapter. Recall how even if hidden out of sight and mind, the card might still exert a pull on the potential borrower. Something similar can be detected in the case of collections devices. James, for example, explained how his wife, Georgina, used to try to regulate the moment of revelation that collections letters portend:

JAMES: [...] there is a drawer over there where she used to hide them. But she would reveal them eventually. She wouldn't keep them forever, but she would try and deal with it her own way – get on the phone to them [...]
JOE: Why do you think she was, do you think she was hiding them from you or from herself?
JAMES: I think she was trying to control it.
JOE: Trying to keep on top of it?
JAMES: Keep on top of it yeah.
JOE: So is it something that would be revealed at one moment?
JAMES: Oh yeah she'd reveal it eventually. And I get the vibes from it anyway.

Georgina's strategy for dealing with these collections letters seems partly directed at limiting their ability to shape the course of household relations. By attempting to render them invisible to James and dealing with them herself when out of earshot, she limits the regularity of their intersection in the relationship between her and her husband. It is a way of limiting the moments of familial intensity described by Eve, involving the bodily irruption of anxiety, worry, and guilt, as debt comes, in that moment, to occupy the centre of their lives. However, this strategy is fragile. A drawer is no barrier to the letter's effects: James detects what he calls its 'vibes', co-articulated through it and her. These particular technologies of debt collection thus become partially folded into the socio-material fabric of the home, while at the same time unavoidably resonating outwards and towards its inhabitants.

It must be remembered, however, that while the potentially damaging impacts on family or emotional life resulting from the coming together of debtor, debt, and collector may not be the explicit aim of collections technologies, what is, is securing the attachment of the debtor to their debt. Although legal attachments do part of this work, these can exert a surprisingly weak hold – the reasons for this will be explored in Chapter 4. The problem the collector faces is thus not to generate *new* attachments to the debtor, but how to strengthen and (re)generate value from sets of market attachments that already exist. As in all market spaces, the aim is to shape the conditions of calculative engagement to the advantage of the 'producer' (here, the creditor). In the case of consumer credit default, this involves making the optimal use of the anticipatory landscape of default as *a space for the generation of calculative attention*. If the collector makes the most of the affordances that this intimate domestic landscape offers, and convinces a debtor to at least start engaging with their debt, perhaps also to start repaying, then it would have succeeded in transforming a market attachment that was previously perhaps fragile into one that is far more secure.[39]

At this point I want to return to Eve and to unpack her description of one moment in which an emergent state of anxious anticipation holds the potential to become converted into a moment of calculative focus:

> as soon as it comes I have to open it … at least it's for me to know what is there in [*sic*], I start preparing my mind or whatever towards it. The first thing, as soon as I open the door [and] I see any letter, the first thing, before I even take off my coat anytime, I just open the letter and see what it's all about. *If it's one I have to panic [about], I start panicking*. If it's one I just have to put away…. If it's one I have to make a phone call, immediately I just make a phone call.
>
> (Emphasis added)

Eve is describing a process of product qualification (see the book's introduction): she needs to evaluate the letter and decide what should be done with it. If it is a collections letter and she opens it, reads it, takes note of the contents, this will in turn contribute towards the requalification of the particular credit product the letter concerns.

The register through which this process of qualification occurs is, however, quite intimate. Eve begins by 'preparing' her mind towards the letter. She gets her mind/body into a necessary state of calculative and emotional readiness to be able to deal with whatever actions she feels the letter demands. The most mundane, least problematic outcome is if the letter's contents are informational; if so, it is read, then put away. But she describes two further potential outcomes that come to matter if and when the letter is understood as demanding an immediate response: the first is panic, the second is cognitive engagement. An unfolding state of anxious anticipation holds the potential to become calculation *and/or* emotion (or indeed some other entity – that does not concern us here, however).[40] The bifurcation of affect into calculation and emotion is not as a result of the precise contents of the particular letter in hand, but in anticipation of a familiar but yet to be unveiled future. This anticipatory state has been both enfolded prior to the arrival of the letter and produces the emergent conditions for the strengthening of the bond that connects debtor to debt. As it unfolds into calculation, the attachment of Eve to her debt becomes reinforced.

As a number of writers on affect have sought to clarify, emotion needs to be understood as a particular *manner* in which affect becomes something else. Affect is not equivalent to emotion. It is rather that emotion is one way in which affect congeals into an entity that is more bounded and, potentially, amenable to categorisation and human analysis – as occurs here with Eve, in her reference to her own panic (see Grossberg 2010, p. 316; Massumi 2002, pp. 27–28). Emotion, as Ben Anderson puts it is 'qualified personal content'. It emerges from the affective while at the same time inevitably feeding back into it (Anderson 2014, p. 83).

Crucially, though, the processes through which affect congeals into something else do not necessarily just relate to emotion, *but can also apply to calculation* – holding in mind once again that calculation is invariably at least partially qualitative, or 'qualculative'. In this case, these qualculative processes might include those that surround and stem from putting the letter away or making a phone call. What Eve is describing is the very potential for affect to bifurcate, to emerge and then to become abstracted in and through quite distinct, but always related, registers. Panic and clearly-defined calculative action – body and mind, put crudely – need, according to Eve's account, to become separate and distinct entities. Both briefly coexist in a state of unrealised existence, each ready to become fully realised as required once the letter is opened.

It is certainly the case, as the economisation programme suggests, that in such instances a debtor's cognitive capacities are being equipped and translated through the socio-material device of the collections letter. The product, in turn, undergoes a process of requalification. But to this account we can add a description of the way in which certain forms of requalification depend on the unfolding of embodied process. This is what Brian Massumi calls the 'capture' of affect (Massumi 2002).

Attending to affect in economic settings directs attention towards how markets need to keep changing not just the material infrastructure and equipment used by buyers and consumers, but also *the intimate attachments* surrounding them. For instance, in the cases of Eve and Georgina and James, a defaulting debt becomes tangled up in their attachments to one another, affecting their conditions of interaction. Georgina becomes deceitful (even if simultaneously caring) while James becomes suspicious (even if perhaps willingly ignorant). Eve's many and varied household attachments (to care, to protect, to the need to earn a wage, etc.) become, at crucial moments and even if only briefly, secondary to the market attachments that stem from her debt, while for Angela and Julie, the security of their attachment to an identity they have grown to become familiar with, their sense of who they are, can feel close to rupture. We have also seen how in Georgina and James' case such shifts in the domestic fabric of attachment are not simply a side effect of markets, or market 'overflows' (Callon 1998a), but rather wrapped up in the production of moments of calculation. It is when 'vibes' can no longer be ignored that letters are brought out and dealt with. In Eve's case, the panic that spreads into household relations *also* becomes the basis for calculation.

There is a further point to be made here: sociology has often been far too quick to arrive at conclusions about the damage that the apparent encroachment of market forces may be doing to the domestic and the personal (see Zelizer 2002a, 2002b, 2005). However, when it comes to the encounter between debtor and collector, we need to recognise that damage is happening: debtors' worlds are likely to transform, it is a process that is likely to be painful, and they are likely to prefer it was otherwise. Indeed, the very success of most collections letters depends on this, for instance on the existence of an uncomfortable state of anxious anticipation. It is such states that act as affordances for product requalification, but also for the congealing of affect into calculation and emotion.

The degree to which domestic life will be affected by its routine encounters with collectors will vary according to the particularities of people's lives. This includes the ability of debtors to know how to deal with collectors. It also includes their embodied and emotional capacities and the distribution of such capacities amongst other household actors (although we haven't seen it here, potentially to include the non-human, e.g. computerised technologies of financial planning and accounting). For some people, therefore, attachments may well become 'stickier' than for others. To examine this further, I want to focus down on the challenges faced by a single debtor, whom I will call Jane. In thinking through the importance of affective attachments that 'stick', I hold in mind related work by Sara Ahmed (2004, 2010) and Rebecca Coleman (2009, pp. 166–194).

Living with sticky attachments

At the point at which we met, Jane was in her early 60s, living in a rented house in a village in the West of England. In the mid-1990s (Jane couldn't remember when exactly) she and her husband David decided to start their own cleaning business after seeing an advert in the local paper advertising a franchise. Jane described how the business had ticked over for the first few years, even if not making large profits. However, in the late 1990s, the costs of the business started to rise, due in part to the introduction of the minimum wage. It was at this point that the couple started to borrow, with some of the debts being taken out jointly and some solely in Jane's name. Then a number of further issues started to affect the business, including most notably being defrauded by the franchise owner to the sum of approximately £10,000. The couple were, however, unable to pursue this money, because – being a business – they were unable to obtain legal aid. As well as the costs involved, this event also marked the end of the franchise. The result was that, having used both the business and the personal bank overdraft, a personal loan, and some hire purchase borrowing, including on her husband's car, Jane and David had borrowed in excess of £35,000 across nine credit accounts (three of which were held by the same creditor). Despite much of this being used to directly support the business, these debts were thus still personal, consumer credit debts. As sole traders, Jane and her husband were liable for these debts to the same extent as if they had borrowed them for non-business uses.

For a while the couple dealt with these consequences together, with David trying to get a new IT business started from home. However, a year prior to our interview David was diagnosed with terminal lung cancer, which finally led to his death in December that year. Meanwhile Jane had long been struggling with her own health issues, after being diagnosed with ME[41] in the early 1990s, which had meant she had to leave her job as the manager of a sheltered housing scheme. This meant that Jane was not only living alone, but was also largely alone in dealing with both her illness and the debts that she was still liable for – now standing at around £24,000 – with her only income coming from her state pension. She did have some support from a third party money advice service, National Debtline, who were giving her ongoing telephone advice on how to deal with her creditors.[42] This meant that, with this advice and their letter templates, she had managed to successfully come to agreements with all but one creditor. They had stopped charging her additional interest and had agreed, as a holding measure, for her to pay them each a £1 'token payment' every month. (This is a payment demanded by the creditor, effectively as a repeated legal acknowledgement of the ownership of the debt). She was also getting some support from a grief counsellor and a local grief support group, with whom she met up regularly. Jane has a large family, including many grandchildren.[43] However, she tended to see these rarely, with most living outside the local area.

I want to begin by following an analogy that Jane herself draws, between two apparently different states of affective anxiety: severe indebtedness and grief. In the case of both, she tells me, others can *empathise* but they cannot *understand*. She continues:

> I mean the bereavement is completely different to what I was expecting, even though I was expecting it.... There's so much more to it. And I suppose the same with [the debt] ... *there's so much more to it than just getting those letters.*

> (Emphasis added)

Later she turns to her debts:

> I think it holds me back in a lot of ways, and I feel I can't sort of move forward and I feel trapped, very trapped and it's funny isn't it. You sort of can go out and socialise and, it's sort of like putting a face on, but there's this other thing going on. It's hard to put into words really. I suppose if you spoke to someone else that was going through the same thing.... And it's gone on for so long it's just embedded now, you know, just I suppose even if I cleared it, it would still take a while to get rid of the.... It's just been around, I mean it's going to be what nine, coming on nine years, that's a long time.

As with her grief, she asserts the difficulty of being able to articulate her experience of being in debt to those that have not been through 'the same thing' (it being 'hard to put into words'). The debt is, as she puts it 'embedded', to the extent that even if she is able to clear it (our previous conversation had turned to the option of bankruptcy), 'it would still take a while to get rid of the ...'. She tails off, but the absence she leaves is tempting to fill – perhaps by drawing on her next sentence: rid of the feeling, perhaps, of it just 'being around'? Either way, it is clear from this extract that Jane and her debt have become so tightly bound together, that she struggles to even imagine life without it.

Echoing Ahmed's analysis of the social role of pain, introduced briefly at the start of this chapter, Judith Butler has shown how one of the effects of grief is to reflexively *display* relationality (Butler 2003, p. 13; see also Bell 2007). Our often-unacknowledged dependence on attachments to others is exposed when, in the case of death, the bonds between two living bodies, each of whose presence is so familiar as to be deeply woven into the life of the other, are sundered. Left are the embodied memories of the survivor, themselves in the process of being reshaped by the absence of their object. In the case of debt, however, it is not a forever absent Other that displays relationality to a debtor, but an Other that becomes *ever-present*. As with many debtors, Jane's home is being filled with an ever-increasing accumulation of the material paraphernalia of technologies of debt collection. The burden of living with debt comes from having to live near-daily with relations – in the form of material debt collection technologies – that attempt to make sensible the (market) attachment a person should feel to his/her debt.

Where debt and grief are similar, however, is the way that, for some, they become so deeply folded into the individual, so deeply embodied/embedded, that, as Butler also highlights, verbal articulation falters. This is of course one of the features of relations of affect: at best they can exist only, as Raymond Williams put it, 'on the cusp of semantic availability' (Williams 1977, p. 134; see Seigworth and Gregg 2010, p. 21). They are not transferrable into a realm of signification without becoming something potentially quite different (as we saw, previously, in relation to the congealing of affect into emotion and calculation). The mundane unfolding of affect usually poses little problem to the conduct of daily life. However, some affective relations feel so personal, so utterly different from those other people seem to experience, that pushing them to unfold into registers of signification feels more reductive and unsatisfactory than usual (see Gibbs 2010, p. 201).

The parallel between grief and default points to how intimate the affective enfoldings of defaulting debt can be for some debtors. Others may not realise it, but Jane carries her debt with her, which then continues to resonate into her routine social interactions. To 'socialise' she has to go out with 'a face on': she has to try to prevent the personal, individualised issue of default leaking into her encounters with others. Because she feels that a lived experience of debt default and debt collection is a precondition for both conversation with and understanding from others, Jane is left trying to deal with her debt largely alone (with occasional assistance from a debt advisor).

Market attachments have therefore achieved the capacity to endure; they have become, in other words, *sticky*. They have become sticky by becoming intractably wrapped up in attachments that operate through different registers and have ostensibly different, non-market, objects. This stickiness should by now be familiar, even if the degree of attachment varies: Eve's children realise that the attachments of default were stuck to her when she moves anxiously towards opening a recently arrived letter; both Angela and Julie realise the relations of debt are stuck to them when they feel debt becoming part of who they are; James feels debt to be stuck to Georgina when her practices of concealment resonate out into the household. In Jane's case, it also affects both how she moves into public spaces and the modes of articulation that she permits herself. Perhaps once there were clear boundaries between consumer credit, a particular market assemblage, and the situated assemblage of her everyday life. Now, however, those boundaries have become blurred.

Part of understanding the politics of default is thus to understand its onto-logical character (see Marres 2009; Mol 2002; Woolgar and Lezaun 2013; Woolgar and Neyland 2013). That is to say, 'a politics that has to do with the way in which problems are framed, bodies are shaped, and lives are pushed and pulled into one shape or another' (Mol 2002, p. viii). In pointing this out, the aim is not simply to draw attention, for its own sake, to what might be termed 'ontological multiplicity' – that is the existence of multiple realities which might become relevant to social life (indeed, to all life – but, as a sociologist, it is social life that concerns me above all). As John Law puts it, ontological multi-plicity matters as 'some [realities] will be preferable to others' (see Law 2008, p. 637).[44] For many debtors it clearly *would* be preferable for their debts not to be part of 'who', or 'what' they are, to put it in the terms Angela used earlier (the blur between the human and the non-human here is in itself interesting). And yet, as the case of debt default shows, this can be unavoidable: as they enter default, both debtors and their worlds – which are, after all, more or less insepar-able – can become unavoidably different.

In Jane's case, market attachments become particularly sticky by their inter-section with a quite specific non-market attachment: her ME.[45] Like many other ME sufferers, and on top of her feelings of fatigue, Jane variously attributes to the condition frequent acute headaches (which, in distinguishing it from migraines, she refers to as 'the ME headache'), joint pains, problems with con-centration, and depression. Yet, as her accounts reveal, this interferes with the kinds of bodily and cognitive authority that repeatedly dealing with technologies of debt collection demands. For Jane, what causes her particular difficulty is the endless stream of paperwork she is required to complete.

Even before being in debt, Jane's ME had meant that completing paperwork had been a challenge. But because of her long-term defaulting debts, she now has to bear a new administrative burden. In part, this involves the domestic man-agement of the high volume of correspondence she is routinely receiving. For her protection, she keeps and files any significant letter she receives, to the extent that there are archived boxes of papers in her loft, newly arrived documents in a cupboard in the living room, and filed papers in folders upstairs ('I keep every-thing. Just anything'). She also sometimes adds her own notes onto these docu-ments, including recording the details of relevant conversations she has had over the phone. As an example, Jane shows me, and permits me to photograph, one of the ambiguous collection letters (perhaps more akin to a 'postcard', although it is sealed and needs to be opened up) she had received and annotated, in this case from Mackenzie Hall (Figure 2.2), a debt collection agency.[46] As part of the ongoing management of her debt she is also required to routinely fill in income and expenditure forms, on which Jane has to justify her continued inability to repay. An edited reproduction of one that she was about to send off is shown in Figure 2.3, with a section enlarged. This document reveals in more detail some of the labour Jane is putting into filling in these forms. The form has been meticulously reconstructed by hand, most likely from an existing template. Each cost is carefully worked out and sometimes carefully corrected.[47] The consequence of having to fill in these forms is a persistent anxiousness, a feeling she feels increasingly unable to live with:

> What I'm finding at the moment is getting all these letters every six months from every company that I owe money to. Asking me to sort of pay more and having to do all these finance forms with them all. You know, it's not like doing one off. I mean, I just got another one this week. And I'm getting tired, you know, I'm finding it really tiring. I'm getting to the stage I feel I just, I'm not going to be able to do this much more. So it would be easy for me to be bankrupt and clear of it because it's the stress of all this coming through and I need to deal with it all. I mean it's every couple of weeks I'm getting a, having another one to do, you know.

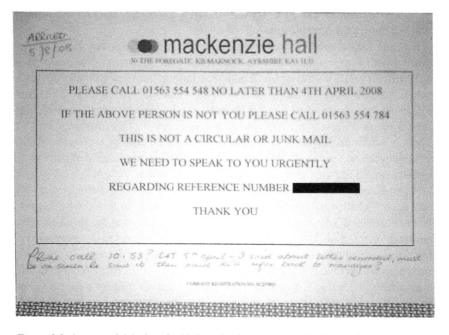

Figure 2.2 Annotated Mackenzie Hall collections 'postcard'. Handwritten text reads: 'Arrived: 5/8/08'; 'Phone call 10.53? SAT 5th April – I said about letter recorded, must be on screen. he saw it then said he'll refer back to manager?'

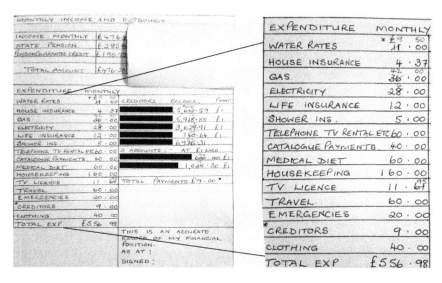

Figure 2.3 Income and expenditure form.

Jane's worries about her debts are compounded by the stress of the administrative burden that accompanies their ongoing management, including having to correspond with multiple creditors (six, owning nine different accounts). In addition, there is always the possibility that even where a stable arrangement has been agreed, the debt can be sold on, or the creditor can pass the account to a different collector, in which case the cycle will begin again.

The cumulative result of a process that had been going on for nigh on a decade, and compounded by her ME, means that she feels exhausted. As she puts it, a significant contributor to what she calls the 'stress and strain' of her situation comes from 'the pressure of trying to keep up with everything'. Meanwhile, her ME means that it often feels like 'your body is sort of wanting you to switch off … [but] that's not always possible, because sometimes you have to keep going'. For Jane, the anticipatory anxieties that have become folded into her life are not simply a result of *being* a long-term defaulting debtor; rather they stem from having to manage the *process* of long-term debt default, with a body that is not equipped to 'unstick' the attachments of debt default from her life, from her body, from her sense of psychic well-being, from, in other words, the other attachments that co-define her.

The most obvious unsticking mechanism would be bankruptcy, however even here Jane finds herself constrained. Going bankrupt would mean having to close her bank account and open another. Yet there is only one bank branch in her village. She cannot drive, so to pay her bills means long bus trips into the nearest city, something she dreads. Her attachment to debt is thus amplified by its entanglement with her attachment to a variety of local infrastructures, including her bank account, her village, and her dependence on public transport.

Conclusion

Consumer credit is a financial instrument that is designed with attachment in mind. Perhaps the most obvious object of attachment is temporal: the moment a borrower borrows, they instigate a connection to their own future that includes a new entity: the credit product. The problem for the borrower is that however well she or he might be able to predict they way in which they live with this attachment, the precise *manner* in which it grips hold of the range of other forms of connectivity that compose everyday life will be ultimately unknowable. Within the social sciences, talk of risk and uncertainty rarely captures this lived, embodied unknowability and contingency. However wide calculative or 'qualculative' frames are stretched, the character of the utterly intimate, personal life alongside the effects – good or ill – of past action will likely remain a murky best guess. For many defaulting debtors the sequences of past purchases and moments of expenditure that combined to create their outstanding debt will be similarly indistinct, perhaps similar to the memories of Michael Hamburger, appearing in W.G. Sebald's book *The Rings of Saturn*, who describes his memory of a Berlin childhood as 'a darkened background with a grey smudge in it, a slate pencil drawing, some unclear numbers and letters in a gothic script, blurred and half wiped away with a damp rag' (Sebald 2002, pp. 177–178). The difference for the defaulting debtor, however, is that the sum total of these moments are gathered together and made to haunt the present.

This points to a shift in how we might understand what a market attachment *can become*. As we have seen, certain market attachments can come to be very attached indeed, sticking to a range of embodied and domestic affordances, wrapping their tendrils tight around other attachments. There is an ontological politics to this process, as bodies are pushed and pulled one way and the other. Some are perhaps flexible enough to stand the strain. Some, however, will be brittle.

Although market attachment may feel 'constantly threatened' (Callon *et al.* 2002, p. 205) from an organisational perspective, this way of describing the forms of connectivity established within markets can obscure the multiple and potentially intimate registers through which processes of attachment can operate and interact. The fact that, for a defaulting debtor, market attachment can feel inescapable is because of the very real forms of connection that are established to the range of other bonds, other potentially inescapable attachments, that shape the relations between household members and between an individual and their bodies, psychic states and the physical infrastructures of their homes and localities. In the process of attempted market attachment, it is thus not just the product that is transformed and 'requalified', so too is the qualifier: the debtor/consumer.

Attending to the potential intimacies of market attachment also helps to clarify the relationships between affect, emotion, and calculation. Too often, calculation is thought to be the outcome of rational deliberation. At the same time, too often, affect and emotion are used interchangeably, as a way of describing that aspect of life that is felt and embodied. However, given that calculation is just as felt and embodied as emotion, it is unsurprising to see it stem from, or more precisely to unfold from, affective states. Calculation is, as the economisation programme has argued, constituted through socio-material process; this insight remains unchallenged. However, what has tended to be missed is that some of the most intimate of the socio-material domains can matter greatly to the formatting of action in markets, including that of embodied life. Indeed, we have begun in this chapter to see hints of what, in later chapters, will become far more explicit: that, when it comes to successfully connecting with defaulting debtors, the debt collections industry understands that intersecting with the affective dimensions of life is of crucial importance in the quest to generate a debtor's calculative attention.

There is also room to build on the accounts of attachment with which we began this chapter. Take, for example, the attachments of cruel optimism, as outlined by Lauren Berlant (2011), which I described as being characterised by a relationship of desire towards an object, however problematic or harmful. Some of the forms of attachment we have seen at work in this chapter could be described in those terms – it is possible to detect relations of desire and cruel optimism at work, for instance, in Jane's commitment to performing herself as a competent economic despite the personal costs. These forms of attachment, however, may well come to coexist with other modalities of attachment. To be in default is to encounter technologies designed and organised in such a way as to *elicit* attachment, to pull attachment out of people and out of their situated domestic lives, irrespective of whether or not an attachment is the object of desire. In the case of debt default, this operates at the intersection of the mutual unfolding of debtors' anxious, anticipating bodies and technologies of debt collection. If we are to understand, as Berlant invites us to, the production of the present, we thus need to understand the precise and directed formatting of this in-between space. The present chapter began this process by looking at debt default through the eyes of the debtors. This needs to be complemented by seeing default from an organisational perspective. It is to this, and to the work of the creditor and the collector, that the book now turns.

Notes

1 It can thus be seen as sitting in dialogue with the long-standing sociological interest in the everyday as an important empirical site for the study of social relations (see de Certeau 1998; Goffman 1959; Lefebvre 1991; Gardiner 2000). In attending to the role played by affect within this domain, and in addition to some of the writers cited below, I draw particular inspiration from Kathleen Stewart's (2007) beautiful and compelling exploration of the politics of ordinary affect. Works by Fiona Allon (Allon 2010, 2013; Allon and Redden 2012), Paul Langley (2008b) and Randy Martin (2002) on how the everyday become an important mediator of forces of financialisation are also important reference points. Finally, in their exploration of the intersection between the domestic and devices as vectors for experimentation and/or forms of engagement, Ann Kelly's (2012) and Noortje Marres' (2012) work were very much in my thinking while writing this.

2　As later chapters will explore, this figure should be held to include work undertaken both by creditors, and third party agencies working on their behalf to collect debts.

3　As such, I follow Stengers – who invites us to think with Whitehead and to undertake what she calls a 'speculative adventures', which do not begin by assuming whether or not something 'matters', but is instead interested in questions such as 'how does it matter?' 'does it really matter?' 'what if I accepted that it does not matter?' (Stengers 2005, p. 54).

4　As explored in more detail in Deville (2014).

5　There are echoes of an empirical imbalance within economic sociology more generally, which has shown itself hesitant to explore the personal and the intimate, as explored in depth by Viviana Zelizer (2005, 2002a, 2002b). See also Deville (2014).

6　Some of the exceptions to this are explored in the book's introduction.

7　Including the work of Sara Ahmed (2004, 2010), Jane Bennett (2001) and Judith Butler (1997).

8　These are themes that have also been explored within STS by Emile Gomart and Antoine Hennion (Gomart and Hennion 1999; Hennion 2007, 2013). Although they do not engage specifically with questions of affect, their work on how the intimate interfaces between bodies and environments are mutually constituted has been influential in my thinking and sits in the background of the above discussion. Miranda Joseph (2010, 2014) should also be acknowledged as one of the first to draw out in detail the significance of Berlant's work for the consideration of consumer credit borrowing practices.

9　In their accounts of processes of attachment, Butler, Ahmed and Berlant all to varying degrees draw connections to psychoanalytic theory, in which the concept of attachment has been highly influential, an influence that can be traced back in part to John Bowlby's work (1969, 1973). While this isn't a particularly relevant point of reference to the present study, in part given the latter's attention to the socio-material composition and distribution of social and emotional relations, this heritage should at least seen as pointing towards a usage that speaks to the implication of actors in embodied, emotive relationships – which speaks to at least some understandings of what affect is and does. Furthermore, I would like to thank Robbie Duschinsky, whose exploration and development of a Deleuzian account of processes of psychic and bodily attachment, via Bowlby, and in particular his account of the socio-material distribution of attachment, proved helpful in clarifying some of the similar questions that this chapter seeks to explore (Duschinsky 2014; see also Rojas 2014).

10　For instance when Butler explores the subject that 'will attach to pain rather than not attach at all' (1997, p. 61).

11　Affect is less a reference point for Butler than for Berlant, or indeed for Sara Ahmed, whose work I will discuss in due course. This characterisation is hence a gloss, of sorts, that attempts to bring together a distinct but related body of work.

12　This is a dialogue which Ahmed herself prefigures in her analysis of status of Deleuze and Guattari's work within feminist theory (Ahmed 1998, pp. 69–78).

13　Deleuze's work in this respect builds on and critically engages with the description of processes of folding (even if in a more representational manner) by both Heidegger and Leibnitz.

14　Processes of folding also need to be understood as deeply intertwined with processes which are 'withdrawn' or 'virtual': that is to say, that which in a given situation is *present* but not *actualised*, what Deleuze also calls the 'plane of consistency' (a concept initially developed in his book *Bergsonism* (1988a)).

15　Creativity is here understood as related to the production of novelty. See Halewood (2011) on this meaning of creativity, as in fact coined by Alfred North Whitehead.

16 Quarterly data, not seasonally adjusted.
17 On the associations between care for others and indebtedness see Berlant (2006, 2011) and Han (2012).
18 See for instance: CCR-2 (2012, p. 30), Still (2010).
19 Metropolitan Collections Agency, letter dated 24 December 2008.
20 Moorcroft Collections Agency, letter dated 23 July 2009.
21 Metropolitan Collections Agency, letter dated 24 December 2008.
22 Lowell Financial, letter dated 27 May 2008.
23 Marlin Financial Services. Letter dated 15 April 2009.
24 MBNA. Letter from November 2008 (precise date unknown).
25 Angela, David, Eve, Jane, Julie, Kathy, Lauren, Mary, Peter, Richard.
26 The UK regulator does not prescribe the amount of phone calls that are considered 'unreasonable'; this is left for collectors to decide and to be prepared to justify (see Office of Fair Trading 2012).
27 What follows is based on an amalgam of collections conversations overhead while sitting next to debt collectors at 'Alpha' collections agency.
28 In my analysis of the importance of anxiety to collections practices, I build on Paul Rock's work which also connected the two, including the exploitation by collectors of '[t]he uncertainty and anxiety which surround enforcement' (1973, p. 11; see also p. 100).
29 A concern expressed by multiple interviewees. Since 6 April 2014, most bailiffs in England and Wales are now referred to as 'Enforcement Agents' (The Sheriffs Office 2014)
30 See Fitch *et al.* (2011), Meltzer *et al.* (2011, 2013), Mind (2007, 2011), Richardson *et al.* (2013).
31 Jane, Julie.
32 Again, expressed – in different ways – by multiple interviewees.
33 Angela.
34 Eve.
35 Pete.
36 Gary.
37 Ruth.
38 David.
39 I draw here and elsewhere in this chapter on analysis presented in Deville (2014).
40 These are not of course wholly discrete, however they are different enough to be identified as distinct embodied states.
41 Myalgic Encephalopathy, also known as Chronic Fatigue Syndrome or Post Viral Fatigue Syndrome.
42 National Debtline is a free service, funded by a mixture of private donations and government grants.
43 Jane's experience of default is in some ways more extreme than faced by many defaulting debtors. However, looking at the struggles that someone faces that may, for many others, not be present helps to shed light on the particular sets of alignments that produce that which is straightforward or 'normal' in the first place, a lesson from STS-informed currents within disability studies (see Galis 2011; Moser 2006, 2009; Moser and Law 1999; Schillmeier 2010).
44 A brief side note on questions of preference: one of the things about being in default is that preference in the present is to a significant degree determined (a heavy word, but chosen deliberately) by preferences in the past. This conclusion, of course, is only tenable as long as we retain a healthy scepticism both about the very idea of preference being a wholly autonomous, self-determined form of action and about whether 'preference' really describes the forms of action that were involved in accruing the debt in the first place.

45 ME is a condition that is still contested in some medical circles (Cairns and Hotopf 2005; Ranjith 2005). Its most visible and agreed upon symptom is a feeling of extreme fatigue, often after periods of either physical or mental activity. A range of other physical symptoms is reported as being connected to ME (The ME Association 2010) (although on these, the medical profession does not always agree).

46 Using collections postcards including personal information that might be readable to others without a letter having to be opened would be in breach of the regulator's guidance for UK debt collectors (Office of Fair Trading 2012).

47 It also documents the fact that, according to her current estimates, and despite only making £1 a month payments against each of the nine credit accounts, she appears to still be living above her means – her £556.98 stated monthly expenditure exceeding the stated income by £80.78.

3 The discovery and capture of affect

A history of debt collection

[T]he debtor is an individual with his [*sic*] own hopes, fears and feelings. No matter how much debtors may have in common or how much information we gather about the 'average,' the problem of debt is a very personal one for each individual. It has a meaning to that person which is different from its meaning to others. The artistry in collecting lies in the ability to add to a general knowledge of debtors a sensitivity to the uniqueness encountered in every individual.

E.H. Barnes, psychologist and debt collector (Barnes 1959, p. 19)

Up to this point, the book has explored the lived character of default, that is, how default is experienced and how debtors grasp the lures of the collector as they encounter them in their homes and everyday lives. In the process, debtors' own accounts have provided some valuable insights into the industry, showing how the predominant routes into their lives tend to be via the twin technologies of phone and letter.[1] This insight into the world of UK collections broadly tallies with what we know about the way in which defaulting consumer credit debts are collected in many other countries. This includes the US, which we will also visit in this chapter.[2] Collection agencies are therefore now companies whose business involves, above all, the art of making and managing contact remotely. As with a number of financial industries – lending as much as banking – face-to-face interactions between company and defaulter are increasingly the preserve of more niche areas of the market.[3]

In order to trace these organisational processes further, this chapter and the two that follow move away from the everyday, experiential domain of defaulters and towards the day-to-day business of debt collection. This will involve unpacking the particular strategies, approaches, and technologies used by collections organisations to try to strengthen the attachments that connect them, and the credit products they work with, to defaulting debtors.

Making this empirical and analytical move brings particular demands, both of the reader and the analyst. Domestic, everyday spaces – the way they are made, lived, and organised – are more or less familiar to us all. The domain of the collector is, however, much more unfamiliar. Very few of us will have found ourselves implicated in the fairly unique work of debt collection whose character is summed up in the above epigraph by E.H. Barnes, a figure who we will return to later in the chapter. Depending on one's role, this work can involve emotional labour – having the conversations and (now, as we will see, much more rarely) physical confrontations involved in convincing people to repay – or the organisational, bureaucratic labour of managing and profiting from portfolios of overdue or defaulting debt, potentially consisting of thousands of individual accounts. This difficulty leads to the question of how this domain might be approached analytically. In particular, following on from themes explored in the last chapter, how exactly might the affective become present and operationalised within organisational processes, in attempts to secure, or re-secure market attachment?

This chapter proposes that the contemporary business of debt collection can be far better understood by placing it in dialogue with its past. First, this will involve venturing into some of default and collection's 'last 3,000 years'.[4] While the experience of default and the practice of debt collection (broadly defined) are as old as debt itself, I am interested here in the genealogy of some quite specific mechanisms and techniques, some of which retain a continuity with the present, others that the present has explicitly set itself against. Building on arguments developed in the last chapter, I will look at how this has, sometimes quite explicitly, involved the 'attachment' of a debtor to their debt. In the last chapter we looked at the connections that bind people to markets – market attachments – come to intersect with, and draw from, attachments that people have to a range of other people and things. In this chapter we will encounter a further modality through which forms of market attachment have historically sought to operate: through the physical attachment of a debtor to a debt. This mode of attachment works less through processes of affective enfolding and unfolding, than on the very material 'stuff' of the body. Whether through bodily incarceration, dismemberment, or the development of specific legal mechanisms, the body has routinely been used to stand in for a debt in the case of non-payment.

However, this modality of attachment became increasingly unavailable to collectors from the mid-nineteenth century onwards, as debtors' prisons started to be abolished. The chapter documents the responses to this shift and how these in turn became intertwined with developments in the consumer credit lending industry. In the process we will move to the US to see the early development of technologies that would eventually be exported around the world. This involved turning to a range of resources, including psychology and experimental methodologies, in the collector's quest to 'capture' affect. The result is to transform the ontological basis of collections work and to lay the groundwork for tendencies that will only fully come to fruition as we move, in the next chapter, into the twenty-first century.

The long history of body attachment

The extension of a debt from one person to another is generally dependent on one of two potential responses being available to the creditor should a debtor fail to repay as agreed: either a socially agreed mechanism that allows the creditor to reclaim from the debtor some property of equal or greater value of the debt, or being able to mobilise this mechanism in the form of a threat. The former, in turn, might be underpinned by conventions of law or, as in the case of 'loan sharks' and other informal money lenders, for example, the threat of violence being directed towards debtors, whether enacted by the lenders themselves or those at their disposal.[5] Alternatively, the creditor may demand a continuing claim over a particular piece of property, as depended on by forms of pawnbroking.[6] Such socially agreed frameworks also need to be able to respond to situations when the asset on which the loan was extended will no longer cover the loan, when this asset becomes lost or otherwise unavailable, or when debts are extended without a strict relationship to an asset in the first place. Each of these situations is deftly covered in perhaps the most famous legal document of them all: the Magna Carta, issued in June 1215. This is the ninth of 63 points in the document:

> Neither we [the King] nor our officials [in some versions 'bailiffs'] will seize any land or rent in payment of a debt, so long as the debtor has movable goods sufficient to discharge the debt. A debtor's sureties [guarantees] shall not be distrained upon [seized] so long as the debtor himself can discharge the debt. If, for lack of means, the debtor is unable to discharge his debt, his sureties shall be answerable for it. If they so desire, they may have the debtor's lands and rents until they have received satisfaction for the debt that they have paid for him unless the debtor can show that he has settled his obligations to them.

To put it in Michel Callon's (1998b) classic terms, this document, and the many and ever more complex national apparatuses designed to regulate the use of credit that have followed in its wake, are state-led attempts to manage any overflows a credit transaction might generate, in order to provide the stable frame necessary for the conduct of that transaction. As with all such laws, the aim is at least twofold: to provide a set of practical mechanisms available to a creditor should a debt not be repaid, as well as to outline to debtors the consequences of not repaying. The latter, in turn, can be deployed by creditors as threats in order to secure payment. As we will see, it is the threat of legally instigated proceedings that ultimately becomes more significant for the debt collections industry than these proceedings themselves. To stay momentarily with the Magna Carta, we find that it puts three main mechanisms at the creditor's disposal: two are contained in the above extract: first, the claiming of 'lands and rents' as payment for the debt and, second, the ability to continue to do so over time. The third mechanism, an extension of the second, is contained in the next set of points, which address the possibility that the debtor might die. The important principle it reveals is that responsibilities can potentially extend over generations, even if we learn that there are certain dispensations available to wives and to 'under age' inheritors.

What such laws delimit are the degrees to which the state can exert control over the defaulter. In the above example, this is discussed in terms of control over a debtor's property. It can also be explicitly directed towards the debtor's body.[7] In a central piece of Roman legislation, we find 12 legal 'tables' dedicated entirely to the regulation of debt, which detail in turn the increasingly severe consequences of non-payment. After stipulating repayment periods available to the debtor after successive court appearances, the third of these tables outlines a succession of ways in which the debtor's body could be held as forfeit for an outstanding debt. These include the possibility of his (it is likely the debtors would have been male) incarceration by the creditor (who, at a certain stage may take the debtor away with him, in chains), the potential to be physically forced to endure public humiliation (later in the process, the debtor is to be brought to the forum on three successive days to have their debt announced in public), with the process culminating in the debtor either being turned into sheer bodily value as he is sold into slavery or even being physically dismembered by the creditors 'if they desire to do so', with the apportioning of body parts between them (here of course, creditors clearly receive little in return apart from the presumed satisfaction of seeing this particularly brutal form of punishment enacted; any deterrent effect is for the benefit of future creditors) (see Scott 2001, pp. 63–64).[8] The transformation of debtor into slave was also a mechanism employed in certain Ancient Greek societies, at certain points becoming the object of popular uprisings (see Finley 1964; Austin and Vidal-Naquet 1977, pp. 70–71). Both debt-bondage and imprisonment for outstanding debt appear to have been features in Ancient Egyptian society at particular historical moments (Graeber 2011, p. 219), with both also featuring at a number of points in the Bible.[9]

Non-repayment of debt was, then, a matter to which the very severest consequences of the legal system could be applied. It is the body's fleshy materiality – its torture, its debasement, its punishment as public spectacle – that is an object of penal control, very much in the mode presented by Michel Foucault in his classic work *Discipline and Punish* (1975). These technologies of the body provided the debt collector with an important resource: should a debtor not repay what they owe, it was their body, its liberty, its safety, which becomes debt's ultimate guarantee. This gave the debt collector an ultimate, terrible threat to deploy if it became necessary: that the debtor's very flesh could be forced into a violent relation with their debt. This is Shylock's famous threat, in *The Merchant of Venice*: Antonio should prepare himself to hand over a pound weight of his own flesh should he not be able to repay what is owed.

While some of these practices, including debt slavery, may have been particularly characteristic of the ancient world,[10] a central principle was carried over into the Middle Ages and the modern (but not, by and large, the contemporary) era: that the body of the defaulting debtor could be physically compelled to stand in for the debt. This is rendered explicit in early English legislation concerning the state sanctioned imprisonment of non-paying debtors. The Statute of Marlbridge, passed in 1267, permitted a creditor to force those without the means to repay their debts to appear before the local sheriff (Vogt 2001, p. 341).[11] In the statute we find the origins of an enduring legal formulation that established beyond any doubt the relationship between a debtor and their body, in which a debtor without access to funds to repay their debt may be first 'distrained' (seized), before being '*attached by their bodies*, so that the sheriff ... shall cause them to come make their account' (cited in Vogt 2001, pp. 341, n56; emphasis added).

As we also know from Foucault (1975), the arrival of modern mechanisms of criminal justice shifted the object of address of the penal system away from the flesh of a perpetrator towards the criminal 'soul'. On the one hand, rather than bodily revenge, punishment should be concerned with the transformation of the criminal: their mind, their practices and habits would, through the application of techniques and technologies guaranteed by the new criminological sciences, be reformed. On the other, punishment became increasingly concerned with what Foucault calls the 'social body'. Crime becomes generalised. Individuals are now constituted as 'citizens' and in exchange are provided with a distinct set of 'rights'. By breaking a law an individual is breaking the implicit social pact that accompanies these granting of rights. This new formulation required similarly generalised techniques of punishment. Punishments should be judged by their effects on society as a whole – whether by reforming criminals or sending messages to future potential law-breakers. Finally, given their broader effects, punishments should be meted out carefully and precisely so as to maximise their transformative effects, both on the criminal and the social body as a whole.

This did not render the 'stuff' of the criminal body irrelevant, however. It is rather that the individual body comes to matter less for what is done to it directly. As Foucault put it:

> [t]he body now serves as an instrument or intermediary: if one intervenes upon it to imprison it, or to make it work, it is in order to deprive the individual of a liberty that is regarded both as a right and as property.
>
> (Foucault 1975, p. 12)

It is this that provides the context for the rise of debtors' prisons, which were employed particularly widely across Europe in the eighteenth and nineteenth centuries. On the one hand prisons offered the promise of an institution that could reform the recalcitrant debtor. After all, the new capitalist economy depended on the security and dependability of the debtor-creditor relation;[12] as Foucault argues, one of the ambitions of the modern prison was to reconstitute the criminal as a fully rounded economic subject, an *homo economicus* (1975, pp. 122–123). On the other hand, the core principle of using the body as an ultimate material guarantee for a debt, a principle that had underpinned the credit economy for so many centuries, could be transferred into the modern era, even if in altered form: bodily freedom, newly considered as a both *right and property*, could now be made to stand in for the property (the debt) that was, by right, due to the creditor.

This new, amended principle was also eminently portable. The pathways of Empire meant that debtors' prisons were quickly transferred to British America – one of the first instances of a transatlantic transfer of specific technologies for dealing with defaulting debt. Although there were variations in the specifics of their legal arrangements, every British colony and subsequently every US state allowed the use of imprisonment for outstanding debts (Mann 2002, p. 79).[13] This transfer included the relevant legal mechanisms, although in the US the idea of 'attaching' the debtor's body in lieu of their debt became arguably yet more explicit: while in the UK it appears that 'writ of attachment' came to be the most commonly used legal formulation, in the US 'body attachment', as well as its legal twin 'body execution', found common usage (the latter is a legal term and does not refer to capital punishment).[14] These powers were used to compel the defaulting debtor to appear before court and, if they could not find (either themselves, or from relatives/associates) the funs require to cover the debt (a 'security', held until the case had been resolved), they would be confined to prison until a debt was repaid (Mann 2002, pp. 24–25).

Over the course of the nineteenth century, however, something changed. The identity that had served creditors for so long, between a debtor's body and a debt, could no longer be sustained.[15] In the US, the state of Kentucky began the steady march of abolishing debtors' prisons in 1821. Federal debtors' prisons were abolished in 1833 and most states had followed suit by the 1920s (Peebles 2013, p. 702; Vogt 2001, p. 345). In Europe many countries did the same, mostly towards the end of the nineteenth century.[16] In the UK, the imprisonment of defaulting debtors was formally abolished in 1869, although prison continued to be used as a routine, if exceptional, sanction for defaulting debtors right up until 1970[17] – the difference being that debtors were not criminalised for their failure to repay the debt, but for the 'contempt' understood to be being exhibited by a debtor's non-adherence to a court order to repay (see Finn 2003, pp. 187–188; Rock 1973, p. 222).[18]

The imprisonment of defaulting debtors is an ostensibly powerful weapon in the creditor's armoury. The fact that creditors were potentially able to constrain a debtor's liberty until the debt was repaid could act as a powerful incentive for a debtor to put pressure on friends and family to find funds to allow their continued freedom (Mann 2002, p. 25). Perhaps more importantly, it served as a threat that could be mobilised against a debtor to convince them to repay without the need for court proceedings. Given the deep interrelationship between the rise of personal credit and an ever-expanding capitalist global economy, this backstop of the nascent consumer lending industry might have become ever more relevant. The abolition of debtors' prisons, however, suggests otherwise. How, then, can we account for their demise?

Part of the answer is that, while the rise of the modern prison may have been, it its own right, an ethical project, when it came to debt *in particular*, its use came into conflict with the claims being made for another ethical project, which it both coincided with and undergirded: capitalism. As Gustav Peebles argues, many in the British reform movement of the nineteenth century believed that the legal relationship between creditor and debtor, a relationship that was (and still is) at the heart of capitalist accumulation, 'had yet to rise beyond its supposed barbaric underpinnings'. He continues:

Specifically, the explicit right of the creditor to seize and sequester the body of the debtor, and the corresponding implicit right of the debtor to flee his debts and thereby 'swindle' the creditor out of his assets, allegedly created the same dark Hobbesian world that reasoned capitalist trade should eradicate.

(Peebles 2013, p. 701)

The fact that the very entity at the core of the capitalist endeavour – the extension of and profit from capital – seemed to be relying on the bodily incarceration of the debtor, undermined its ability to claim to be not simply an economic project, but also a moral one.

Peebles, in a study that looks in particular at the British reform movement, identifies a number of factors that played into this argument, many echoes of which can also be found in the corresponding US reform movement, as documented by Bruce H. Mann (2002). Of central importance is the fact that the imprisonment of a debtor for debt seemed to actually prevent him or her from being, or becoming, a productive economic citizen. As suggested in the previous extract, prisoners in the UK were, for the duration of their stay in prison, protected from having further assets seized towards the repayment of a debt. This led many critics of debtors' prisons to see them as a something of a haven, an escape from the responsibilities that accompanied the conduct of a 'proper' life within this new, rapidly emerging commercial world. This claim was reinforced by the fact that, if prison did not ultimately convince a debtor to repay their creditor, in certain instances there existed a set of 'specific legal rituals' that some debtors could ultimately undergo to 'wash' the debt away (2013, p. 717). While there were some circumstances where debtors could earn a meagre income in prison (see Finn 2003, p. 144; Woodfine 2006, p. 5), not only was this likely to make little impact on their debts, quite deliberate attempts were made to separate debtors from the broader commercial world (Peebles 2013, p. 712). In the US case, the self-evident fact that the incarceration of a debtor was often of little practical benefit to the creditor led many colonies to permit insolvent debtors to be bound to their creditor as, in effect, indentured servants, being made to work to pay off their debts for as long as seven years; as one debtor himself put it, 'the gaol [jail] will pay no debts' (Mann 2002, p. 79; see also Countryman 1976, pp. 812–813).

The reform movement was also cut through with concerns about the moral implications of using the debtor's body as a debt's ultimate guarantee. Christianity was highly influential in the movement and this fed into a discomfort with the equation of the body with finance. As Peebles notes, in reformers' discomfort about the seizure of the debtor's body in lieu of repayment, we see a connection to Viviana Zelizer's (e.g. 1985; 2005) work, which provides an analysis of the long history of the social and economic unease about the potential bleed between the body and finance; 'If the soul was priceless, then it became abhorrent to treat its vessel, the body, as a mere thing that could be seized as collateral like a piece of cheap property' (Peebles 2013, p. 705).

Finally, in the context of the application of rationality and categorisation towards an ever-broader range of entities, there was an increasing discomfort with the homogeneous, undifferentiated form of punishment represented by the use of imprisonment for unpaid debts.[19] In the US, for instance, focus shifted to the lack of differentiation between unfortunate debtors and the broader criminal class: 'misfortune is no crime', as it was put in *Forlorn Hope*, a newspaper set up by a lawyer and campaigner for prison reform William Keteltas (Mann 2002, p. 104).

We could connect the ultimate dissolution of the debtor's prison to a host of more recent developments. There are for instance parallels between the eighteenth and nineteenth century attempts to redistribute responsibility for the reform of the debtor away from the criminal justice system and towards the debtor themselves – now seen as the prime agent for effecting the bodily transformation necessary to become a well integrated economic citizen – and Foucault's (2007, 2008) later attention to how forms of governance become enacted through biopower and 'apparatuses of security'. This includes the new problematisation of debtors as a diverse, heterogeneous 'population' and the associated shift towards techniques of prevention rather than punishment. We could also draw an ancestral line between this and those contemporary moments when debtors are addressed as ideally entrepreneurial figures, tasked with managing and being responsible for their own finances (see Chapter 1; see also Langley (2008b, 2014), Marron (2009, 2012)).

Interesting as it might be to pursue these avenues, I want to remain focused on the practical outcomes for the work of debt collection implied by the removal from the scene of that ultimate material guarantee that had, for so long, stood in for a debt if it was not repaid: the body.[20] The principal result was to radically change the adverse future consequences that could be deployed by a creditor in the direction of the debtor in the form of a *threat*. Threat has long been the collector's most potent weapon, even when prisons were available as a sanction. As Mann documents, many US creditors knew that prison would, on its own, do little to secure repayment, while legal action could drag on for years (Mann 2002, p. 18). In the UK we see how supporters of imprisonment for defaulters drew attention to the importance of the 'unerring ability of the *threat* of incarceration to distinguish between the industrious and the idle poor' (Finn 2003, p. 216; emphasis added; see also Peebles 2013, p. 711). Such threats were no longer available to the twentieth century collector. At the same time, collectors were about to enter a world characterised by the explosion of consumer credit. Their response to this twin problematic, in a move that continues to shape the contemporary consumer collections industry, was to begin to better mobilise affect in the service of attempts to secure market attachment. What we will see is not a radical break, however, but rather the flowering of existing tendencies. Mann provides the eighteenth century example of Emphraim Kirby, a young Connecticut attorney who was trying to change the mind of a client determined to take legal action: it would, said Kirby, 'be best in most cases to endeavour to secure the debts by friendly negotiations' (Mann 2002, p. 20).

Precisely what practices and approaches were covered by 'friendly negoti-ations' we can only guess. However, already here we see the recognition of the need for collectors to connect with the debtor, to solicit their attachment, through registers not limited to the disciplinary or the juridical. In this sense, it is a foretaste of what is to come.

The transatlantic transfer of consumer credit technologies

After centuries in which a debt collector could threaten the debtor with, at the very least, imprisonment, the twentieth century debt collector would be left having to redefine the very business of debt collection. No longer could the debtor be addressed, be threatened, in relation to their fleshy bodily substance.

The resulting process of redefinition was by no means instantaneous, taking until around the mid-1960s until a distinct form of expertise started to crystallise into a set of methods and approaches that continue to be developed and refined to this day. However, whereas the principal technologies of debt collection from the previous era – including the debtors' prison and its associated legal instru-ments – had been exported from Europe to its colonies, the twentieth century saw the US export its technologies outwards and back to Europe, including to the UK. The main reason for this reversal is simple: technologies of debt collec-tion are inevitably deeply intertwined with technologies of credit lending – and the form of credit lending that had the most significant impact on the work of the collector in the twentieth century was consumer credit. This is a technology that was refined, experimented with, and embraced in the US far earlier and to a far greater extent than in any other country. For this reason, before we examine exactly *how* the collections industry responded to the changed landscape of credit and debt the world confronted at the beginning of the twentieth century, we need to look at *where* the most significant developments occurred.

In the US, consumer credit not only happened earlier than anywhere else, it also happened on a far larger scale.[21] It began to make major advances in the 1930s, stuttered briefly in the 1940s,[22] before marching more or less relentlessly forward from the 1950s onwards. Key to its ascendency was the rise of revolv-ing credit that, in contrast to instalment credit, allowed the debtor to repay according to a potentially variable schedule. It would of course be the credit card that, from the 1960s onwards, exploited the potential of revolving credit more than any other instrument.

It is testament to the power of consumer credit to capture the imagination of both businesses and politicians in the US that it seemed to possess the power to knock out of the way any and all attempts by government to control its growth. The 1940s hesitation was in part because of the introduction of a form of credit control known as 'Regulation W', which put restrictions on the credit businesses were able to extend, in particular during the Second World War. In the period following the end of the war, and in part because of pressure from retail lenders, this regulatory apparatus was significantly watered down, before being eventu-ally abolished in 1952 (Hyman 2011, pp. 99–131; Marron 2009, pp. 70–71).[23]

When President Jimmy Carter tried to reintroduce credit controls in 1980, the experiment lasted a mere two years, again wilting under the pressure from businesses and lenders, with many (perhaps unfairly) holding credit controls at least partly to blame for the then faltering economy (Marron 2009, pp. 95–96).

However, it is worth keeping in mind how relatively unique this early history of US consumer credit is. If we look across the water to Europe, not only were many European countries far slower to embrace consumer credit, in many cases this embrace remains, to this day, significantly less enthusiastic, as Figure 3.1 shows. A notable exception, recently at least, is the UK: as the same chart indicates, in 2010 its households relied marginally more on consumer credit than even their US counterparts. This is, however, a relatively recent state of affairs. Well into the 1970s, the very kinds of credit controls that the US had tried, but failed, to institute, constricted consumer lending in the UK. It was only in the 1980s, when the Thatcher government came to power, that many of these controls were lifted,[24] paving the way for the real acceleration of consumer credit lending throughout the decade and beyond.[25]

Because of this somewhat delayed embrace of consumer credit in the UK, for much of the period leading up to the 1980s specifically *revolving* consumer credit, which had long been so important in the US, was more or less absent. Consumer credit was instead limited to instalment credit: to bank loans extended to generally well-off middle or upper class borrowers, or, towards the lower middle and working class end of the market, largely either to mail order and retail credit and to hire purchase credit extended against particular high value items – household appliances or cars, for instance. In the so-called Crowther report,[26] published in 1971, which paved the way for the beginnings of the

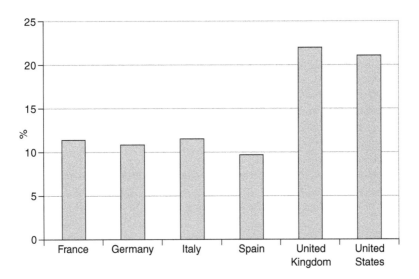

Figure 3.1 Consumer credit as a percentage of household disposable income, 2010 (source: Adapted from Magri *et al.* (2011, p. 23)).[30]

deregulation of the British consumer credit industry three years later,[27] we find a revealing snapshot of the pre-deregulation state of affairs. It provides data for 1969, which shows that bank lending was more or less matched by mail order, retail and hire purchase lending (see Figure 3.2).[28] It also includes figures for check-trading – a form of doorstep finance which has been analysed in some detail by Liz McFall (2014). Credit card debt is, at this stage, a negligible 0.1 per cent of the market. When it comes to the slightly different measure not of credit extended but outstanding at the end of the year, credit card debt made up only around £5 million, or around 0.04 per cent of the total £13 billion then owed by British borrowers. By contrast in the US, of the almost $123 billion worth of consumer credit outstanding by the end of 1969 (almost six times as much as in the UK), credit card debt made up almost $15.3 billion, or around 12.5 per cent (Weistart 1971, p. 1488).[29]

The important consequence of this, from the perspective of the UK, is that the movement of consumer credit lending technologies has followed a consistent geographic trend: from the US to the UK. Of these movements, it is perhaps the trajectories of technologies associated with consumer credit lending that are most familiar. For instance, in the US, the widespread issue of unsecured personal loans by banks started in earnest in the 1930s (Hyman 2011, pp. 73–97), whereas in the UK it was only after the government removed the 'ceiling' on bank lending in July 1958 that we find banks starting to adopt the practice (Wadsworth 2013 [1973], pp. 216–217). In the UK, when the Barclaycard, the UK's first mass market credit card, launched in 1966, it was dependent on technology licensed from Bank of America (Martin 2010, p. 181; see also Anon 1966). By this stage the US consumer had accumulated over a decade's worth of

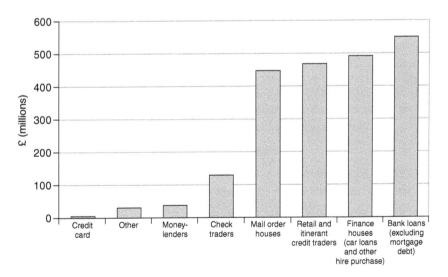

Figure 3.2 UK unsecured consumer credit debt extended during the year, 1969 (source: Adapted from Crowther (1971, pp. 57–58)).

familiarity with these devices, given that experiments with the earliest mass market bank and credit cards can be traced back to the early 1950s (Hyman 2011, p. 145; see also Chapter 1). Similarly, while the development of quantitative credit scoring practices began in the US in the mid-1950s, these practices would not be fully embraced in the UK until the mid-1980s (Leyshon and Thrift 1999; Poon 2007; Wainwright 2011).[31] We thus find the Crowther report constantly looking over the Atlantic towards developments that it expected to soon arrive on British shores. For instance, with respect to credit cards, it notes that although they

> do not as yet appear to have given rise to problems in this country, it is to be anticipated that the inevitable expansion of this form of credit will produce at least some of the difficulties that have already been experienced in America.
>
> (Crowther 1971, p. 341; on credit scoring, see p. 376)

Less well understood is that the same broad set of trajectories can be observed with the transatlantic movement of debt collection technologies. In the next chapter we will see how the UK's recent embrace of debt purchase – that is, the purchase of large portfolios of defaulting debts from a creditor – stemmed from what was originally a US innovation. This movement is also to be found in the older history of UK collections. We thus find that the use of the telephone for collecting consumer credit debts only starting to be adopted in the UK in the 1960s (perhaps even as a result of a direct transatlantic connection – although coming in this case from Canada, not the US (Scully 1983)).[32] In talking about the rise of what he called 'direct debtor contact', Steven, a retired collections company director that I spoke to, with decades of experience in the business, told me that previously 'it was all letters and litigation, although we might have made visits' and that the use of telephone collections was 'a major breakthrough [...] oh yeah. It was a new innovation'.[33] In the US, by contrast, we find in the industry publication *The Collector* (from which much of the following information stems) detailed discussions about the use of the telephone as a collections tool as far back as the early 1940s.[34] By way of an example, take the following extract, from an article published in 1943 titled 'The use of the telephone in effecting collections':

> People drop everything to answer the phone. Take advantage of that fact. A collector using the phone is always under your eye. He is worth more money. He will develop fast. You are right nearby. With a Talk Card [a predetermined set of responses to objections and excuses] he is hard to beat. Specialize in the use of your phone for a month. You will soon find that you have probably been neglecting the most important, economical and efficient method of communication you have. Overcome your dislike for it. It can be made your best collection accessory in short time.
>
> (Turner 1943; see also Gibbs 1942; Kane 1947; Peterson 1943; Poswa 1941)

Already, then, we see explicit discussions of the particular type of interaction that conversations mediated by telephone afford, in contrast to other mediums. By 1945, we find a full-page advert in *The Collector* for a collector's 'manual', in which it proclaims the telephone, the solicitor, and the letter to be the 'inseparable trio' of collections (Figure 3.3). The recognition of the importance of harnessing multiple different collections techniques together, including here the letter, telephone and litigation, pre-empts discussions that would continue in the industry over the course of the next 60 years. As the anonymous author puts it in the accompanying text, '[t]he amount of your profit or the extent of your loss will depend entirely on how this TRIUMVERATE is managed and coordinated' (Henry S. Fulks, Publisher 1945; original emphasis).

As with the broader credit industry, the US collections industry also embraced the full promise of automation far earlier than the UK, assisted by the far greater economies of scale of the US consumer credit market.[35] In the UK, up until the 1980s, when computerisation transformed the face of collections, most of its work seems to have been manual, although perhaps assisted from the 1970s by some, by comparison, relatively rudimentary duplication machinery to assist in filing work.[36] By contrast, by the 1960s in the US, a new breed of larger collections agency was using sophisticated automated processes, both to assist in their back offices and in their communications with debtors. This made eminent financial sense given the significantly increased scope of collections work available as credit card lending, and thus credit card default, took off from around 1960 onwards.[37]

One such company was the Credit Bureau of Greater Syracuse (CBGS). It claimed that in the 1960 to 1961 accounting period its new business was worth $3 million.[38] This figure was a sixfold increase from the previous year. And yet company secretary Newton D. Bartle insisted that no additional staff needed to be taken on because of the automated processes they had instituted. Bear in mind that, five years later in 1966, only £1 million (a roughly equivalent figure at the

Figure 3.3 The Inseparable Trio (source: Detail from Henry S. Fulks, Publisher (1945)).[39]

a

b

Figure 3.4 Using various IBM machines to assist in the collections process.[40] Original captions, for Figures 3.4a abd 3.4b above: a) 'As new accounts come into the office, work cards are punched on an IBM 26 printing card punch. One girl can now prepare punched cards in a shorter time than three girls working manually'. b) 'An operator loads punched collection work cards into an IBM 403 for automatic preparation of collection notices at the rate of 1600 per hour'.

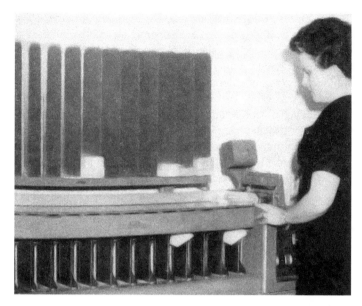

c

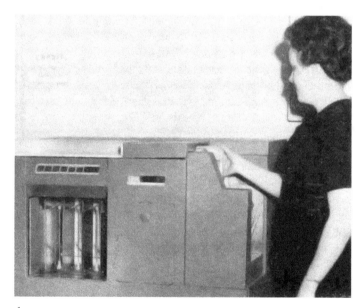

d

Figure 3.4 Original captions for Figures 3.4c and 3.4d above: c) 'At the end of each day, the entire collection file is processed through an IBM 82 sorter. The sorter drops out accounts which are to receive a second, third, or final follow-up notice the next day'. d) 'Cards out of the file each day are processed on an 085 collator and interfiled into their proper place. This operation was also done manually previous to the machine installation'.

time) would be lent on credit cards to the *entire UK population* (Crowther 1971, p. 52). This US collections company did not even operate nationally, but only in the state of New York. In particular by using IBM punch card machines, CBGS claimed that automation provided numerous benefits, including helping in the automatic preparation of collections notices, managing follow-ups, and in preparing forwarding notices to other collection agencies to enlist their help in retrieving the debt (i.e. when a debtor had travelled out of the collector's area of operations). He continues: '[t]oday, one girl [*sic*] can handle 1,300 new accounts in two days. This includes preparation of work cards, acknowledgement lists, original notice and the alphabetizing of the work cards for filing' (Bartle 1962, p. 9) (see Figure 3.4). The overall economic gains of this increased efficiency were significant: pre-automation CGBS' average amount collected per employee was $2,500 per month; post automation this had increased to $6,200 (1962, p. 11). A typical US collections agency at the time, by contrast, likely to own a company with perhaps half a dozen employees, just operating in a local area, was collecting a mere $1,500 a month.[41] The rise of this new breed of large collections agency, vastly more efficient and profitable, would in time emerge as a major threat to these smaller companies.

Not only was the UK industry less technologically sophisticated, it was also far less cohesive. While in the US a nationwide body, the American Collections Association (abbreviated to ACA; in 2001, it changed its name to ACA International), had been founded as early as 1939 to represent the interests of consumer credit collectors, in the UK a comparable organisation only emerged in 1980s, first as the Collection Agencies Association and later, following a merger with the more trade-focused National Association of Trade Protection Societies in 1988, as the Credit Services Association.[42] An interview with a debt collector, conducted by Paul Rock in the mid-1960s, reveals the US association's incredulity at this apparently fragmentary British industry:

> American Collectors' Association, I had them in here a little while ago, and apparently all the debt-collecting associations in America have got an association. And he came over here: he'd no idea of how the work was over here, he couldn't understand why we were all individuals and not joined together. And I explained to him, I said 'an Englishman is a very different type to an American. He is prepared to work on his own [...]'. But they couldn't see it at all.
>
> (Rock 1973, p. 79)

For much of the twentieth century, then, the UK debt collections industry was playing catch up with its US counterpart, with the gap only closing in the 1980s, as consumer credit boomed and computerisation took hold. To really locate the early debates and exploratory, experimental practices that would later become accepted as part of the collective 'know-how' of the global collections industry, thus means turning our attention to the US (although I will refer back to the UK when relevant).

Having now established where to focus our attention geographically, we may wish to recall where we have ended up after our trip through some of the last 3,000 years of credit, collections and default. The situation can be broadly summed up as follows. The US collections industry was faced with a twin problematic: on the one hand, the growth of consumer credit from the 1930s onwards meant that collectors were ever more in demand; on the other, the sanctions available to them had been watered down significantly over the course of the previous century, in particular by the removal of the threat of the physical attachment of debtors to their debts. As we have seen, part of the response to this problematic was technological: embracing the promise of the telephone, of automation, as well as of simply working together as an industry. However, this tells only part of the story. To really understand what changed, we need to look to something else. That something, I want to propose, is the industry's increasing understanding, mobilisation, and exploitation of affect.

The mobilisation and exploitation of affect

When Emphraim Kirby, the eighteenth century Connecticut attorney we met earlier, suggested 'friendly negotiations' as an alternative to litigation, he was mobilising an aspect of his contemporary collections expertise. We can speculate that this was a form of knowledge or 'know-how' obtained through a mixture of personal experience and knowledge passed down through the profession, in which the challenge becomes how best to use this knowledge to exploit what Mann calls 'the rules of the game' (2002, p. 23). This included knowing how and when to 'bluff' a debtor (ibid.). In Kirby's case, this know-how told him that a form of well-managed, interpersonal interaction may, in this particular case, be the most efficient method to use for a creditor looking to recoup their outstanding debt.

Attorneys and lawyers have long existed in a highly formalised professional domain, which has in place a range of structures to allow such expertise to move between its members. This includes the system of professional training and certification, which is of course part of what lends this profession its social legitimacy and authorises the knowledge it produces. It also includes routine encounters with other members of the profession working on similar issues. This might occur within particular legal practices, in court cases, via forms of associational affiliation, or in the potentially frequent range of informal encounters with others in the profession.

However, in the early days of debt collection in the US, collectors operated in a far more isolated domain. In an interview in *The Collector*, Fred Schmitz, a Milwaukee collector with more than 30 years experience in the industry, recalled how, when he first set up his collections business in 1931 (initially on a part-time basis) 'anyone could be a collector and almost anyone was' (Zimmerman 1966, p. 6). His own entry into the business came when, facing a particularly expensive dentist's bill, he jokingly offered to collect the dentist's other outstanding debts in order to pay off his own. The dentist promptly took him up on the offer, marking Schmitz's entry into the collections business. He would in due course extended his work to a range of local dentists and medical practices and, eventually, to a range of types of debt. Like many collection agencies at the time, this was a husband and wife operation, with the work of collections being largely face to face; Schmitz said he 'spent most of my day pounding on doors. The people I called on were generally anything but receptive to my request for payment – of any kind!' (ibid.).

Another example can be found in the semi-fictionalised memoirs of Preble D.K. Hatch, titled *Don't Shoot the Bill Collector* (1950).[43] The book begins in 1929, with Hatch unemployed and financially responsible for his wife Emily and their two children. One rainy evening, he came to a decision:

> I recall sitting by the window for an hour listening to the steady pattern of the rain against the glass while my wife hurried about, caring for two feverish and very uncomfortable children. Abruptly I called out to her.
> 'Emily, I'm going into business.'
> 'What business?' she demanded, in a tone heavy with skepticism.
> As I replied, my grin was as cheerful as that of an undertaker in a healthy town.
> 'Bill collecting. Northrop over to the hardware stores says that they have a lot of overdue bills on the books. He thinks he could collect plenty of them, if he only could get the time to go see these people. Well, I've got the time. And lots of other stores must be in the same fix'.
>
> (Hatch 1950, p. 2)

By the next morning, Hatch had bought a second hand desk, a small card file (for under 10 dollars), rented a typewriter, installed it all in the front room of his house and was good to go as a debt collector. This is how easy it was to set up a collections operation, with many states not requiring licenses at least until the late 1930s, some much later.[44] The book then follows him, again helped by his wife, as he learns his trade on the job over the next nine years (although he brought some experience with him – in his previous job he handled credit collections for a furniture company (Hatch 1950, p. 1)), up until the point when he sets up a credit bureau alongside his collections operation.[45] Hatch provides a series of light-hearted vignettes, each of which see him getting into his car (or even onto a motorcycle), travelling to the debtor's home and encountering him or her face to face, getting into a variety of scrapes along the way. In the process, he collects debts on items as varied as a sewing machine, a milking machine, an outboard motor and a horse, as well as on overdue bills for department and general stores, a doctor's practice, and for a newspaper subscription.

This nascent industry thus involved an army of small collections agencies, addressing individualised debts and debtors, with collectors building up their expertise as they went. In Hatch's case we see him learning the art of handling difficult debtors, experimenting with different types of letters and different ways of phrasing these letters. In some cases, letters are carefully personalised to try to improve the chances of soliciting a response from a particularly troublesome debtor (Hatch 1950, pp. 38–39, 66–67).

During this early period of the industry, the accumulation of debt collections expertise was thus to a significant degree dependent on the accumulated knowledge gathered and retained by either individual collectors or larger, but still quite regionally specific, collections companies. We could therefore characterise the particular set of specialist expertise being mobilised within the collections industry as *experience-based* (see Collins 2007; Collins and Evans 2002).[46] A set of contingent encounters is enfolded (to echo the terms of the last chapter) into embodied experience, which is then unfolded and drawn on as a resource in their formation of qualitative judgements – qualculations seems a particularly apt term here (see Cochoy (2008) and Chapter 1) – about how to act in a particular situation and which techniques or tactics to roll out and when.

In this respect, it seems the US scene in the 1930s and 1940s very much mirrored the structure of much of the UK consumer collections industry up until computerisation changed the face of the industry in the 1980s. Similar to the US, much consumer credit in the UK was offered by retail stores (a service provided by finance houses, later in the 1970s), which tended to undertake a lot of collections work in-house, before passing particularly difficult to collect debts out to collectors. As Paul Rock notes, UK collection companies were fairly isolated from one another, were highly protective of the information about the local debtors they had on file and rarely communicated with one another about their methods (and I've already pointed out the absence of a national association representing collectors of consumer credit debts[47]) (1973, p. 79). Like in the US, this external collections work might also be undertaken by individuals, given that, as Rock puts it about debt collection in the 1960s, it 'requires almost no capital and very little expertise to establish an agency' such that a collector might just be a 'solitary individual working from his suburban home' (1973, p. 76). While there might be broad continuities in the knowledge deployed by those within the industry (what Rock at various points calls an industry 'mythology'), for instance about the rough 'types' of debtors one might encounter, the knowledge about how *exactly* to proceed when confronted by a given situation was very much experience based: the truthfulness of the defaulting debtor is detected by intuition, by hunches, by 'feeling', by the gradual development of a 'knack', with the interpretation of what a default on a debt might actually signify about the debtor and their propensity to repay potentially varying significantly between different organisations (1973, pp. 62–63, 65). The same can be said about decisions on whether legal action should be instigated or not, or whether to accept an offer of partial repayment (1973, p. 97). While in 1970s Britain, with the gradual rise in the volumes of consumer credit, there was a move away from sole operators towards dedicated collections companies, the role of experience-based calculative judgement remained. As one industry figure[48] told me:

> It was very much up to the company, and often you and your boss, how frequently you contacted a customer, whether this was by phone or by letter,

or indeed the times when you would go out and see a customer, or the customer could come and see you. All that was manually organised. It wasn't done in the way that of course computers starting doing [...]. You were very much in control of what happened and when and how.

In the US, by contrast, from a very early stage the collections industry was looking for resources that might help supplement and reorganise this experience-based mode of expertise. This was frequently connected to a desire for the industry to 'modernise' and to improve the perception of its work amongst both the general public and their clients, the creditors.

The formation of the American Collectors Association in 1939 undoubtedly helped the pursuit of this goal, by bringing together individual collectors to discuss shared matters of concern as an increasingly cohesive and self-reflexive industry. So too did the numerous national and state-level meetings and conventions which are documented in the pages of *The Collector*. Both at these events and in the pages of this publication specific techniques and the latest ideas of the day were routinely discussed and scrutinised. One valuable new resource during the 1940s, then, was simply being able to share knowledge amongst likeminded individuals.

If increased organisational collaboration can be characterised as a resource internal to the debt collections industry, then a specific external resource was, during the same decade, embraced with particular enthusiasm in the industry: psychology. Articles that deal with the question, and promise, of psychology appear in the pages of *The Collector* regularly in this period, including some which are reproductions of conference addresses. Sometimes this interest is made explicit in the article titles. We have, for instance, 'The New Psychological System of Collections' (O'Brien 1941) (an excerpt of a new book of this same name), 'Psychology in Collections Letters' (Miracle 1941) (also the prize paper at the 1941 Joint Convention in San Francisco), 'Psychology and its Use in the Collection Office' (Lesman 1946) (also delivered before the 1946 American Collectors Association Convention), 'Psychology: Its Use in the Collection Business' (Lusk 1946), 'Psychology as a Collections Tool' (Lockman 1948) (also delivered at the 1946 Central States Convention in Fort Wayne) and a reproduced Associated Press report headlined 'Bill-Collecting Field Uses New Psychology Methods' (Anon 1948). What we see in these and other articles are not, however, detailed discussions of the specifics of academic psychological practice, but a rather loose interpretation of concepts and methods used within the discipline. What was becoming mobilised, therefore, was a broad set of principles and claims associated with psychology. Most obviously, this includes the claim that human subjectivity is at least partially knowable and amenable to categorisation and that, on the basis of this knowledge, the grounds for action and interaction may be modified.

As McFall (2014, pp. 121–169) argues, markets have at their core, a practical heart. Debt collectors were less interested in the possibility that psychology might reveal to them the deep mysteries of the human soul, than in its potential to provide them with a way to modify and render modifiable their relationships with debtors. It is for this reason that we see psychology acting as what Nikolas Rose calls an 'intellectual technology' (1996, 16). This is psychology 'not as merely a body of thought but as a certain form of life, a mode of practicing or acting upon the world' (ibid., 16, 90). When applied in a non-academic setting, this intellectual technology is of course not disconnected from the various 'psy' disciplines (e.g. psychology, psychiatry, psychoanalysis, psychotherapy) whose prominence and influence over social life has increased over the course of the twentieth century. It is rather that its claims can retain their power even when such connections are loose. The claim is to provide a *way* of speaking about and understanding human subjectivity. (Indeed, we all have to recognise our complicity in this: when I refer to the role affect, emotion and anxiety play in collections work, for instance). Like the legal profession, psychology is also accompanied by institutions and technologies that authorise the knowledge it produces. The most notable are those that ground its claim to be empirically and methodologically 'scientific'.

What 'psychology' might actually *do* for collections work becomes clearer when we move into the specifics of these articles. The earliest reference to psychology in *The Collector* that I have been able to find comes from an article published in July 1941.[49] Its author is Thelma Ray Osborne, co-owner of the Masemore Adjustment Company of Wichita, Kansas.[50] She writes:

> Acting as both representative of the client and intermediary for the debtor, the collector is in a position to be of real service – protecting his client against loss and ill will, and his debtor against ultimate defeat and disaster. It is still necessary to be firm and at times severe with many debtors, but the modern collector, having made a study of psychology, gets to know his debtors and acts accordingly. Thus the man who deserves courteous kindly treatment receives consideration. The debtor who responds to and understands only more severe methods is handled accordingly. The important point is that debtors, instead of being lumped together and treated with contempt and abuse, are segregated according to their attitudes, their ability and desire to pay, and handled psychologically, with the end result that the collector becomes in many cases both friend and credit counsellor.
>
> (Osborne 1941)

Osborne sums up the 'lure' of psychology for the collector fantastically well. The enfolding of experience as a basis for qualculative action (as a collector 'gets to know' and 'acts accordingly'), is situated in relation to this new approach to understanding the world (the 'study of psychology'). An old model, where all debtors were treated uniformly ('lumped together') is contrasted to a 'modern' approach in which debtors can be differentiated ('segregated') not only according to the particularities of their economic circumstances ('their ability ... to pay'), but also according to the expression of their personality ('their attitudes', their 'desire to pay'). This is what it means for the encounter to be 'handled psychologically', with the outcome characterised not by aggression and enmity but friendship, in which the collector becomes a kind of therapist (a 'credit counsellor').

A second article is worth looking at in greater detail. It is a reproduction of a conference presentation given by R.H. Lockman, from a collections company in Indianapolis. At the conference, Lockman appears to have begun his presentation by handing out a sheet on which were printed a variety of psychological terms including, amongst others: 'Reactions', 'Emotion', 'Sensation' and 'Intelligence'. The aim, he says, is to 'attempt to tie [these terms] in with our thinking and work'. He then proceeds to explain himself:

> We are in business to give or render service and, in so doing, make a reasonable profit for ourselves. To achieve this end what do we do? We write letters, make phone calls and conduct personal interviews in which we try to create the desire to pay the account. They are the stimuli. The reaction desired, or the response, is the payment of the account. The letter, phone call or interview must appeal to the emotions. Emotion means a 'stirred up' state of mind. Included are Joy, Sorrow, Fear, Anger, Amusement, Disgust and Curiosity. There is where your psychology enters in.
>
> (Lockman 1948, p. 33)

Lockman then proceeds to outline how this might apply to both collections letters and collections telephone calls. Letters should be 'short, to the point', '[t]he way must be left open for the debtor to pay or explain why' (ibid.). He continues:

> Many or shall we say, most people have a tendency to place a taboo on words that recall to them a sense of shame or wrong-doing. So they resent words that remind them of these feelings. They get angry, another emotion. By approaching the situation in a more friendly light the other emotions are reached and the proper response elicited. For example: the word 'important' may not get a reaction, but use the word 'urgent' and see what happens. 'It is urgent you come to our office' 'It is urgent you phone Market 9000'.
>
> On the phone a straight-forward appeal will usually get the desired response. If that fails, subterfuge must be used, in which you play your intelligence against that of the debtor. To get answers you have to build up confidence. That can be accomplished by modulating your voice and the use of proper timing.
>
> (Ibid.)

These extracts encapsulate what psychology is doing for collections in the 1940s. Initially we see Lockman undertaking 'translation' work (see Callon 1986a): he tries to make psychology, a distinct academic discipline with its own sometimes impenetrable vocabulary and concepts, relevant to the practical work of the collector. In so doing familiar collections techniques – letters, phone calls, personal visits – become reborn as 'stimuli'. The same happens with familiar situations: a debtor's response becomes a 'reaction', their anger is an 'emotion' that is potentially a product of a range of unconscious drives (more negatively, shame and resentment or, more positively, those 'other emotions' that result from friendly modes of address). This work also involves demystifying psychology. In Lockman's article, as in many others, this means attempting to render collections as *already* concerned with psychology, irrespective of whether or not the collector is aware of it. He opens his talk by pointing out that we use psychology 'every day. In our work, at home, on the bus and at the bowling alley, but do we realize it? And when we do know it, do we follow through?' (ibid.). Another author refers to his 'liberal' interpretation of psychology, arguing that '[o]ne need not be a psychoanalyst or a doctor of medicine in order to practice this science. No, an ordinary collector may achieve acclaim and success by proper application of this aptitude' (Lesman 1946, p. 26). Others assert that the good/modern collector is either 'a past master in psychology' (Sease 1947) or a 'first-class practical psychologist and an alert student of local conditions' (Kean 1947, p. 23), or even that 'three-fourths of [a] collector's procedure is based on the fundamentals of psychology' (Lusk 1946).

The promise of such translation work is twofold: on the one hand, to turn collections work into something not equivalent but similar to the academic discipline of psychology – in other words, to transform debt collection into a 'science' – on the other, to create a form of industry specific knowledge. As one author puts it, encapsulating both aspects, '[c]ollecting money from slow-paying people is not the work of an amateur. It is a science with principles as clear-cut and definite as those of any other business or profession' (Lane 1941, p. 7). The promise, in other words, is to move away from an experience-based mode of expertise towards a form of *technical expertise*, one characteristic not just of a generic practice but also of a *profession*.

With this translation complete, the categorisation of emotion can begin. Lockman, as we have seen, identifies seven emotional categories ('Joy, Sorrow, Fear, Anger, Amusement, Disgust and Curiosity'). Other articles undertake similar processes of decomposition and delineation: one lists a grand total of 11 'destructive' emotions collectors have drawn upon (in the past, the author emphasises. They are: 'fear, worry, anxiety, terror, dislike, anger, resentment, inferiority feelings, weakness, shock, and torture' (O'Brien 1941)), another an open ended four ('anger, disappointment, sympathy, pleasure, etc.' (Miracle 1941)). Another author looks to the efficacy of appealing to positive emotions including 'fairness, honesty or pride', which need to be set against the dangers of arousing 'contempt' in the debtor (Lane 1941; see also Elder 1942).

Importantly there are practical outcomes to this new attention to emotion and debtor psychology: in Lockman's case the letter and the phone call become populated by variables that can be adjusted in order to achieve the desired result. In letters this might be the specific words that are used, in phone calls this can be a vocal tone, or the timing of a collector's intervention into the conversation. Another author warns against the 'superfluous and unnecessary' overuse of threat in the body of a letter, given that the very letterhead does most of the work of communicating the collector's intention; the danger is that it makes 'too much of a show of force and arouses antagonism and is apt to kill the flickering intention and desire to pay' (O'Brien 1941, p. 15). Another discusses the 'applied psychology' involved in deliberately printing the name of the collections agency on the exterior of an envelope, or sending letters 'care of' a friend or employer: 'This, when used strategically will embarrass the debtor into paying the bill just to stop those letters from coming' (Lusk 1946). Another, also on the topic of letters, advises against an overly formal approach – '[i]n order to obtain results a collection letter must carry with it a spirit of human interest in the other person' – before going on to highlight the power of curiosity in letter design: '[e]ach letter must be so constructed as to arouse curiosity sufficient to lead the reader from word to word, line to line and paragraph to paragraph' (Miracle 1941).[51] From yet another we learn that apologising, threatening and insinuating that a debtor is dishonest are three 'attitudes' that are 'psychologically wrong' (although the author later shows himself to be hardly averse to the use of threat; it just depends on the person: some must be threatened, he says, 'and some must be forced') (Lane 1941, p. 6).

There are many more examples that I could provide, in which psychology is explicitly drawn into relation to the intimacies of collections work during the 1940s, including in discussions about collections undertaken face to face, over the telephone, and by letter. These examples would multiply yet further if I were to bring into the fold instances where these terms are mobilised more implicitly. The central point is that psychology provides the intellectual architecture upon which to hang and develop industry-specific discussions around the inner motivations of the defaulting debtor.

This had two important consequences. The first relates to the long history of debt default. Recall earlier how the abolition of debtors' prisons changed the problematic of collections. Gone, apparently, was the possibility of the collector being able to tie a debt to the debtor's body, that ultimate material guarantee, in turn significantly changing the character of the threats available to the collector. Given that collectors could do little about these changes themselves, the attention of the US collections industry turned to how threats might be better formatted, as well as to how threats – a quite particular mode of engagement – might be situated in relation to different modes of engagement. What psychology offered was an opening up to detailed scrutiny of the emotional registers through which these interactions were occurring, with the potential that they could be adapted so as to achieve more successful outcomes, more of the time. This included an understanding of the deep connection between the emotional state of the debtor and the approaches deployed by the collector.

I suggest that this marks a crucial symbolic moment, even if it is not articulated in these terms: the moment in which *affect is formally 'discovered'* by the debt collections industry. Of course collectors had long tailored the modes of interaction they might use in their dealings with debtors, including whether, for instance, threat or friendly discourse might be most effective. However, previously this had largely been done on an ad hoc basis, with an individual relying on his or her own embodied expertise to make decisions about which approach to use. What was discovered, then, was a way of talking with more precision to each other about what was previously a rather indefinable collections 'know-how'.

The second consequence follows from the first: the discovery of affect by the collections industry, their expanded focus on the debtor's emotions and thought processes, resulted in its attention turning, once more, to the debtor as an embodied economic subject. What the abolition of debtors' prisons had seemed to render immaterial for the conduct of collections work, thus comes back into the picture. However, this turn back to the debtor body is marked by a significant ontological shift: previously, it was the debtor's fleshy substance that was important, by providing the credit industry with an ultimate material guarantee. While this guarantee could not be restored by the discovery of affect, what it does is render important not fleshy substance but inner drives. If these unusually unseen, immaterial forces could be rendered visible and understandable, then the industry would have discovered a significant new mechanism for securing a debtor's attachment to their debt.

There was, however, a problem: what *exactly* was the best way to do this in practice? While in the 1940s it was increasingly realised that the success or failure of a particular letter or a particular way of interacting with a debtor was almost certainly a result of its ability to connect with their varied emotional landscape, discussions about how, precisely, these could be adapted remained rather limited – certain combinations of words or phrases, or certain demeanours, seemed more effective than others, but *how* effective exactly? How might these compare to other combinations? What other variables might be in play? And, crucially, could any of these effects be *measured*?

The industry would, in due course, be far better able to answer these kinds of questions. Before I outline how they began to do so, we should track what happens to explicit discussions on the connections between the discipline of psychology and debt collection following the 1940s. As we move into the 1950s, such discussions continue, usually in relation to specific collections techniques – for instance letter design, telephone manner, and the use of telegrams (see Anon 1951a, 1951b; American Collectors Association 1956b, 1956a, 1956c; Bailey 1959; Byler 1951; Linam 1956; Watts 1953). However, they now proceed with less revelatory intensity. It is not, it seems, that the relevance of psychology as a framework for thinking about collections decreases, but rather that it starts to become institutionalised. This is reflected in the fact that many of the discussions of debtor psychology concern how to provide collections workers with the 'basic' training necessary to be able to better undertake their work (American Collectors Association 1956b, 1956a, 1956c). Simply asserting that collections work is involved in the intimacies of emotion and human subjectivity is no longer in itself startling, but becomes increasingly rather self-evident. The translation work has already been done. This had been achieved in part by the authors in the pages of *The Collector*, certainly, but also most likely by the sheer fact that psychological terms and concepts had been proliferating throughout society at the time. Indeed, we have to bear in mind similar developments in parallel fields: the 1950s was a decade in which consumer psychology was promising to give advertisers deep insight into the mind of the consumer, building on work that had started some decades earlier (see McFall 2014, pp. 19, 95; Odih 2007, pp. 94–101; Schwarzkopf 2009a, 2009b). The claim that market-oriented encounters might be mediated by, and manipulatable in relation to, consumer psychology was, therefore, by no means unique to the credit collections industry.

As we move from the 1960s to the present day, explicit discussions of psychology in the pages of industry publications come to be increasingly limited to those that address the daily work of telephone collectors.[52] In the 1970s, for instance, we learn that ACA has 'schools for collectors' in which one of the subjects is the use of 'basic psychology' (American Collectors Association 1974). In another article, ACA instructor Al Rasher focuses on how a good knowledge of 'sales psychology' and 'personal motivation' will assist in telephone collections work. Similar pieces populate the magazine from that point forwards (e.g. Fagin 1985; Goodyear 1986; Hartmann 2003; Trezza 1998; Remley 2006; Rosso 2013), including in a four part refresher series provided by the American Collectors Association in their 'Collected Wisdom' series (ACA 1995a, 1995b, 1996, 1997). Demonstrating the degree to which the US and UK industry have come into alignment in recent years, these concerns are also on display both in the pages of UK industry publications and at recent industry events (e.g. Bailey 2010; Credit Services Association 2011; Fleming 2010; Kiely 2011; Syron 2012; Willcox 2012).

One of the principal reasons for this shift, I suggest, is that an intellectual technology that continued to be drawn on in the training of debt collectors, came to be increasingly supplemented with technologies that academic psychology had itself long relied on: experimentation and testing. Indeed, there are two sets of interlinked moments in the history of the US collections industry that stand out in this respect, in which we see these two technologies come into direct dialogue.

In 1959, a certain Eugene H. Barnes wrote an article in *The Collector* on the topic of anxiety in debt collection, an article that also provides the epigraph at the start of this chapter. Similar to some of the articles on psychology in the 1940s, his piece begins by undertaking some translation work: he describes anxiety as a specialist psychological term, defined as 'a feeling of fear ranging all the way from a mild apprehension to acute dread' in which 'the person experiencing anxiety is motivated to some action which will relieve the feeling of distress' (Barnes 1959, p. 6). He connects this particular affective state, which we have already observed in the previous chapter, to procedures of debt collection: '[i]t is obvious', he says, 'that the collector is trying to arouse anxiety when he suggests that the creditor may institute [a law-]suit or when he mentions the possibility of taking the matter up with the debtor's employer' (ibid.). The article goes on to argue that this is also the case when the collector threatens damage to the debtor's credit file, or their standing within their family or community. It also discusses the particular variables that might matter to anxiety. One of these is time: anxiety, argues Barnes, decreases the further away a feared event is, and increases as it gets closer. This means that

> [t]he threat of a bailiff at the door this evening produces stronger anxiety than the threat of a repossession next month. Likewise, the promise of 'drastic action if we do not hear from you in three days' has somewhat more motivating force than the same appeal with a five-day grace period.
>
> (Ibid.)

Another variable is the 'certainty of consequences' – the greater the certainty, the greater the degree of anxiety that will result. 'It follows, then', says Barnes, 'that the collector should exert an effort to convey the inevitability of results if the debtor persists in non-payment' (1959, p. 14).

Even if Barnes' introduction of the specific concept of anxiety to debt collectors was new, so far, so familiar one might say. However, part of what is interesting about Barnes is that he had a doctorate and had worked briefly as a research psychologist (and had published three articles on experiments he had undertaken with tests for personality disorders (Barnes 1955, 1956a, 1956b)). He had, however, left his academic life behind to work as research director of National Accounts System, then in control of seven collections agencies in the Chicago area (Black 1961, p. 53). In this role he was able to put his theories on the basis of debtor motivation to the test within the collections business. He claimed, in a conference presentation[53] reported by Hillel Black in his book *Buy Now, Pay Later*, that by using his techniques he had succeeded, over the course of two years, in increasing the amount his organisation was collecting from $50,000 a month to $170,000 a month (Black 1961, p. 54). He also claimed the highest recovery rate in the country (ibid.).

More interesting still, is that there is direct evidence of his impact. Almost two years later the owner of a collections company called Coast-to-Coast Collections Service, a certain R.H. Carder, comes back to Barnes' article. The beginning of the article is worth quoting at length:

> We have been concerned over the past several years [with] defining a maximum collection demand system. What we wanted was a system of demands that would be psychologically effective ... something that would, through a psychological effect on the average mind, automatically create a maximum average money reaction.
>
> To us the first big breakthrough came from the pages of *The Collector* in an article entitled 'Anxiety' by Dr. Eugene Barnes. Just prior to this, the physical facilities of a large IBM installation with a very substantial accounts receivable inventory came under our control. Our tab supervisor created a remittance analysis board for our IBM 407 machine, giving us a low cost means of tabulating the payment responses from the delinquency

notices. These responses are tabulated both in the number of individuals responding and in the total dollar response. These categories are further divided by the odd or even terminal digit of the account number. In testing a notice form, the new notice would be sent on the odd numbered accounts; the even numbered accounts receiving the old notice. Thus we had a direct, and we believe, extremely accurate comparison. Total responses tabulated exceed 180,000 individual remittances as a result of over 640,000 notices sent.

(Carder 1961, p. 6)[54]

Coast-to-Coast had therefore moved into the business of *experimentation*. After lavishing more praise on Barnes ('We are completely convinced from what we have seen this past year that Dr. Barnes was very much on the right track with his anxiety theory ...' (ibid.)), Carder proceeds very much in the style of an academic paper, to outline a series of tests that the company had conducted with its collections letters: what was done, what worked, and what did not. This involves setting up a control group and a test group, in order to test a sequence of seven letters, each spaced 15 days apart. This letter sequence was for a 'pre-collection' service: in other words, collections work done under the name of a client company, by an external collections organisation.

Coast-to-Coast was by no means the first collections agency to run experiments with collections devices. Recall, as an example, Hatch's rudimentary experiments with different ways of phrasing his letters. As one mid-1960s article notes, '[t]he scientific study of the effectiveness of collection letters, and the various ways to use them, is nearly as old as the haphazard use of the same' (Johnson 1966). We thus find throughout the pages of *The Collector* various references to 'tests' and the use of 'trial and error' with different collections devices, with more specific examples including a 1947 trial of various collections 'post cards', which are discussed in terms of differences between their average returns (Reiter 1947), or early 1950s experiments with the collections returns generated by new form letters to be used in medical collections and the sending of telegraphs to debtors (McGinnis 1953; Watts 1953). In the UK in the 1970s and 1980s, alongside personalised letters, most debt collection companies would also informally test out different letters and different letter styles.[55] It would thus be surprising, given his background in experimental psychology, if Barnes was not undertaking formalised experiments with his letters. However, in terms of their scale, sophistication and the rigour of their method, Coast-to-Coast's early 1960s experiments seem to be in a different league.

Their real challenge, writes Carder, was 'properly building up the anxiety pressure with each step' (ibid.). Initial experiments with different emotional appeals ('honour' compared to 'pride' compared to the threat of instigating a 'secondary process'; how exactly such categories translated into the specifics of collections letters we can only guess) were insightful in isolation (the threat of a 'secondary process' came out on top) but did not help define an ideal sequence.

This the team solved by focusing not on emotions but drawing on one of Barnes' other categories, *inevitability*. This is operationalised in 'an appeal consisting of the double concept that the bill must be paid *or* inevitable disaster will occur' (ibid., original emphasis). Carder then outlines the ideal trajectory of inevitability:

> It can be described as making the debtor feel as though he were standing on a railroad track with an express train on its way. In the beginning he sees or feels only a hint of a shape on the horizon and is disturbed by only the faintest sound. From this beginning the whole disaster builds from a vague shadowy outline, relentlessly coming closer and closer, faster and faster until, in the final minute, the debtor sees the full power and form of the disaster bearing down on him.
>
> (Carder 1961, pp. 6–7)

Further analysis was conducted on the income received for each letter. While this broadly showed that, as expected, repayment amounts gradually decreased over the course of the seven letters, there were some letters that recouped more than expected and some less so. The format of letters was then adjusted to achieve a smooth decrease, in order to maximise the amount collected at each stage (with the exception of the very last letter, whose recovery percentage increases slightly by comparison with the previous). The letters, in sets of seven letter sequences, are then forensically analysed for the benefit of readers. In sum:

- Letter 1: this is all about making contact effectively; to do so it aims to get the reader's attention through 'color, cartoons and friendliness'.
- Letter 2: 'shows the first sign of our 'inevitability' campaign as it slowly moves into gear' – particularly effective has been 'a small cartoon with bright red letters', which grabs attention with 'an initial concept 'some things just won't wait', with 'Second Notice' in a thin-lined boxed at the top of the letter; the colours, meanwhile, 'are sharp black and red on a sparkling white card'.
- Letter 3: the letter heading is changed to indicate the debt has been passed to the client company's internal credit department. This is an area, writes Carder, 'where many creditors, we believe, either over-accelerate and get tough, or fail to achieve any increase in anxiety at all'. Coast-to-Coast achieves a balance by opening with an inevitability theme: 'your account is now 45 days due'. This is softened with an understated 'honour' appeal: 'write in 10 days', for instance. The body of the letter includes specific motivating words: 'payment', 'all obligations', 'must', 'finally', 'failure', 'compel', 'resort'. Then the 10-day schedule is re-emphasised in caps.
- Letter 4: the text is similar to the third, but 'harder', including new motivating phrases: 'go further', 'final recourse', 'since you must eventually.' The paper is however different – grey, not white, with the header in just a single colour, not two.

- Letter 5: it abandons the tweaks in text that have characterised the previous two and instead changes format. The letter becomes smaller; a size somewhere in-between A5 and A4, looking to grab the reader's attention with red bold letters stating 'Final Notice'.
- Letters 6 and 7: these are discussed only briefly. Both now come from the client's attorney, while still avoiding 'everything specifically antagonistic or with bad taste'. (Carder 1961, pp. 7, 11)

Given the longer history of experimentation in the industry and the rapid adoption of automation during the period it is extremely likely that similar work was being done, perhaps cruder, perhaps more sophisticated.[56] Further, given that the approach is, in terms of its ambitions, near identical to techniques employed by many contemporary agencies, some of which we will see in the next chapter, what is particularly important is the historical precedent that is being marked. Perhaps for the first time, we see the coming together of three distinct developments not just in the early- to mid-twentieth century US collections industry, but in the longer history of debt default.

The first is technological: mid-twentieth century automisation and computerisation allowed the issuing of hundreds of thousands of collections notices as well as for the amounts collected as a result of these notices to be collated and subject to detailed analysis. As I have already observed, this capability would not arrive in the UK collections industry until the 1980s and it would not be fully exploited there until the 2000s.

The second is psychology as an intellectual technology. Barnes' deconstruction of the drivers for anxiety, building on a long-standing interest in psychology within the industry, provides Coast-to-Coast with an ambition: the construction of a steadily increasing 'journey' of anxiety. This journey, in turn, consists of a set of waypoints, each of which can be tailored for maximum economic effectiveness. This turns the humble collections letter into a potentially sophisticated technology, composed of a near infinitely modifiable bricolage of variables. These include the precise words and phrases that are used, how these are emphasised or not, how they are ordered, what colour and imagery is used, what paper size and type is used and, of course, how letters are linked to one another.

The third is the role of large scale testing and experimentation. The reason that, from the 1960s onwards, discussions of psychology in the context of US debt collection come to be increasingly limited to how telephone collectors are trained, is because people are particularly difficult to fit into tests and experiments. The approach one collections worker will use – whatever their training, whatever script they are made to work with – will be quite different to that used by their neighbour. The best a collections agency can hope for is to standardise those aspects of telephone collections work that they can, while harnessing the most productive aspects of each collector's own unique approach; perhaps, here, the intellectual technologies of psychology will provide some assistance by allowing the drivers and thought processes of debtors (and indeed collectors) to be reframed and decomposed. Letters, by contrast, fit very well into experimental methodologies. They lend themselves to standardisation, to duplication and to large scale monitoring. In Coast-to-Coast's case each letter is able to carry a unique identifier and a large body of letters can be divided into a control and a test sample. It is this that allows the detailed analysis of letter efficacy and the optimisation of their ability to generate financial returns. The empirical bases for these experiments are the lived responses of the debtor; these tests are, in other words, *in vivo* experiments (see Çalışkan and Callon 2010). It is the combined sum of hundreds of individual responses to individual letters arriving through letterboxes and becoming actors in hundreds of everyday lives that is the territory on which this experimental work is conducted and which it seeks to understand.

If translating the intellectual technology of psychology into the world of debt collection marked the moment at which affect can held to have been 'discovered' by the debt collection industry, the embrace of the *in vivo* experiment marks the moment in which affect begins to be rendered far more amenable to being 'captured'.[57] Through the generation and quantitative analysis of data about debtors as a *mass*, what was previously an opaque and somewhat mysterious quality of human existence is boiled down to tendencies to respond to the prompts of the debt collector in either one way or another. To return to the terms used in the previous chapters, the collector becomes far more able to understand the affective basis of the lures it is proffering. The unique problematic of market attachment that the collections industry seeks to respond to thus becomes redefined.

Conclusion

> A bill collector probably sees more of life in the raw than any other person you could name. At least, that has been my impression. Some of it seems humorous (afterward), some of it pitiful, much of it just plain cussed. But all of it has carried a banner of human interest.
>
> (Hatch 1950, p. 1)

We have already met Preble Hatch and heard his company's origin story; this is how he opens his memoirs. Like many early twentieth century debt collectors, Hatch claims privileged knowledge about the human condition. The work of debt collection then involved a routine of intimate, face-to-face encounters with people that operated through registers of interaction that were less bound by social nicety. It is after all, now as then, something of a taboo for a stranger to enter a home and, with little in the way of introduction, ask its inhabitants for money. The collector was thus in the position of having to perform repeated mundane breaching experiments, whose results laid much of life bare for the collector in all its rawness, in all its messiness. This was conducted on the porches of debtors, in their kitchens and living rooms, with negotiations continuing amidst the hurly-burly of everyday life – a world composed of curious children, sharp clawed tom-cats, snoring grandparents and fights between a husband and a wife, where the collector, after the culmination of his business and finding himself far from a bed, might have to pluck up the courage to ask a debtor if she would rent him a room (Hatch 1950).

We can speculate that, if we were able to observe the work of the very earliest debt collectors, we would find much that was very similar. To find a debtor, you need to find their home. To claim that debt, you needed to go to that home. This would have applied as much then as now. Further, even in the days of debt slavery and debtors' prisons, it has often probably been far easier for a collector to obtain what he wanted through negotiation and entreaty, rather than taking possession of the debtor's body as a guarantee against repayment. Debt collection, we might therefore say, has likely always been concerned with the domestic and the intimate, with a domain which blurs the boundaries between the personal and the economic, between passion and calculation. Debt collection, in other words, has always been concerned with the exploitation of affect.

There was, however, a crucial difference between Hatch's work and that of his predecessors: Hatch could not threaten defaulting debtors with either state-sanctioned violence, or slavery, or imprisonment. He had gained one additional lever – the debt collections letter – but most of all had to rely on his charm and persistence. In the ancient game of debt collection, then, the twentieth century collector seemed to be holding a far weaker hand.

Yet, in particular in the US, where the early expansion of consumer credit had made the work of the collector ever more important, the very reliance of the industry on the efficacy of its very human dealings with debtors focused its attention on this previously indefinable domain. By translating some of the epistemological apparatus of psychology into the world of the debt collector, attention could shift away from the fleshy stuff of the debtor, towards their inner world. This was the promise that marked what I've called the 'discovery' of affect. Accessing this inner world, understanding it and moulding it to the collector's advantage might provide the collections industry with a crucial new edge.

The act of discovery, as so problematically demonstrated by colonisers of their so-called 'New World', is also an act both of naming and laying claim. What psychology did for collectors was, on the one hand, to allow them to categorise and define what they were doing. The abstract, indefinable quality to collections work suddenly could be talked about, deconstructed, and tied down. On the other, it allowed the collections industry to lay claim to their practice and their expertise – that seemed so different to that possessed by so many other occupations – as *distinct*. Few other professions, it could now be asserted, had this degree of insight into the emotional territory that unfurls around the debt collector upon his or her demand for money. It could now be said that what the experienced collector knew better than anyone else was which emotional register to address a defaulting debtor through: should it be pride, perhaps? Or shame? Or fear? Or curiosity? The same collector could also claim to know when these different registers might be differently deployed and, once a debtor reacts to an initial address, which register to shift into *next*.

Affect, even if translated into the language of emotion and seemingly rendered amenable to being cut up and categorised, is a slippery fish. Just because think you can see it, just because you think you can name it, doesn't mean you can catch it. Collectors may now have believed themselves to be adept practical psychologists, but the routine work of debt collection changed only slightly as a consequence. The hopes collectors had for psychology would only begin to be more obviously fulfilled with the arrival in the industry of automation. Specifically, it opened up a new promise: that, by coupling automation to rigorous, experimental methods, the inner drives of a defaulting debtor could be discovered as *effects*. While psychology might provide a master-narrative for this work – including helping to work out hypotheses to be tested – ultimately what mattered most was not whether a particular effect represented the interaction between a collections device and a particular emotion, but rather that a collections device, for whatever reason, had become more effective.

Here we are, again, at the practical heart of markets: the collections industry was only interested in understanding the inner drives of the debtor so far as it gave them some greater purchase on the debtor – some way to strengthen the attachments binding the debtor to their debt. The basis of this attachment could no longer be the debtor's corporeal matter. The solution to this problem was to look beneath the surface of the debtor – what they found were attachments that might be secured as readily through the capture of affect as they could through the capture of flesh.

As we move in the next chapter from the mid-twentieth century to the beginnings of the twenty-first, we will see that, supplemented by ubiquitous computing and technologies of statistical modelling and econometric analysis, new forms of experimentation will emerge within the debt collections industry. This will mean that it can in some instances dispense altogether with a coherent master-narrative about the reasons behind a debtor's reactions to its prompts. On these occasions, what comes to matter far more is that reactions can be identified, differentiated and quantified. In these cases, we will see how experiments come to be conducted not only with the daily lives of debtors, but also with their pasts and their tendencies towards future action. *In vivo* experimentation will, thus, come to be combined with experiments that are *in vitro*.

Notes

1 Although these are increasingly being supplemented by electronic means of communication (notably text message (SMS) and email).

2 The picture in the UK has been confirmed to me in various ways: in the observation of the collections practices of three companies, in interviews with industry figures, and from observing discussions on a debtor's online forum: Consumer Action Group (available at: www.consumeractiongroup.co.uk/forum). In the US, as in the UK, industry discussions tend to simply assume that letters and phone calls are a natural part of collections, even as they are being increasingly supplemented by forms of digital communication (Carlson 2011; Jarman 2011; Rosso 2012; Stephens 2011). Presentations that I have observed at three iterations of the UK's major debt collections conference, CCR-i, indicate that this is also likely the case in many other

European countries, both in Western and Eastern Europe, including the Czech Republic, Greece, Portugal, Slovakia and Spain. Although of somewhat dubious academic merit, a recent survey by the Federation of European National Collection Associations (FENCA) may at least provide some further indicators. It lists the primary methods of collection in a handful of countries as follows: Germany (phone calls and letters), the Netherlands (phone calls), and Russia (phone calls, letters, face-to-face collection and SMS) (FENCA 2010).

3 Despite some moves towards outsourcing beyond the UK, it still remains the norm for debt collection operations in this country to have their call centres based in the UK. As one company director writes, most UK credit management departments have tended to see outsourcing as a short-term, tactical measure, preferring to keep their operations in-house (Purvis 2010).

4 I am taking a lead here from David Graeber's book: *Debt: The First 5,000 Years* (although the book goes 2,000 years further back!). The earliest example in my far more modest overview is a reference to a debtors' prison from the reign of the Egyptian pharaoh Pharaoh Bakenranef, who reigned between 720 and 715, taken from Graeber's book itself. Hence the (roughly) 3,000 year figure.

5 See Carruthers and Ariovich (2010, p. 99) and Marron (2009, pp. 24–35) on its varied history. For a fictionalised account, see Elmore Leonard's *Get Shorty* (1990), as also analysed by Margaret Atwood (2008, pp. 132–134).

6 For the history of pawnbroking in the US, see Marron (2009, pp. 18–20). For the UK equivalent see Hudson (1982) and Tebbutt (1983).

7 This section can be seen as sitting in dialogue with David Graeber's (2011) analysis of the techniques and forms of violence involved in transforming persons into commodities within credit relations, as well as Maurizzio Lazzarato's (2012) extension of Nietzsche's analysis of the forms of bodily violence depended on by the formation of the debtor subject.

8 There has been some dispute over this literal interpretation although, whatever the intention of the law, as Scott notes, a number of Roman writers themselves understood it in this manner (Scott 2001, p. 64).

9 See for instance 'The Parable of the Unforgiving Servant' (in Matthew 18, English Standard Version) or 'The Widow's Olive Oil' (2 Kings 4, English Standard Version). Both available at www.biblegateway.com [Accessed 17 February 2014].

10 Although we cannot, of course, ignore the varied credit relations, including forms of state sanctioned debt peonage and indentured labour that underpinned both feudalism and the various European colonial projects, including those that characterised the Atlantic slave trade (see Graeber (2011)). Indentured labour was central to the early US colonial project in which English and European subjects, including those with limited means and convicts, were made to work for years to repay their passage and subsistence costs. As we will see, indentured labour may also have been used as an alternative punishment to prison for defaulting debtors (Countryman 1976, pp. 812–813). Finally, it should be noted that unofficial and illegal forms of debt bondage are still widespread (see International Labour Office 2012).

11 Also known as the Statute of Marlborough. A further important milestone is 1350, when Edward III passed the 'Debtors Act' (Morris and Rothman 1998, p. 271).

12 Peebles (2013) in particular draws the connection with industrialisation and capitalism. Some indicative figures for the UK: in the 1770s the prison reformer John Howard undertook a tour of a range of prisons at the time. The total number of prisoners he counted during this tour was 4,084. Of these, 2,437 were debtors (Milman 2005, p. 73). Between 1830 and 1834 between 12,000 and 15,000 debtors were thought to have been sent to prison for their debts (Manchester 1980, p. 132). See also Finn (2003). It was not possible to obtain specific figures for Europe – however given the vociferousness of the campaigns for the abolition of debtors' prisons, as documented by Peebles, across a range of European countries, we can infer

that their use was widespread. Marcus also mentions the use of imprisonment for the non-payment of debt in Aleppo, Syria in the eighteenth century (1985, p. 119).

13 Although, as Mann makes clear, a distinction needs to be drawn between the dedicated British debtors prisons and the use of more varied forms of imprisonment in the US (Mann 2002, p. 85).

14 'Writ of attachment' was also used in certain US states (Mann 2002, p. 24). Body attachment and body execution are also sometimes used with reference to their respective Latin legal equivalents: *capias ad respondendum* (you may seize (the person) to (make him/her) answer the charge) and *capias ad satisfaciendum* (you may seize (the person) to (make him/her) satisfy (the claim)) (Merriam-Webster 1996). On the history of body attachment in the US, see Anon (1976) and Countryman (1976).

15 Contemporary exceptions include Hong Kong and China (Tze-wei 2009) and Saudia Arabia (Al-Jassem 2013), in which debtors may still be sent to prison for unpaid debts. LeBaron and Roberts (LeBaron and Roberts 2012; Roberts 2014a) have also documented the way in which there has been something of a return to debtors' prisons in the US in relation to a range of debts, including in relation to the collection of consumer credit debts. They cite the increase in lawsuits brought by the collections industry and a rising number of arrests in relation to collections work. This indicates, then, that the history of debt collection is by no means progressive and/or linear.

16 France in 1867, the Northern German Union in 1868, Austria and Belgium in 1871, Denmark in 1872, Switzerland and Norway in 1874, and Finland in 1895 (Peebles 2013, pp. 702, n5).

17 When the Administration of Justice Act finally put a stop to the practice (Milman 2005, p. 8).

18 The report of the Payne Committee, which was set up to look into the issue, estimated that in the 1960s around 3,000 people a year were being sent to prison because of their debts, even if many only ended up staying for a short period of time (Milman 2005, pp. 8, n40).

19 Peebles quotes the governor of Whitecross prison: 'I divide debtors into only two classes, honest and fraudulent.... it is monstrous that the same sentence should await the guilty and the guiltless' (2013, p. 706).

20 The new and revised bankruptcy laws, which in both the US and the UK followed the formal abolition of debtor imprisonment and which were subject to a process of repeated redefinition over the course of the twentieth century, only complicated the picture: however much creditors and their representatives pushed for these laws to favour them rather than debtors (see Countryman 1976; Carruthers and Halliday 2000), one of the very purposes of these laws was to impose limits on the material assets that could be reclaimed by creditors from an insolvent debtor. For more on the history of US and UK bankruptcy law see Countryman (1976), Di Martino (2005), Duffy (1985), Duncan (1995), Mann (2002), Nadelmann (1957). The question of bankruptcy will be returned to in the book's conclusion.

21 There is no need here to retell a complex history that has already been told many times before, in a number of different ways. Particularly rich historical accounts are provided by Lendol Calder (1999), Louis Hyman (2011) and Donncha Marron (2009). Martha Poon's (2007) historical account of the rise of the FICO score in the US is a further important contribution, and can be complimented by Thomas Wainwright's (2011) analysis of the adoption of similar methods in the UK in the 1980s. On the role played by securitisation in this process see Johnna Montgomerie's (2006) work. See also Paul Langley's analysis of the role played by the financialisation of everyday life as a driver for the consumer credit boom (2008b, 2008a).

22 As Marron documents, this sat alongside a range of other forms of attempted macro-regulation of consumer credit, including at the state level.

23 Louis Hyman (2011, pp. 108–113) shows that ultimately the regulation may in fact have played a significant role in increasing the take-up of revolving credit, which for

a period enabled retailers to avoid the regulation's strictures. This, of course, is the type of credit that, in particular through the increasing take up of credit cards, would shape the course of the consumer market for years to come.

24 These include: the abolition of exchange controls in 1979, the removal in 1980 of the so-called 'corset' from banks (formally the Supplementary Special Deposit Scheme – explicitly designed to constrain lending, this required clearing banks to deposit additional funds with the Bank of England when their lending exceeded certain predefined thresholds (Mullineux 2012 [1983], p. 32), the abolition of fixed reserve requirements in 1981, and the entry of building societies into the unsecured lending market in 1986 (I draw here principally on Cobham (2002, p. 56); see also Devlin and Wright (1995), Mullineux (2012) and Payne (2012, p. 112)).

25 Credit card transactions grew rapidly over the course of the 1980s then stalled during the recession of the early 1990s, before picking up again and climbing rapidly over the course of the late 1990s (Knight 2010, p. 18). The mid-2000s saw a fall in their use: the number of credit cards in circulation peaked at 71.5 million in 2005, falling to 58.9 million by end of September 2012. Borrowing figures mirror this decline: this peaked at £67.4 billion in 2005 and had decreased to £56.1 billion at the end of November 2012 (The UK Cards Association 2013, p. 15). See also Montgomerie's (2007) comparative analysis of the growth of consumer credit lending in the US, the UK and Canada and Marron's (2009, pp. 84–85) analysis of the US case.

26 Based on an investigation chaired by Lord Geoffrey Crowther (1971).

27 In the passing of the Consumer Credit Act in 1974.

28 It also provides data for 1966, for which the picture is very similar. This has been omitted for the sake of clarity.

29 Based on an exchange rate of 1.67, as accurate for 31 December 1969.

30 End of period data. Sources include respective national banks, the Federal Reserve and Bureau of Economic Analysis. European countries include consumer and producer households and include bad debts, whereas the US data includes only consumer households. Includes data on consumer credit granted by both banks and financial companies, with the exception of Euro area countries, France, Germany and Spain, although these make up only a small proportion of the total consumer credit being lent. For a full list of sources see Magri *et al.* (2011, p. 23).

31 In his study of credit granters in the 1960s, Rock finds some evidence of early experiments with quantitative credit scoring practices, in one of the hire-purchase companies in his study. This company was drawing on technologies employed by its US parent company although, as Rock writes, 'the firm's credit manager was unsure about their applicability to Britain' (Rock 1973, pp. 46, n13). All the other companies in his study employed what he calls 'intuitive judgement' in making their credit assessments.

32 The article cited speaks of 'one particular transatlantic organization'. Although the identity of the company could not be confirmed, one industry figure suggested this might have been a Canadian company that opened up a branch in London, with employees subsequently leaving to set up their own firms.

33 This corresponds to Paul Rock's observation about debt collection in the UK in the 1960s in which he observes that 'debt collection is usually based on letters alone' (1973, p. 80). In the book as a whole we only find one explicit mention of the use of the telephone in collections (1973, p. 109). Dominic, a collections industry spokesman I interviewed, who had spent many years working in the consumer credit industry, came to a similar conclusion: '[t]elephone collections as know it today, was not heard of in the 1960s and 1970s and collection was mostly undertaken by letter or doorstep visits' (email correspondence).

34 Apparently coinciding with the increasing number of women coming into the industry. This seems to have been mirrored, albeit later, in the UK (interview with Steven). Part of the reason seems to have been their sheer effectiveness, sometimes to the

surprise of their male counterparts, with one author citing 'the staying qualities that are so essential: patience, persistence, tact, firmness, directness, persuasiveness, to mention a few' and that '[t]hey appear to be more even-tempered' (Kane 1947).

35 There is not room here to provide a full history of the take-up of automation within the US collections industry. The Credit Bureau of Greater Syracuse example provided below should not be taken as fully representative of the state of automation within the industry as a whole at the time, although similar practices were widely discussed within the pages of *The Collector* at the time (e.g. Anon 1962; Campbell 1966; Osborne 1964; Schoeing 1965; Walsh 1966; Zimmerman 1966). Well into the 1980s, numerous smaller collections agencies continued to exist, many of which used predominantly manual methods, including systems of index cards for keeping track of information about debtors; by 1983, 16 per cent of ACA members were reporting they had access to computers, a proportion which would of course grow considerably in the years that followed (Rosso 2008, pp. 25–26).

36 Dominic mentioned the 'Kalamazoo' machine, for instance. Both Steven and Dominic confirmed that, prior to computerisation in the 1980s, the majority of collections work was manual, with no mention of automation made in Rock's *Making People Pay* (1973). The early British credit card lender Barclays was computerised as far back as the late 1960s (Martin 2010). Access, its competitor launched in 1972, almost certainly was too. The exact role computerisation played in any internal collections processes these lenders had in place (other than the automated issuing of credit statements (Martin 2010, p. 113)) cannot, however, be ascertained.

37 The death of the small, local collections office was a major concern in the industry in the 1960s (see American Collectors Association 1989, p. 109; Schoeing 1965), leading one experienced industry figure to observe in 1966 that 'with the increased amount of business available and more of it on a national credit card basis, we are seeing a trend toward larger, centrally located offices with more collectors, automation and offices geared to handle extremely large volumes of business. I'm afraid the small office is dying out' (Zimmerman 1966, p. 7).

38 The company name is not given in the original article. However, his apparent relative Glen D. Bartle appears later in the publication listed in association with the company (H.L. Steiner Organization 1966). They are both listed together in a newspaper article from 1949, the former as company president, the latter as secretary (Anon 1949).

39 Every effort has been made to contact the copyright holders for their permission to reprint these images. The publishers would be grateful to hear from any copyright holder who is not here acknowledged and we will undertake to rectify any errors or omissions in future editions of this book.

40 Every effort has been made to contact the copyright holders for their permission to reprint these images. The publishers would be grateful to hear from any copyright holder who is not here acknowledged and we will undertake to rectify any errors or omissions in future editions of this book.

41 The comparison is to income reported, in the same article, by members of the American Collectors Association.

42 The exact founding date of the Collections Agencies Association is unknown. The earliest reference to its existence I have been able to find is contained in *The Collector* in March 1983 (Scully 1983).

43 The author changes the names of persons and businesses, as well as 'the locations, plot procedure and physical characteristics'.

44 For a similar account see Schmidt (1949). By the late 1930s, some states started to require debt collection companies to have licences or 'bonds' with the state including both Wisconsin and Colorado in 1937 (Zimmerman 1966, p. 6; Colorado Department of Regulatory Agencies Office of Policy and Research 1999). Issues of the *The Collector* in the early 1940s saw the association push for the licensing of agencies within states, in order to improve the image of the industry. In its pages agencies highlight

their licensed status in states including California (July 1941, p. 12), San Francisco (March 1942, p. 8), Michigan (June 1942, p. 27), and Indiana (Feburary 1944, p. 16). An article written in 1944 on the evolution of the collections business in the Pacific Northwest refers to the rise of state licensing in at Oregon and Washington in the preceding years (Fearey 1944). In 1948 one article refers to the problem of the continued absence of such laws in many states (Campbell 1948, p. 33), one of which a later article confirms as New York (Lee 1949).

45 The forerunners of credit reference agencies, credit bureaus give information on debtors to potential creditors – as Hatch puts it, '[t]he two businesses go hand in hand' (1950, p. 209).

46 There is no need here to rehearse the long-standing debates within science and technology studies about the different roles expertise plays in different social and material settings, or how there is variously conferred legitimacy. For overviews of some of these debates see also Irwin and Michael (2003), Jasanoff (2003) and Wynne (2003).

47 Trade-oriented collectors were also heavily dependent on experientially grounded expertise, although many at least had the benefit of wider institutional support in the form of Trade Protection Societies, whose origin can be traced back to the late eighteenth century (see Bennett 2012; Finn 2003).

48 Interview with Dominic.

49 *The Collector* was first published in 1934 as the publication of the California Association of Collectors (CAC). The ACA, founded in 1939 negotiated with the CAC to take over the publication, with the first ACA produced issues appearing from September 1940 (American Collectors Association 1989, p. 4). It is only the latter which are publicly available (in the Library of Congress).

50 Thelma Osborne is an interesting figure. Later during the 1940s she became one of the only, if not the only, female member of the board of directors at the ACA (it is hard to be sure given that some member listings only include initials and surnames) and, in the 1950s, would become the chair of public relations. She continued to write articles in *The Collector* up until the mid-1960s on a number of topics, ranging from changes in the collections industry, to specific technological developments, to the role of women in the industry. Although most authors in *The Collector* were male, Osborne is by no means the only female contributor. Another, in fact, is her business partner Lena Schmidt, who, in 1949, gives an account of their 13-year career together (Schmidt 1949).

51 See Franck Cochoy's (2011) detailed analysis of the power of curiosity in market settings.

52 Although it is not necessary to go into here, it seems that what partially replaces the specific concern with psychology from the 1950s onwards is a more generalised concern with what it takes to 'motivate' a debtor to repay, which we find in its various forms throughout *The Collector* and, in the UK, in recent editions of *Credit Collections & Risk*. See Kurt Danziger's (1997, pp. 100–123) excellent analysis of the rise of motivation research and the increasing interest in questions of motive in popular discourse, and in particular within business circles.

53 Hosted by the National Retail Merchants Association. The year is unknown but it is certainly before 1961, given the publication date of Black's book.

54 Minor edits regarding the use of capitalisation and italics made to maintain typographical consistency.

55 Based on email correspondence with Dominic.

56 We saw earlier, in the case of the Credit Bureau of Greater Syracuse, just how much more profitable a large agency could be compared to a small agency once it had instituted automation. As a result of these economies of scale the 1960s and into the 1970s saw the US industry change significantly, with large companies expanding and often buying up smaller collections companies, in part in order to obtain access to local markets (Rasher 1970). Like Coast-to-Coast these companies were heavily dependent

on automated processes (see Campbell 1966; Zimmerman 1966, p. 7). Certain large credit card providers even handed over all their data direct to collectors on punch cards, with the customer information able to be translated into the collector's own systems (Campbell 1966, pp. 7–8). However, whether these companies were using this automated technology in the manner reported by Coast-to-Coast is unclear because their precise techniques are not reported in *The Collector*, which remains one of the few historical records of the collections agency in this period. This is because the publication's audience was, and to some extent still is, the smaller collections agency, which would likely have been unable to have the capital or the scale of operations to install these kinds of automated processes themselves. My focus is thus on the logic implied by such developments and how they parallel and pre-empt far more recent technologies.

57 I will expand on this further in the next chapter, in which I will put into dialogue work by Franck Cochoy (2007), including his concept of 'captation', and Brian Massumi's (2002) work on the capture of affect.

4 The strategic management of affect

Venturing inside the collections company

In collections, it's not what you say, it's how you say it. Boost your returns by improving relationships.

Twitter post (Experian Data Analytics 2009)

The art of debt collection has long been concerned with how, precisely, to secure the attachment of a debtor to his or her debt. As we have seen, over the course of its history, the industry has increasingly directed its attention to the unfolding affective affordances of life. These have become the object of its technologies and its investigation, in some cases, through forms of experimental intervention.

These practices are indispensible components in the 'production of the present', to recall the terms used by Lauren Berlant (see Chapter 2). They are encountered, in their different forms, and in different ways, by untold numbers of debtors more or less anywhere that has embraced the now almost ubiquitous apparatuses of consumer credit. Very little is, however, understood about the organisational processes that sit behind them. This chapter, and the chapter that follows, seeks to remedy this by moving into the contemporary debt collection company itself.[1]

To do so, it draws on research undertaken in the call centres and offices of three UK collections companies: Alpha, Beta and Delta.[2] Exploring debt collection as it is practiced by these companies will not only open up organisational processes, it will also contribute to further developing the argument that I have been making throughout this book: that the intimate and the affective matter to markets. That we have shifted from the terrain of the everyday and the domestic into the seemingly more impersonal world of the organisation does nothing to change this fact. As we will see, affect is a generative force that is distributed and acted upon far beyond the boundaries of the home or the body. Even if it is not referred to as such by organisational actors, affect is at the very heart of the way collections companies arrange their operations, the way they talk about debtors, and they way they talk *to* them. In the previous chapter, I suggested that debt collectors have become increasingly interested in the process of 'capturing' affect. This is a formulation that I draw from the work of Brian Massumi (2002). It is an analytical resource that I will this explore in more detail in what follows, while suggesting that it can be put into dialogue with an analysis of what Franck Cochoy (2007) calls processes of 'captation'. The relevance of bringing both terms to this empirical setting can, however, only be appreciated by understanding the particular problem of market attachment confronting the contemporary debt collector.

Before moving on to this, however, it may be helpful to situate the account that is to follow with a brief description of the place that Alpha, Beta and Delta occupy with the UK collections industry, as well as how we are to understand the UK industry's place within the broader global flow of collections expertise.

Contingency collections, debt purchase, and the global collections industry

Venturing into Alpha, Beta and Delta allows an insight into distinct but connected aspects of the debt collections industry. Alpha and Delta are both large, well established 'contingency' agencies. Creditors employ contingency agencies, to collect defaulting debts on commission (the legal ownership of the debt remains unchanged). As such, they fulfil particular functions for creditors, tending to be used to collect on debts once they have reached a degree of seriousness where the creditor deems that any internal collections operations they might have in place are insufficient. It is also commonplace for contingency companies to specialise in particular aspects of collections: Alpha, for instance, tends to collect on accounts with relatively low balances, on which attempts had often already been made to collect on the debt, either by other contingency agencies, or via creditors' own internal collections operations (the latter will be addressed in more detail in the next chapter). Delta tends to work debt at a relatively early stage in the collections cycle, with much of the outstanding balances being relatively high.

Beta, by contrast is a 'debt purchaser' and one of the largest in the UK. As will be explored in more detail in the next chapter, debt purchasers have come to occupy an increasingly significant role in the collections marketplace. Rather than collect from a creditor on commission, debt purchasers buy a portfolio of debt, composed of potentially many thousands of individual accounts, outright. The ownership of the debt moves from the so-called 'original creditor' to the debt purchaser, now the new creditor. Some purchasers acquire these 'bad' debt portfolios with the intention of sending them out to contingency agencies, often after having undertaken an analysis of which accounts are more likely to generate a return (to which the chapter will return to in due course). In these cases, the function of the debt purchaser is to manage the collections process. However many debt purchasers buy defaulting debts with the intention of 'working' these accounts *themselves*. It is the latter business model that informs Beta's operations. Debt purchasers like Beta are therefore companies that, like contingency agencies, specialise in collections, with the key difference being that they retain the ownership of the account and will therefore potentially collect on that account for a far longer period. Accounts are usually only passed by a creditor to a contingency agency for a limited period of time (this forms part of a deliberate strategy, as the next chapter will examine), tending to be a few months.[3] Debt purchasers, by contrast, as the (new) creditor, themselves take on the responsibility for collecting on that account potentially up to the point of making the decision as to whether to either write off the amount entirely, or to instigate legal action. This process could take many months, or even years.[4]

The focus on the UK offers an insight into one of the world's most techno-logically sophisticated collections businesses. While for much, if not all, of the twentieth century, collections practices in the UK tended to belatedly adopt those being deployed by the world's largest industry in the US, as it has moved into the twenty-first century the UK collections industry has become, in some aspects at least, more advanced even than its US rival. This is despite the economies of scale that still pertain to the US collections market (and even with the UK's posi-tion as perhaps the most enthusiastic embracers of consumer credit in Europe (see Figure 3.1, previous chapter)).

The reasons for this are instructive as the comparison renders clear both what is distinct about the work being undertaken by collectors in the UK, as well as how this maps onto tendencies within the global collections industry. The first relates to the distinct regulatory regimes in UK as compared to the US. In the UK, collectors are particularly vulnerable to a recent requirement that all UK companies have had to be ready to demonstrate, if required, that they are 'Treat-ing Customers Fairly'.[5] With the industry having noted with some trepidation the strong regulatory action taken in other domains in relation to this require-ment,[6] one of its effects has been to limit some overtly aggressive and/or mis-leading styles of collections; another is the introduction, in particular in larger companies, of fairly detailed systems of monitoring the compliance and behaviour of collectors.[7] The second reason, related to the first, is that it often makes less sense for collectors in the UK to use the courts to recover their debts. In the US, not only is the legal process quicker than in the UK, but also it can be instigated *en mass*, with industry increasingly turning to the controversial prac-tice of so-called 'robo-signing'. This involves the filing of thousands upon thou-sands of lawsuits against debtors, in particular in small claims courts.[8] One US industry consultant recently claimed that, while in 2008 only 15 per cent of col-lections revenue had come from some sort of legal process, in 2011 this figure had risen to just under 50 per cent (Dressen 2013, p. 48). In the UK, the propor-tion is likely far smaller.[9] These two factors have meant that UK collectors have had to learn to work particularly hard to collect debts without easy recourse to legal action while being subject to closer regulatory scrutiny than their trans-atlantic cousins.

This does not, however, mean that the UK collections industry is exceptional. The US is a country with a legal system arguably particularly skewed in the col-lector's favour. However, this is by no means a default option. The aforemen-tioned industry consultant was not pointing to the high rates of litigation in order to suggest it as a blanket option, but because he wanted to sell his company's specific brand of expertise. This involved deploying the very kind data analytics that this chapter will document, which are designed to suggest to collectors which *types* of debtor should be subjected to which *types* of collections action.[10] This is a form of expertise that is increasingly global. As it moves into different national markets, the biggest question the collections industry faces is thus not whether to litigate or not, but *where to draw the line*. This is a question increasingly informed by a resolutely pragmatic weighing of the costs of deploying a particular collections technology against the economic benefit to the collector of so doing.

Problems of market attachment, 'captation' and capture

We have become increasingly used to thinking of things of all kind as 'multiple'. People, their bodies, the objects that surround them: what any of these things are and how they become fixed as one thing or another, depends very much on who, or what, is doing the fixing (see Mol 2002). Debtors are no exception. In Chapter 2, I suggested that both borrowers and defaulters might be seen as hybrid figures, amalgams of particular people with particular socio-economic technologies. In the case of defaulters, we saw the degree to which technologies of collection can come to inhabit everyday life and fold into the bodies and routines of both debtors and other household members. It is in and through this encounter that attempts to make debt 'matter' to the defaulter are played out, which often involve the debtor's struggle to avoid become overwhelmed by the attempts to secure their market-involvement – by these attempts at market attachment, in other words.

But, in this process of ongoing ontological transformation, there is little sense that debtors still see themselves as 'customers' of the credit industry. In what sense could they be characterised as such? Defaulters do not enter the collections industry looking to buy anything – not in the conventional sense, anyway. At the same time it is likely to be extremely hard for them to 'detach' themselves from their debts, given their financial constraints. Amongst debtors, when they do on occasion refer to themselves as such, this is more likely to be when looking into the past and recounting their journey into debt and their interaction with lenders.[11] *Then*, they assert, they *were* customers of the credit industry. Now, however, they are 'debtors'.[12] From their perspective, the relationship between themselves and the credit industry has therefore changed, from one of potentially fragile, always 'threatened' attachment (Callon *et al.* 2002, p. 205), to an attachment that has a (seemingly) solid grip on them.

However, within the UK debt collections industry, from senior management down to collections call centre worker, the debtor repeatedly appears in the guise of the customer.[13] Garry Stran, the chief executive of Clarity Credit Management, a leading collections agency, addresses this tension directly when he asserts that, because his company values the 'quality of the conversation' between his staff and 'the customer', it is 'just like almost all other customer service organisations'. But, he cautions, '[i]n our case *the term "customer" is slightly misleading as ordinarily the people we are talking to are debtors* who, for whatever reason, have not met the terms of the contract that they entered into' (Stran 2008, p. 29; emphasis added).

Are debtors customers or not? Stran seems unsure. As he notes, their relationship to the collector seems to be defined by their past actions: when they were borrowing and meeting the terms of their contract *then* they were customers; now, however, what they *really* are, are defaulting (contract breaking) debtors. The Chief Executive of Lowell, a major UK debt purchaser, also pointed to this tension: 'customers do not choose to give us their "custom" and they do not have the option of taking it elsewhere if they do not like how we treat them' (Bartle 2011). This debate was continued in the industry's latest revision of its 'Code of Practice', with discussions centring on whether to name the targets of collections activity as debtors or customers. In this case, a decision was made to stick with the former, the stated justification being that it matched the language of the regulator (Credit Services Association 2012a, 2012b).

As the collections industry thus seems well aware, this does not seem to be a conventional market encounter, characterised by competition between providers, with producers attempting to secure attachments with customers by entreaty. Perhaps calling defaulters 'customers' rather than 'debtors' is simply more pleasant? Perhaps it speaks of a desire to communicate a certain business ethics? This is undoubtedly part of what is going on here, in particular given the rise of the 'Treating Customers Fairly' regulatory culture described above. Another collections executive described how '[w]e banned the word "debtor" ... including any mention on our systems, calls, correspondence and all internal workings – and firmly replaced it, without exception, with "customer"'; this was, we are told, partly for the reason that the former was seen to be 'derogatory' (Court 2011). Leaving aside the question of how the term 'debtor', which seems a fairly accurate descriptor in this instance, comes to be seen as more derogatory than 'customer', which seems peculiarly inappropriate, this tension is nonetheless revealing. It points towards the central problematic faced by the creditor that has to deal with the defaulting debtor: that, despite the way in which the forms of market attachment surrounding debt default feel, from the borrower's point of view, very powerful, when viewed from the perspective of the creditors, they can seem very fragile indeed.

The first source of fragility concerns one of the most common fears articulated by debtors in the UK: that bailiffs are a potentially immanent presence, about to force their way into the home in order to reclaim property from the debtor as payment for their outstanding debts. In most cases, however, this is a distant prospect. In the UK, for a creditor to obtain permission to have a bailiff enter a debtor's home in order to seize possessions in order to recoup all or some of the outstanding debt, there is a relatively lengthy legal process that needs to be undertaken.[14] Equally significant are the costs involved in litigation and the fact that many defaulting debtors will have very little in the way of seizable assets with significant resale value. We saw in the last chapter how litigation has historically been something that collectors would often avoid. In the UK, this applies just as much now as it ever has, in particular if the outstanding balance is low (see Credit Management Research Centre 2008, p. 109). This second weakness, rarely fully comprehended by the debtor, thus operates around the relative lack of legal sanctions available to collectors. These constraints led one solicitor in the industry to begin an article by repeating a sentiment he claims is commonplace in the industry; that it is 'a debtor's world', concluding that, protected by regulatory frameworks, the debtor has been 'elevated into a very advantageous position' (Kirton 2010). On one hand, such claims are a tactless exaggeration, in light of the degree of distress and anxiety that actually living 'a debtor's world' entails, as documented previously. On the other, it can be seen as pointing towards a frustration emerging from an industry whose key revenue source does not feel secure in its grasp.

There is one further reason for the fragility of the tie between debtor and debt. This is related to the significant level of competition that exists between collectors. It is common for defaulting consumer credit debtors to owe money to multiple creditors, in the UK often over half a dozen.[15] Given the debtor will likely have access to an extremely limited amount of disposable income, the collections market thus plays out not in the attempt to attract new customers, but to convince existing debtors to pay *you* over others, *before* paying others, for as small an outlay as possible. This problematic is one that is near universal to contemporary debt collections practices.

The particular problem facing these debt collectors can therefore be summed up as follows: how to (re)generate value from consumer credit assets (existing market attachments), from non-paying individuals with constrained financial resources, when legal instruments are insufficient, too costly, and/or too slow, where multiple other collectors are engaging in similar petitions, while relying on ostensibly mundane technologies of mass contact.

Following the attempts by collectors to secure market attachment can be considered, after Franck Cochoy, as following the work of attempted debtor 'captation':

> it is a matter of studying the actants and the *dispositifs* (devices) which allow the opposite poles of the organization and the market, the institution and public space to be brought together, and of trying to understand their modes of articulation. We aim to show how and by what means a regulated context, dominated by management or administrative procedures, attempts to exert a hold on these less understood, more fleeting, more fluid, collectivities that we know as citizens, users, electors, buyers, consumers, clients (Cochoy and Grandclément 2005). To do this, we shall focus upon … the 'captation of the public'. By *captation* (a French word which has no satisfactory English equivalent), we mean the ensemble of the operations which try to exert a hold over, or attract to oneself, or retain those one has attracted.
>
> (Cochoy 2007, p. 204)

In many respects, this description fits the pursuit of collection practices well, speaking to the problems that the collector faces in attempting to encircle debtors. This includes the work of securing and retaining debtors: assembling relevant devices in and around the (life of the) debtor, to bind them to you over others. It also involves organisational procedure (management, recruitment, training, administration, infrastructure, and so forth). And it speaks to the *difficulty* of this work: as we saw in the last chapter, the defaulting debtor has long been understood to be fleeting, variable, and difficult to understand.[16]

But there is an aspect of market relations that is only at the margins of Cochoy's account: 'the capture of affect' (Massumi 2002). We have already encountered this formulation in the last two chapters. Focusing on affect in this way directs attention to how one market actor (here the creditor, more generically a 'producer') attempts to establish or reshape the relationship between themselves and another market actor (here the debtor, more generically, the 'consumer'), by intersecting with and directing the latter's emergent and distributed 'body-in-everyday-life' (Michael 2006, p. 44). This means paying attention to human action that may often not have a clear-cut relationship to human perception, understanding, or consciousness (see Clough 2009). Nigel Thrift writes, for instance, that

> increasingly, commodities are thought of as interfaces that can be actively engineered across a series of sensory registers in order to produce positive affective responses in consumers.
>
> (Thrift 2007, p. 39)

And that, as he puts it, a 'new version of efficacy' (p. 50) is 'gradually being foregrounded' (p. 49) in which

> what is being attempted is to continuously conjure up experiences which draw customers to commodities by engaging their own passions and enthusiasms, set within a frame which can deliver on those passions and enthusiasms, both by producing goods that resonate and by making those goods open to potential recasting.
>
> (Thrift 2007, p. 50)

These extracts do capture some of the character of some of the socio-economic intersections between defaulter and collector. However, given the problematics of collection, the challenge for collectors is less to 'draw' the debtor towards them, as to 'renew' customers' relationship to their commodities. At stake, for both collectors and defaulters, is not the simple presence and absence of (credit) attachments, but the *quality* of these attachments: for both parties, this operates around whether they are able to reshape existing attachments between debt and creditor to their advantage. The reference to the production of 'positive' affect is not inappropriate (even if 'enthusiasms' is): there is always the potential for the collector to stimulate positive affective responses if it can provide the debtor with some form of resolution (relief or gratefulness, for example). However, at the same time, debt collection practices also incorporate the frequent stimulation of 'negative' affective responses – we saw in Chapter 2, for instance, the crucial role played by forms of anxious anticipation. And finally, while – as we will see – the harnessing of debtor databases and the tailoring of communications strategies accordingly has some significant overlap with Thrift's attention to dynamic product 'recasting', although conducted more in this instance by the 'producer' than the 'consumer', I prefer to avoid claiming that contemporary debt collection cleanly fits with a 'new' or different epistemic regime.[17] Writing on debt collection back in 1973, for instance, Paul Rock had already identified that one of the key methods of consumer debt collection involved creating what he referred to as 'controlled anxiety' (1973, p. 70).

What emerges with these edits made, along with some other syntactical changes, is a definition of what I propose the variably successful enactment of debtor and debt, in and through debt collection practices, involves. It goes like this:

> Defaulting consumer credit debts can be thought of as interfaces that can be actively engineered by collectors across a series of sensory registers in order to produce *predominantly negative affective responses* in debtors. What is being attempted is to *iteratively* conjure up experiences which *refresh debtors' existing attachments* to their debts by engaging their own passions, set within a frame which can deliver on those passions both by producing good that resonate and by *subjecting those goods to acts of* potential recasting.
>
> (Key edits highlighted)

On the one hand, the form and much of the relevance of Thrift's argument remains. On the other, however, given the need to impose these changes, debt collection can at least be considered as a peculiarly inverted case of the kind of operations he describes. In what follows, I propose to explore the collections process in greater detail, as a way of opening up some of these peculiarities.

Listening in to collections conversations

In order to understand the enactment of (the attachments between) debtor and debt in and through technologies of debt collection, there is much to be gained from looking at the precise ways in which the interaction between debtor and collector can come to be played out. Aspects of this will be examined in greater depth in the following chapter, which centres on debt collections letters and the interaction between creditors and collectors. But here I want to begin by focusing on the human-to-human interaction that occurs between defaulter and collector, focusing in particular on the role of collections call centre workers and the conversation between them and debtors.

Alongside the collections letter, the collections call centre worker sits at the forefront of the full range of discursive interactions between collector and collected. As such, they can, in a similar way to Liz McFall's (2011) door-to-door insurance agents, be seen as (mostly) human 'market devices', which are absolutely central to collections industries all over the world. As I discussed in the book's introduction, their status as device is a product of their implication within a network of social and technological prostheses: most importantly, this includes the autodialler. Depending on the sophistication of the technology being employed by the collections company, this either enables the call centre worker to him/herself automatically make outgoing calls, or, increasingly, to respond to a mixture of automatically generated outgoing calls along with incoming calls from debtors.

The particular role a call centre worker will play will depend in part on the technologies with which they work. Also, as will be discussed, the nature of the role to a significant degree varies according to the place of the particular collections operation within the industry. There are also the inevitable differences in the particular history and culture of the company being worked for, including the extent and types of training on offer.

Alpha and Beta, the two call centres I visited (in the third, I listened to calls remotely at their head office) are composed of a mostly young workforce, spending a significant portion of their days undertaking activities that might be familiar to many people that work in call centres in less controversial industries. This includes tasks such as taking monthly payments, dealing with queries, and updating records. The frequency of calls they have to deal with varies – at times the volume would increase markedly, in one agency prompting the team leader to corral his team in order get them to hurry through their calls. But there are also times of relative calm, which collectors often use to chat with their neighbour. Of course, it is the collections conversations making up the rest of their time – those in which collectors try to convince debtors into paying – that makes their job a somewhat different and certainly more controversial proposition than others. And it is the case that, in both Alpha and Beta, some conversations do become heated. However, not only is this not the norm, but, after being able to listen in to an excess of 100 calls, across the three companies I visited, with numerous different collections call operators, including recorded conversations that I chose at random, one commonality stands out: that only rarely do they approximate to the degree of emotional intensity debtors express in their interviews in talking about their debts.[18] This mirrors the situation that Jeanne Lazarus found when encountering the debt recovery unit of a French bank (2013b, pp. 243–244). This becomes less surprising once you understand the work of contemporary debt collection: it involves practices operating precisely in and through the crossing point between mundane and intense modes of (inter) action.

To illustrate this, I will begin by introducing Juliet, a collections worker at Alpha. Juliet is a somewhat older, more experienced collector than some of her colleagues, having been at Alpha for nine years. Whilst she is clearly good at her job, it does not seem to particularly enthuse her. This is not apparently because of any major unease at having to routinely ask defaulters for money, or any concerns about the personal emotional impact of repeatedly having to make these calls. It appears more, as she says, because she feels 'a bit like a robot'. It is clear what she means: her calls are fairly standardised and similar to one another, with little room for personal expression. This is not meant to imply either that her job does not involve pushing for money or that her calls are devoid of emotional content – the latter will be addressed shortly. However, her work also needs to be understood in relation to how Alpha's particular business model relies as much on its volume of calls made and accounts being worked as emotive input from individual agents. Listening to Juliet is thus to listen to a collector who maintains a steady tone and rarely gets flustered.

Juliet is good at her job. One of the more successful conversations over the course of the hour I sat next to her was with a caller called Emily. From her tone of voice, Emily is perhaps in her 30s, and has a soft Scottish accent. In this conversation, as with many at Alpha, it is clear that she has dealt with the company on at least one previous occasion. This particular call results from Emily ringing Alpha in order to arrange a payment on a long-standing overdue debt, a call that is directed to Juliet. As Emily later reveals, after a period of unemployment she has recently been working for a temping agency, which means she feels that she will shortly be able to pay back some of her debt.

The conversation begins, as is usual in collections calls, with Juliet confirming Emily's identity, before Juliet attempts to fix the context that should, from her perspective, frame the call, by (re)stating the reasons for Emily's account now being handled by Alpha. Juliet's way of doing so is to describe how the debtor's account has been 'escalated' by the creditor and is now being dealt with instead by Alpha. On the one hand this appears to be a statement of fact. The move from creditor to contingency agency might seem to a debtor to mark a debt as having moved to a new, more serious point in its journey of default (as explored further in the next chapter). On the other hand, however, in terms of the ownership of the debt, nothing has changed: the debt is still owned by the original creditor and the debtor's credit rating – that by this stage, will already in any case have been significantly damaged by being marked by a recent 'default' flag – will not be directly affected by this transfer.[19] In this context, Juliet's reference to a call being 'escalated' therefore can be seen as an attempt, even if understated, to amplify the conversation's underlying affective intensity (see Chapter 2). The message is that the debtor's situation has undergone an irrecoverable shift, and should be now considered more serious, and accorded more focused attention than they might otherwise have given. This is an attempt to focus the debtor's calculative and emotional labour on their debt.

As the conversation progresses, it becomes punctuated by similar understated prompts. These include Juliet asking Emily twice whether she has the funds to pay the full outstanding balance – a figure of just over £3,700 – as well as offering to 'settle' the debt for £3,000, to in other words accept a reduced payment in exchange for closing the account. However, although these prompts are unsuccessful in their own terms, they do have an ancillary effect: Emily, who has called up with the intention of paying £100 off her debt, responds to Juliet's framing of the conversation as a space for negotiation. She revises her initial figure upwards: 'If I came into some money, obviously I would. I could maybe pay £150 today, then maybe £50, £60 thereafter?' After a short pause, Juliet accepts. She reads the offer back, telling Emily that she will call back next month to reassess her situation, before organising the payment. 'That's great, yeah', says Emily, before she thanks Juliet 'very much' for her help, ending with an 'okey doke'.

From a regulatory point of view, this conversation is more or less a model of compliance (see Office of Fair Trading 2012). There is no use of 'misleading' threats to unlikely legal action. Juliet in fact at no point makes any explicit threats against the caller, nor is her tone aggressive. Nor does she appear to mislead the caller. The conversation also seems to close on an upbeat tone, with an expression of gratitude on Emily's part.

But at the same time, from the collector's point of view, the conversation is a considerable success. Juliet may not have succeeded in collecting even close to the full outstanding balance, but this is not surprising: one of the effects of the restrictions on credit available to consumers post-2007 is, somewhat ironically, a decreased ability to pay off their debts by taking out further lines of credit, making large one-off payments increasingly hard to come by for the collector (see Chapter 5).

The conversation is therefore a success for Alpha on three counts: first, a single payment of £150 on a balance of this size is large by comparison to the many much lower payments that were the norm; second, this payment is 50 per cent higher than Emily offers at the start of the conversation; and third, the debtor has committed herself to making future payments. Alpha has therefore seemingly done its job on the creditor's behalf: it has secured some repayment, over and above what the debtor was initially going to pay. And, perhaps more importantly, it has (it hopes), re-instigated a regular transfer of value going into the future. It has seemingly re-secured the attachment of the debtor to the creditor's asset.

So how should we assess this apparently 'compliant' conversation in the context of the apparent disjuncture between the anxious, affective domestic spaces of debt collection and the seemingly depersonalised forms of interaction between defaulter and collector? There are multiple potential answers to this question, of which I will first outline three.

Answer #1: This is to be found by looking *inside* the content of the conversation. Even if in an understated way, Juliet does, like the letters on the debtor's doormat, attempt to generate moments of emotional, focused affective intensity, whether by pointing to the increasing seriousness of Emily's situation, or demanding the full balance. (This is an amount Juliet, through experience, would have known she was extremely unlikely to receive in the recently worsened economic climate). Here, it is the semantic content of the language that does the ontological work: in the course of their interaction, drawing on mutually understood social cues, both Emily's debt and Alpha become filled with 'meaning'.

Answer #2: This is to be found by looking *outside* the content of this conversation, at Alpha's position in relation to the wider credit market (and beyond). As noted earlier, Alpha is particularly expert at dealing with low balance accounts, which tend to be at quite a late stage in the collections cycle – in other words, accounts in which the amounts owed are comparatively low and which have often already passed through other contingency agencies prior to Alpha. As a rough guide, the average balance across 30 calls, excluding one very high balance account (over £14,000) was £1,276.[20] When collecting on these accounts, the focus thus shifts from the semantic and emotive content of individual calls and towards the successful management of a high volume of accounts, in order to generate low margin returns. This means the business operations of Alpha can be seen as drawing on the practices of other related industries, notably those involved in forms of direct marketing. In Alpha's case, collections conversations can therefore often afford to remain mundane, because they are able to run a profitable business by making numerous small returns on accounts – for example, by securing regular payments of as small as £5, or increasing payments from £5 to £10. A key to their success is to be able to do this more often and at a lower cost than many of their rivals. This answer looks towards Alpha's particular socio-economic context, its relationship with its competitors and the wider industry, and the particular way it generates value in contrast to others.

Answer #3. This is to be found by looking *in-between* the content of the conversation. In Juliet's conversation with Emily, despite its mundane quality, and despite it never appearing to be heading towards an emotional crescendo, the affective, anxious landscape that collections calls are often mixed up with, cannot escape the conversation in its entirety. For, despite its absence in the discursive content of Juliet and Emily's conversation, and despite a lack of any explicit acknowledgement of its existence by Juliet, it can, as so often with collections conversations, be traced in the interstices – in particular in Emily's tone of voice. When Emily speaks she is quiet and stuttering. Although she is resolutely polite and occasionally upbeat, the impression she delivers is of a person who is timid, nervous and, perhaps, frightened. The delivery of her final 'okey doke' sums this up. A variation of the phrase has been popularised by becoming the catchphrase of Ned Flanders, the long-suffering neighbour of Homer Simpson, in the animated television sitcom *The Simpsons*. Flanders' 'okeley dokely' has come to sum up his near-constant unquenchable optimism in the face of the challenges delivered by a modern world. In particular, it captures his cheery determination to lead his life by (Christian) values of tolerance and forbearance, even when these principles seem rarely to be reflected back to him by others, nor generate little in the way of return. In Emily's case, however, there are hints of a comparable optimism but it is on the verge of being extinguished: she renders her 'okey doke' in such a sad, resigned tone, that it infects the conversation with a deep pathos; it speaks of a life being lived at optimism's limits (see Berlant 2011). In this version of the answer, there is an attempt to restore some of the emotive, tonal fragments that are not taken into account by Juliet but which nonetheless threaten at the margins. This therefore can be seen as the tracing of an unequal contestation between two modes of articulation; the first is that deployed by Emily, in which she is unable to wholly separate the affective impact of dealing with the collector from the conversation; the second is that deployed by Juliet, in which the emotional landscape of debt default is marginal-ised, being framed as a peripheral concern.[21]

These answers can be seen as respectively emerging out of different analyt-ical traditions. The first approximates to a phenomenologically-informed ana-lysis: it charts the way in which intersubjective understandings between two actors are arrived at, delivered through language. Even if in a tiny, micro-sociological way, this conversation can be seen as drawing on and in turn rein-forcing socially and culturally constituted systems of meaning. Despite the highly constrained and disciplinary nature of the debt collection conversation, it is still a conversation. It is thus still a mechanism, through which real people, in the course of their everyday lives (even if one is at work), create and redefine social and, in this case, socio-economic boundaries. Here, the object of contesta-tion is the degree to which the socio-economic obligation Emily has to her debt translates, in the present, to a transfer of value from her to the collector. Of course, as a research site, this is not ideal for such an analytical approach and, as such could only be the beginnings of a phenomenology of consumer credit col-lections. To understand in more depth the meaning of this obligation to Emily, we might, from this perspective, have to venture more closely into Emily's life, to understand these categories more clearly from her perspective. Within eco-nomic sociology, this analytical tradition might be understood to include, for example, Viviana Zelizer's study of the domestic 'marking' of monies (Zelizer 1994; see also Chapter 1) or Patrik Aspers' phenomenological study of fashion markets (Aspers 2005).

The second answer is not too distantly related to the first; the difference is principally a matter of scale. In this answer, the conversation can be understood in relation to larger scale systemic forces. The debt collection conversation as a site of socio-economic interaction certainly still continues to be understood as a key component of the composition of the debt collection industry, however it needs to be 'embedded' within wider socio-economic norms and practices. As is implicit in using this terminology, within economic sociology, this analytical tra-dition might be understood to include 'new economic sociology' whose most high profile representatives include the likes of Paul DiMaggio (1994), Frank Dobbin (1994), Neil Fligstein (2001) and Jens Beckert (Beckert and Harshav 2002; Beckert 2009).[22] In an attempt to counter economics' explanatory frame-work, which has at its centre the maximising individual, this approach *socially roots* both the individual and the firm.

The third answer can be seen as drawing on a form of post-Foucauldian ana-lysis, which sees communicative interaction as one site through which to trace the enactment of historically specific knowledge practices, through which forms of subjectivity become enacted (Jäger and Maier 2009, p. 34; see also Wodak and Meyer 2009).[23] We could see in the cracks of this conversation Emily dis-playing her painful experience of default as a form of embodied knowledge, but one that is not rendered as legitimate in this particular setting. Rather, she is forced into engaging as a calculative subject, in particular in the negotiation over repayment. This occurs in and through the haggling over the amount Emily will pay back, which at the same time frames her anxiousness as irrelevant to the conduct of this market. Such an analysis might be the beginnings of an attempt to trace the enactment the debtor subject according to modes of contemporary economic governance, compatible with currents in a Foucauldian inspired economic sociology centring around the investigation of processes and tactics of neoliberal governmentality (Rose 1996a; Burchill *et al.* 1991; in relation to consumer credit, see Langley 2008b, 2014; Marron 2009).

I want to propose a fourth answer, one that speaks to and is informed by each of the above, without claiming to be a unifying synthesis.

Answer #4. This operates within the analytical space opened up by the dialogue between the study of process of 'captation' and the 'capture of affect', or what can be called *affective captation*. This is to be found in seeing both the content of collections conversations (Answers #1 and #3) and the relations within and between collections companies (Answer #2) as pointing to just some of the multiple potential modes of ordering to be found in the relationships that make up the assemblage that is consumer debt collection. From this perspective, debt collection is a site for interlinked, variably deployed socio-material market operations. Methodologically closest to the post-Foucauldian approach, this is interested in tracing the precise ways in which affect becomes provoked and captured. It not only does so by tracing these through both linguistic and non-linguistic/material relations, it sees these as variably and differentially achieved. However at times a Foucauldian approach may efface the multiple, processual, not *necessarily compatible, and not necessarily successful* 'modes of ordering' through which entities are enacted (Mol 2002, pp. 61–71; see also Dányi 2011, pp. 15–16; Law 1994; Marres 2012, pp. 62–63).[24] Attending to these requires a renewed focus on the particular quality of the connections between entities and between different modes. It also requires taking the *care* to attend to what we are being confronted with; for Stengers 'this means reclaiming an ecology that gives the situations we confront the power to have us thinking, feeling, imagining, and not theorizing about them' (2008, p. 58; see also Harbers *et al.* 2002; Mol 2008).[25] As Martin Savransky suggests, this demands an attention to 'the actual, messy, multiple and entangled practices that take place in such processes' (Savransky 2014, p. 110).

Bringing this perspective to the previous case allows us to attend to the way in which this particular conversation is a co-production involving a range of market devices (including tried and tested collections prompts designed to coax from the debtor forms of calculative attention, embodied in the appropriately trained debt collector) and affective states, both the debtor's and the collector's (e.g. marginal optimism, nervousness, fear, boredom). How these are combined, how they work together, depends on the very specific ways in which the 'problem' of the debt is made to matter for the debtor and how certain prompts end up being grasped by the debtor. The work of debt collection thus becomes a situated process of affect management, with the collector looking for affordances to which a connection, an attachment, can become established. The production of a form of subjectivity oriented towards, say, neoliberal rationalities may be one outcome, however we may want to hold in mind that this is likely co-present and potentially put into tension with a range of other patterned arrangements. Rather than boiling down a range of diverse responses to one particular mode of ordering, we may want to at least hold open the possibility of alternate modes through which individuals are brought into markets and held there. This is not a repudiation of Foucault, but to see his work as just one specific way of problematising empirical situations.

Let's take another example, this time from a recorded conversation I listened to at Delta, a major UK debt collections agency. The conversation is between Tom, the collections agent, whose tone is always polite and understanding, and Sarah, a debtor from a major northern UK city, owing a total of around £3,000 to the client, a major UK retail bank. At the time of the call she was dealing with her young children who could be heard in the background. She was unemployed, but hoped to be able to find work once her son started school later that year. In the meantime she was claiming a variety of state benefits. Her partner was a taxi driver; as Sarah put it, 'it's no guaranteed wage, so we just pay what we can, where we can. We're just trying to get everything sorted out at the moment'. The extract starts once the agent has established as much as he can about the debtor's situation. Importantly he has established that there is an asset (a property) that he will try to use as leverage over the course of the conversation. This section of the call begins with a veiled (veiled in part to ensure regulatory compliance[26]) threat, combined with a suggestion for how Sarah might respond:

TOM: Now, if you want to avoid any further action against yourself, or obviously against your property, or anything along those lines, all I could suggest, is that you speak to your friends and family, and see if you're able to raise the funds to close this off.

Sarah acknowledges the threat, but suggests she is unable to respond as Tom wants.

SARAH: Right, I don't think ... . I can't see that being able to be possible, to be honest.

On the basis of this, Tom first offers understanding ('I understand. It's a lot of money'), then respite ('What I'm going to do, I'm going to put the account on hold for 2 days for you'), then some degree of flexibility ('I'm not expecting you to come back to me in 2 days time and say, ok, here's almost £3,000, [but] I would expect you to know whether you're in a position to get those funds together'). Then, finally, this package is wrapped up with a more extensive outlining of the specific content of the threat that is in play – which, to be precise, is that the bank *might* try to connect this unsecured loan to the debtor's secured asset: her property (in fact, there are many processes that would need to be undergone first, including being taken to court; for such a relatively small balance, this is perhaps unlikely).[27]

TOM: Now, at that point, I'll have to build up the pre-sue report. I'll have to put down that you own the property, your husband being a self-employed taxi driver, all this, I need to put this down and pass this to litigation dept. As I said, they're not going to be worried about the money. They can see that you've got a tangible asset, it's something that, possibly not in the short term, but in the medium term, or possibly in the long term, they're going to get the money back, plus any charges, plus any court costs.

This conversation provides a good summary of the structure of many collections conversations, in which adverse consequences and possible remedies, veiled threat and apparent empathy are tossed together – a process of affect management which continues as this particular conversation progresses, ending with the agent 'closing' the call:

SARAH: Is there no possible way that I can pay it off equally per month?
TOM: There won't be. Basically, our remit is to give you the opportunity to repay the full balance. If you're not able to do that, we'll pass it onto our litigation department, and they'll decide on the best course of action.
SARAH: Right, ok.
TOM: I'll leave it with you. Obviously, come back to me before 5 p.m. on Wednesday.

It is common for each collections organisation to have its own guideline scripts for sales agents to follow (and adapt).[28] This is part of each organisation's unique 'secret sauce' for collections – a result of trial and error, experience, intuition, and, increasingly, formalised experimentation (to be discussed further on). This collections company specialises in *seeking repayment in full*, from debtors at a relatively early stage of default. This means that, as in the above conversation, the company keeps pushing for a large payment, willing to wait some time, and potentially have a number of conversations with a debtor, before beginning to negotiate a lower or staggered repayment plan. A contrast would be a company like Alpha that operates with more established defaulters, where the creditor (whether the debtor knows it or not) effectively decides that the chance of a full repayment is slight, with the primary aim becoming instead to collect smaller ongoing repayments, of the kind Sarah mentions at the end of the call. In both models, however, the aim – as Zsuzsanna Vargha (2011) illustrates in the conversations that can accompany other forms of financial selling – is to stabilise both the particular product's properties *and* the customer. In this case, Tom's aim is to *solidify and intensify* the attachments that bind Sarah to this particular product, and to individualise this debt in relation to the competition, by making it not just part of the undifferentiated 'debt' which forms part of the background of her life, but also a product that resonates strongly in the present, that needs to be acted on *immediately* – or, more precisely, at least by 5pm Wednesday, or otherwise face the possibility of litigation. As noted, although Sarah has no way of knowing for sure, it is in fact unlikely that this litigation will occur – and certainly proceedings will not commence so soon.

The 'mode of ordering' (in Cochoy's terms, modes of captation) in effect here can be seen as only loosely related to the mode concerned with producing what might be called a form of neoliberal subjectivity. Specifically, the aim is very much not to leave the debtor to her own devices, to self-manage. She is given ostensible choice ('I'll leave it with you'), but this is a largely rhetorical offering: it is clear that if she does not respond by the deadline, she will be contacted again, whether she likes it or not. Indeed, one of the features of collections practices and technologies is that they are only partially concerned with invoking the sovereign self of choice, autonomy, and freedom (see Rose 1996b, p. 4). The forms of attachment, the mode of ordering, being attempted here are pragmatically oriented at what works – and principally that means stimulating and attempting to capture affect, through varied rhythms of threat and empathy – and their potential concomitants fear and relief.

In order to pursue this we have to move beyond the content of the conversations between debtor and collector, however. To really understand the role of affect within contemporary collections practices means looking at the place of such conversations within the overall *trajectory* of collections. This involves moving away from Alpha and Delta and towards Beta, a major UK debt purchaser.

'Green' and 'Red' teams: a view into a collections trajectory

As outlined at the beginning of the chapter, Beta is a debt purchaser that largely 'works' accounts itself rather than sending them out to external agencies or reselling them on to others for a profit. Given that these companies usually seek to collect on an account until they achieve some form of resolution – a process that could sometimes take years – what a view into Beta offers is a view on a collections trajectory more or less in its entirety.

In order to avoid breaching Beta's anonymity, it is necessary to introduce some ambiguity into the description of its operations. Suffice it to say that Beta divides up its call centre into between four and eight different teams. Each team is assigned a different name, and each is responsible for a different 'stage' in the collections process. Each team is managed individually, has its own targets, and performs a relatively distinct role. Broadly, the collections stages represent the proximity of the account towards either legal action or, potentially, being actually or effectively written off.[29] Hence, this ranges from a team that deals with accounts that Beta has just purchased (which I will call the 'Green' team), to one (the 'Red' team) that deals with accounts where debtors are told that they are on the cusp of being passed to Beta's lawyers (although, there are a number of circumstances in which this threat is not acted upon). In-between sits a number of additional teams, one of whose role is to deal with accounts where the debtor has agreed to make regular repayments and to ensure the ongoing successful management of these accounts (as well as boost returns where possible).

These teams are laid out in linear fashion, mirroring the debtor's potential journey down this trajectory. Towards one end of the long call centre is the

Green team, at the other the Red; in-between these are the other teams, in order. The key variable that predicts a debtor's place on this trajectory is time passed: newer accounts tend to be at one end and older accounts at the other (although it is not always so simple, as will be explored below). The result is that just looking at how Beta has chosen to lay out its call centre and partition its staff provides a spatial overview of the temporal trajectory that many defaulting debtors at Beta follow, if they fail to respond adequately to the collector's prompts.

This layout also broadly matches the mode of communicative interaction to which defaulters are potentially subject. Those further away from legal action, hence closest to the Green team, tend to be dealt with more 'gently' and those closest to legal action, and closer to Red, are generally dealt with more 'firmly' – a difference of 'carrots' and 'sticks', as one collector characterised it. This is a variation in (potential) 'affective intensity'. Compare for instance the following extracts from collections conversations at Beta, ranging from earlier in the collections process ...

'... you're in a really good position to get a massive discount on your outstanding balance ...'
'... obviously I understand, it's a recession at the moment ...'
'... I do appreciate your circumstances ...'

... to later:

'... as you can imagine, the situation with this account is now quite serious ...'
'... your account has got to quite a serious point in our debt collections process ...'
'... you need to understand that this needs to be resolved and you're not cooperating with us ...'
'... obviously, this has come on to the final stage—[this needs to be resolved], otherwise it will go to an external agent, or our litigation agency ...'

These are, to return to Cochoy's terms, *different modes of captation*, at either end of a spectrum.

At one end, the debtor is framed as a subject with whom the collector can collaborate in the restoration of their attachment to their debt; the debtor is 'sold' to, being tempted into clearing their balance at a discounted rate. We can thus detect modes of address erring towards the therapeutic, including periods of attentive, uncritical listening. It is this mode of engagement to which a sign that hung over the collections centre presumably refers, which states simply the word 'EMPATHY'. And it is also to this mode of engagement that one team leader is presumably referring when he jokingly instructs his team, 'can we turn off debt counselling please?!'. He feels, in other words, that in spending too much time listening to and/or empathising with their callers, his team was in danger of losing sight of their ultimate aim: to bring in revenue. At this end of the spectrum, there are attempts to enact a debtor that *do* resemble the subject of neoliberal forms of governance, as described by post-Foucauldian governmentality studies. They are more likely to be understood as subjects that retain a degree of capacity for self-governance, even if this latent capacity has to be given a push via quasi-therapeutic modes of engagement. The obligations a debtor has to their debts are reframed as both moral and self-interested *responsibilities*. If the debtor can be seen as a debtor-customer hybrid, at this end of the spectrum, the modes of captation are more oriented towards the debtor as customer.

At the other end of the spectrum, however, the attempts to enact the debtor-customer occur along very different lines. This is the part of the journey of debt default that Paul Rock describes as 'a progress into controlled unpleasantness' (1973, p. 65). It is here that the modes of captation become far more disciplinary. The modes of address directed towards the debtor-customer are far more explicitly directed at the relationships of *legal, enforceable* obligation that construct this pairing: the debtor-customer hybrid is more a debtor(-customer). Here too, there are clear attempts to capture any negative affective responses that might already be circulating in and through the debtor's world (potentially stimulated by prior incursions from collections technologies). However, rather than using them as a way of potentially transforming the debtor into a responsible economic citizen, the strategies of captation move closer towards seeing the debtor as an embodied subject of discipline. More important than empathising with the debtor or activating a latent, self-governing subject is the attempt to impose *the collector's* account of what the situation is, exemplified by collectors instructing the debtor as to what they 'need to understand'. The debtor is less to be reasoned with and understood, and more to be made to feel *more* fearful of their present situation and future consequences.

It is of course highly unlikely that debtors will see or understand any of this differentiation. Being isolated and individualised, the defaulting debtor may, within relatively quick succession, be addressed as both responsible *and* deviant, without any clear logic or proportionality between these different modes of address being rendered comprehensible. Further, these contradictory and potentially bewildering effects will be amplified if a defaulter has to deal simultaneously with multiple different creditors, as is often the case (as outlined previously).

At Beta there is also evidence of the collections industry attempting to create a fit between the dispositions of particular collectors and the role they played in this process. As Arlie Hochschild (1983) argued in her classic study, the debt collection industry depends to a significant degree on the emotional labour of its employees. One manager at Beta, for instance, drawing on a football metaphor, told me how 'you don't play a left back in goal'. What he means is that he, and the company, are actively aiming to match collectors to the variable approaches being deployed across the collections trajectory. This was reflected in the difference in the approaches and hopes of two collectors I met: Sandra and Ian. Sandra is an older collector, perhaps in her 40s, who had only recently joined Beta after her 13-year career as a chef was cut short by a recurrent back condition. She commented upon how difficult she finds it to ask some debtors for money, recalling one instance where she noticed that the date of birth of one debtor meant that she was in her 80s. This left her struggling with her conscience at being required to ask for a repayment; as she told me '[w]ell, I just wanted to say no, you don't have to pay'. However, she recently moved into the team that primarily deals with the management of ongoing accounts, within which she is happier, because it feels, as she puts it, more like 'customer services'. Ian, by contrast, is in his early 20s, and had recently left a real estate agency to work at Beta. He had been assigned to one of the early-stage collections teams. However he told me he feels frustrated at constantly having to 'hold himself back' and remain relatively gentle with debtors. He was, he said, looking forward to the day when he might have a chance to work in the harder-edged 'Red' team. This may to some extent be connected to the greater financial rewards that can potentially come to those working in, or closer to the final Red team, something Ian pointed towards. However, what was clear (and somewhat unnerving) was Ian's personal passion for a job that many might imagine to be not only stressful, but also controversial.

The variable attempts at enacting debtors as payers in and through the collections process are not, however, limited to the content of conversations: across the collections industry as a whole, these can be seeing being operationalised in a range of ways (including via collections letters, as will be addressed in more detail in the next chapter). One is the formalisation of the forms of *in vivo* experimentation explored in the last chapter, what is now often referred to as 'champion versus challenger' testing. Experian explains the process as follows:

> Perhaps the most important improvement an organisation can take is to regularly review its processes and continually evolve its approach to collections *through experimentation*. Champion v[ersus] challenger allows the organisation to *test in a controlled manner the timing, approach, tone, message, and segmentation of the collection process* on a small population of its debtor base in order to understand what works and what doesn't in different circumstances. Results in the *test environment* can be *measured and compared* against the dominant champion strategy. Successful evolutions can then be rolled out across the broader debt portfolio.
> (Experian 2009a, p. 19; emphasis added; see also Deloitte 2009; Experian Decision Analytics 2008)

Very similar to the experiments conducted in the US in the 1960s (see Chapter 3), we see an ambition to marry collections work with the principles of scientific, laboratory-like investigation, albeit using a 'test environment' populated by debtors, unaware of their participation in an experiment.[30] These forms of experimentation can be applied to a range of variables, including method of contact, time of contact, timings between contact, the collections scripts used on the telephone by particular collections agents, and the particular mix of all these (and many more). A newly optimised 'challenger' model is unleashed against a small sample of the debtors, with the aim of assessing its effectiveness against the existing 'champion'. In theory, whichever proves to be the most successful strategy will be rolled out across the collections process.

A further increasingly important tool – including for Beta – one informed by a very similar logic, is the use of econometric modelling techniques in the analysis of debtor behaviour. This is increasingly undertaken by both original creditors and debt purchasers (who, by purchasing the debt, become the new creditor).[31] Data for this analysis can potentially stem from, and combine, two sources. The first is information that has already been collected by a creditor in relation to the particular account in question, that can be passed to a debt purchaser. This might be the particular payment history (e.g. how often payments are made, made late, or missed entirely) or an account of what collection activities, both internal and external, have already been pursued against a given account (see Birkwood 2011). The second is information on individual accounts shared by creditors to credit reference agencies. This is data that gives a more overarching indication of a particular borrower's track record, given that it covers data across all those accounts that report to the particular 'user group' to which the organisation subscribes.[32]

Part of the function of econometric analysis in this industry is to help debt purchasers make decisions as to how to price debt portfolios they are interested in purchasing.[33] Once a purchase has been made, an additional usage in the collections industry is, by looking at the past performance of accounts, to identify what Daniel, a credit reference agency industry consultant, referred to as the 'low hanging fruit' for particular attention.[34] These are debtors with the ability to repay, who have in the past shown signs of being the *kind of people* that are more likely to repay and/or the kind of people who are likely to repay *more* (than others in an otherwise similar situation). These differences operate through emergent, affective spaces of possibility, assemblages of corporeal, dispositional tendencies, formed out of the complex, particular combination of life history and lived body. The collector that can both identify these tendencies and *connect to them* has a major potential competitive advantage.

The person that the collector seeks is that person who, when confronted by a debt collections letter, or when called by a debt collector, is simply marginally more likely than someone otherwise (seemingly) very similar to them, to respond (more) positively. The variables that predict this tendency could be manifold and will vary considerably according to the particular composition of a debt portfolio. As Daniel puts it:

> There will be a lot of different variables. [...] What we would do is take a sample and look at the variables that are appropriate type of predictors. [...]: you've [successfully] collected [from] this person [and] you didn't [successfully] collect from this person. And you'd look at the variables that predict [that]. And it could be a range of 3,000 different variables. So it could be 'Balance to Limit' [the ratio of the account balance to the credit limit], it

could be 'Pays by Direct Debit', it could be 'Has CCJ' [County Court Judgement]. It could be lots and lots of different variables.

In other words, the variable does not particularly matter (to the collector). The analyst – sometimes from a consultant who is selling their services on – will feed as much data as they can into a database and run models on it. Those variables that emerge as most predictive are, an analyst will suggest, those on which selections and decisions should be based.

There are parallels that can be drawn between this use of econometric modelling and the calculus that increasingly surrounds processes of contemporary brand management, as described by Celia Lury (2004). Here, she writes, the econometric analysis of consumer behaviour operates within the marginal differences between preferences: '[t]here is no necessary proportionality between causes and effects here; instead an economic calculus (or rationality) of statistical *probability* is at work' (2004, p. 50; original emphasis). These technologies exploit the affective, emergent dimensions of human experience: in and through the amplification of minute dispositional tendencies, it is possible to identify that group of defaulters who should have more money invested in them, in the hope of generating a return. That is to say, these are the people that a collector will want to both target first (to get to them before other collectors to) and to target more intensively (for example more letters, more phone calls).[35]

One effect of this is to generate a perverse politics of debt collection: pointing the collector *towards* those who respond most readily to the prompts of the collector also means pointing the collector *away* from those who respond the least readily. This logic is made explicit in the following extract, transcribed from a US collections industry online collections 'webinar':

> I'm going to pay more attention to those accounts that are most likely to pay me. I'm going to spend less time on those accounts least likely [to pay] unless [I have resources]. [...] You wouldn't want to be inundating yourself with extra mailings, or [tracing] accounts that aren't looking to pay you a lot of money, or aren't looking to pay you.
>
> (Banasiak 2009, 16:40–17:20)

Those whose past financial history marks them out as potentially more resistant/ elusive/destitute/stubborn than others in an otherwise similar position may be subject to less sustained and/or aggressive collections practices. From the collector's point of view, it simply is not worth wasting money on them (this is a question of degree: less attractive targets will not necessarily be ignored, but rather paid less attention).

This outcome is peculiar. Debtors who have ostensibly *failed* to enact themselves as responsible economic citizens are (more likely to be) left alone, being, from the point of view of the collector, 'rewarded' for their non-normative behaviour.[36] Debtors who perform themselves as closer to this neoliberal ideal, perhaps in the hope that they might profit from the careful management of their personal finances and financial history, become *more likely* to be subject to the attention of the collector. This is therefore a mode and politics of captation steadfastly and mathematically oriented around *what works*. Modes of ordering that appear coherent and stable in other settings thus become vulnerable to the 'disruptions and translation errors' that Knox *et al.* indentify in the parallel world of Customer Relationship Management, 'as the "real" gets processed through the digital' (Knox *et al.* 2010, p. 353).

The use of such analytical technologies is not restricted to the binary identification of whether a debtor is a payer or not. It can, as in the case of Beta, not only shape *who* is targeted for attention, but *how* debtors, of all sorts, are attended to (see Ossandón 2014). This can be explored by reference to a common device in the global debt collections industry: a collections flow chart. These are used to visualise and develop strategy at various scales, ranging from the macro – for example, to provide a complete overview of a company's collections strategy, incorporating the relationship between different divisions – to the more micro, for example as a way of representing the strategy of a single team or group of collectors.[37] An example of the latter is shown in Figure 4.1. This draws on a chart shown to me during my time at Beta, whilst also making a number of changes in order to avoid disclosing details of Beta's particular business operations.[38]

This flow chart shows potential paths along which a debtor might progress if s/he does not respond to the prompts of the collector in a way deemed to be acceptable – usually involving either repaying an agreed amount of the debt, or setting up a future payment arrangement. On this simplified chart, these paths are divided into 'stages': each begins with an action; the debtor enters the next stage if s/he does not respond 'acceptably'. Each stage is also marked by a uniform ten day time frame, indicating the minimum amount of time the debtor will be allowed to respond before s/he will be advanced to the next stage and be subject to the next action.

In this example, the most frequent action is the regular issue of automatically generated letters. The content of these letters varies by degree of forcefulness, here 'gentle', 'medium' and 'hard' (specific examples will be discussed in the following chapter). In addition, if a debtor's phone number is accurate and available, it is common practice to follow up letters by placing debtors 'into the dialler' – in other words, to put the debtor into the queue of calls that have been allocated to the autodialler in that particular period. This represents an attempt to maximise the impact of debtors having recently received a letter, by also being able to talk to them directly.

In many respects, the flowchart mirrors the organisation of staff across the call centre in line with the trajectory of 'controlled unpleasantness'. Although on a smaller scale, again affective intensity is variably and strategically deployed, with 'time passed' (without resolution from/contact with the debtor) being its key axis. There is also the possibility of debtors leapfrogging 'softer' teams if, by some measure, their account is identified as more serious. Here, for instance, after three unsuccessful letters the collector undertakes a CCJ (County Court

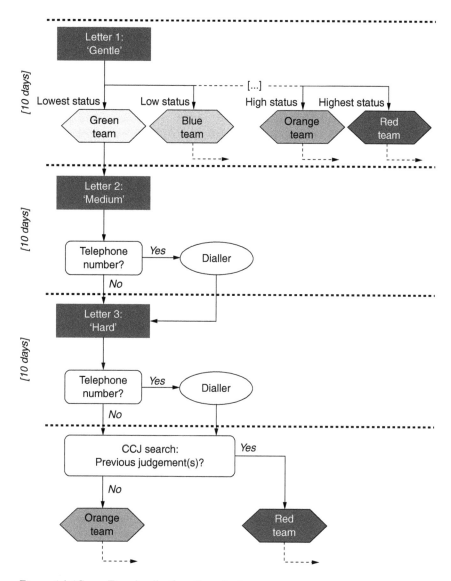

Figure 4.1 'Green Team' collections flow chart.

Judgement) check, moving those that are flagged as 'positive' (in other words, they have had a legal judgement successfully enforced against them by another creditor in the past) straight to the 'hardest' 'Red' team.[39]

It is, however, the introduction of econometric calculus that provides the collector with a far more nuanced range of options. As shown above, after the initial letter, the action to which a particular debtor will be subject varies according to a measure of their overall 'status'. This assessment is a result of the analysis of a range of variables pertaining to their account, which both attempts to capture the likelihood of a positive response by the debtor and the potential income that is at stake. This enables the collector to be able to act pre-emptively. If the initial letter is shown to have been unsuccessful, the individualised assessment of debtor status allows the collector to decide precisely *how* they are to be dealt with. This includes trying to decide quickly which debtors will have to be moved much closer to (potential) legal action.

How exactly such strategies will be deployed will depend on the collections operations of a particular creditor. However, an overarching principle is that 'high risk accounts' – put simply, those accounts judged to have a lower probability of repayment – 'are accelerated automatically to a more intensive collections strategy, increasing the speed and likelihood of recovery' (Experian Decision Analytics 2008, p. 3). *A more intensive collections strategy.* In collections, intensity is partially shorthand for a cost calculation: 'more intensive' collections refers to a greater level of expenditure on recovering debt from some accounts rather than others. However, the term also captures the very material increase in the collections effort: a consequence of increased intensity is almost certainly more frequent attempts at contact, as well as potentially an increase in the modes of attempted contact (options include letter and phone).

The particular mix will vary by collections organisation as well as by the segment being collected from, as summed up by this Barclays collections executive, speaking at a recent collections conference in the UK:

> you apply scoring models, every kind of models that you may have, you will [then] reach the workable accounts [i.e. those worth subjecting to collections processes], you will give [these] to the operations [department], you will decide how you are going to contact and when, and you decide the intensity.
>
> (Coelho 2012)

How and when to contact and the intensity of contact are therefore variables that major consumer credit operations will almost certainly be working into their collections strategies. The results are major differences in how affectively oriented encounters between collector and debtor come to be formatted, in ways in which the individual debtor is likely to be wholly unaware.

The management of the debt collections journey in these ways can therefore be considered as the strategic 'engineering of affect' (Thrift 2007, p. 182).[40] That is, at different points in the collection process and in different ways, the emergent, emotive, bodily and calculative responses of debtors come to be the object of careful, pragmatic management. These attempts will not always be successful, nor will they be uniform. But the clear aim is for the collector to become intimately bound up in the ongoing reconstitution of the debtor and their world.

This thus marks the culmination of an ambition that, as we saw in the last chapter, began to emerge within the debt collections industry in the US in the

1960s: to manage the responses of the defaulting debtor in and through the capture of affect. Experimentation with debtors '*in vivo*' – that is, situating its experimental endeavours in the terrain of their everyday life – was seen to offer a solution to this challenge. These experiments promised to render visible to the collector how exactly debtors would respond to very particular prompts and forms of solicitation. Now these *in vivo* forms of experimentation are increasingly being supplemented by a mode of experimentation operating according to a new distinct logic: that of *in vitro* experimentation (Çalışkan and Callon 2010; Callon 2009).[41] Here, a body of information about the past behaviour of a particular debtor population provides the basis for the prediction of the behaviour of current or future debtors. On the one hand, testing is thus shifted to a more abstract domain: the modelling of anticipated responses of debtors, whether to price debt portfolios or when deployed as part of live collections strategies, to segment debtors and to subject them to different collections models.[42] On the other, it allows processes of affect management to be undertaken over the full span of the collections trajectory. When *in vivo* and *in vitro* forms of experimentation are coupled together, they provide creditors and collectors with the ability to undertake a process of repeated affective 'testing', aimed at discovering what kind of debtor they are and what kind of debtor 'dispositions' they possess (see Cochoy 2007).

Conclusion

The segmentation of collections teams according to the seriousness of debts, the changes in tone of the collections calls within these teams, the strategic deployment of collectors' personalities, and the use of carefully constructed collections trajectories: all point to how market attachment may be secured through the management of emergent, corporeal tendencies. The anxious states of debtors, their life in default, offer the collector affordances that they can seek to exploit, via processes of 'affective captation', including the deployment of both *in vivo* and *in vitro* forms of experimentation. Such attempts are deeply cut-through with calculations of profitability as affect becomes strategically 'engineered' (see Thrift 2007, p. 182). Of course these practices depend on the ability of collections companies to combine technologies of mass contact with call centre personnel capable of increasing the income received. However this is increasingly forming just a part of collections trajectories in which debtors' emergent embodied states form part of a managed process of collections. As the next chapter will explore, this is a process that is sometimes controlled by original creditors, who use both internal processes and external companies to enact trajectories similar to those described above. But at Beta, a debt purchaser, it is possible to view one such trajectory being operationalised within a single collections organisation.

In the process we have seen how variably successful attempts are made to (re) enact the debtor as an economic agent, ranging from being treated as a customer with agency, to being treated almost wholly through their relationships of legal, enforceable obligation. This is the constitution of the debtor according to a spectrum of not necessarily compatible modes of ordering, modes of captation, articulated according to a logic that remains invisible to the defaulter.

It is also worth noting that in this strategic capture of affect, the collector is able to work more or less successfully within regulatory constraints. This is not to deny the existence of practices that break these constraints, but to highlight how econometric, experimental analysis is being used to point the collector to new modes of connecting with the debtor. Rather than the efficacy of collections organisations operating around those procedures that can deliver the strongest threats to the debtor, increasingly their efficacy operates around their ability to be adaptive. That means not only being able to identify those people who will respond to threats and entreaties most readily, but to adapt the organisation of debt collection practices to the debtor's dispositional tendencies. This is not only the formatting by the collector of the debtor's world, the effects of which we observed in Chapter 2, but also the mutual, iterative adjustment of the collector *to* the debtor's world.

At the same time, there is a politics to this, one that evades the attention of regulatory control. Part of this operates around the increasing ability of collectors to map and intersect with debtors' emergent dispositions, to target those who are less able to resist the collector's prompts. But at the same time, part of the politics of debt collection needs to be understood by not only focusing on the relationships within one company, as this chapter has done. A focus is also needed on the relations between companies. It is this inter-organisational relationality – and sometimes the strategic construction of this relationality – that is one important component in understanding both the affective and political landscape that contemporary debt collection practices are involved in. This is the task pursued by the next chapter.

Notes

1 Parts of this chapter draw on an articles published in *Journal of Cultural Economy* (Deville 2012) and *Consumption Markets and Culture* (Deville 2014).
2 As noted in the book's introduction these are pseudonyms.
3 That is presuming the attempt to collect is unsuccessful. If the contingency agency does succeed in generating regular repayments from the debtor against the outstanding balance, the creditor will usually leave them to manage the account, at least for the short to medium term.
4 Another option might include selling on the debt again, although if the debt purchaser has already instigated multiple attempts to collect on the debt without success, potentially over many years, the value of this debt is likely to be very low.
5 The more general regulatory regime in the UK is also arguably tougher, although I would argue that this accounts for less of the difference between the two countries. All creditors are subject to regulatory supervision by a central agency: the Financial Conduct Authority, which has recently taken over from the Office of Fair Trading. This agency provides guidelines for the conduct of collections work that must be followed by all creditors (including both original creditors and debt purchasers) and any organisations working on their behalf (including contingency agencies). Failure to do so may result in the creditor's license being revoked. In the US, by comparison, only companies with more than $10 million in annual receipts from consumer debt collection activities are subject to federal regulation (of course, state regulations also apply).

This omits potentially thousands of companies and around 40 per cent of the industry's annual receipts (see Consumer Financial Protection Bureau 2013a). In practice, the vast majority of enforcement in the US operates through the courts, in which collectors are held to account by debtors for potentially unfair or illegal collections practices. This has been held to be a somewhat ineffective deterrent for collectors (see Bremner 2010).

6 Most notably, the action taken against banks for mis-selling Payment Protection Insurance to customers (ostensibly designed to provide cover to individuals if unforeseen events mean they are unable to maintain their payments on a debt). To date, this has cost the banking industry almost £19 billion pounds (Which? 2013). Because of actions like this, Treating Customers Fairly (TCF) has been the subject of voluminous discussion in the pages of the main UK industry publication *Credit, Collections & Risk*, with companies being routinely advised to embed TCF into the very heart of their operations (e.g. Buckmann 2011; Cleary 2010; Coe 2013; de Tute 2012).

7 TCF requires a range of so-called 'Management Information' to be in place so that a company can clearly and convincingly demonstrate that it is abiding by the six TCF 'outcomes' expected by the Financial Services Authority (2007) (now the Financial Conduct Authority). In Beta, for instance, all collection calls were recorded and were randomly monitored and 'scored' (using a set of categories and a Likert-type scale), in part for regulatory compliance, by a dedicated team (another significant element under assessment was the effectiveness of the call).

8 It is very common for debtors to fail to turn up to see these cases heard by the court, often because they are not properly informed, and, if they do show up, they often do so without adequate legal representation (see Fox 2012; Holland 2011; Jurgens and Hobbs 2010). The large majority of judgements thus tend to go in the favour of the creditor, with the results for the debtor often including the garnishment of their wages or other income direct from the debtor's bank account, or the 'attachment' of any assets they have the debt in question (the question of attachment was explored in the last chapter).

9 No precise figures were available. For a general discussion of this tendency in the UK, see the industry survey conducted by the Credit Management Research Centre (2008).

10 Specifically, he was selling a type of credit scoring aimed at 'late-stage' accounts – that is, accounts that have already been subjected to collections efforts. This type of scoring, as the article informs its readers, 'is designed to help evaluate whether or not to litigate an account', the aim being to 'improve efficiencies and help [collection agencies] work the right accounts in the right manner' (Dressen 2013, p. 48).

11 This claim is based on an analysis of debtor interview transcripts. On only one occasion did a debtor refer to themselves as a customer in recounting their interactions with the collections industry. On this occasion, however, the participant was recounting how he was addressed *by* the industry.

12 This is not to claim that this term is always used by debtors when referring to themselves. However, as in Angela's case highlighted in the previous chapter, this speaks to the way in which defaulters frequently come to see their lives as coextensive with their debt.

13 Drawing on field notes. Of course, a range of terms is used, including 'debtor', 'defaulter', as well as 'customer'. The latter appears, however, to be the preferred, more polite terminology.

14 A creditor must first obtain a legal judgement against the debtor and only when this is broken will the court appoint a bailiff. Slightly different processes apply to the three different legal jurisdictions. In England and Wales, the court order is called a County Court Judgement and in Northern Ireland it is a Money Judgement (StepChange 2014a). The role played by bailiffs in the UK is undertaken by persons termed Enforcement Agents (StepChange 2014b). In Scotland, the debtor can apply for a

'Time to Pay Direction', which, if granted, will prescribe a repayment schedule. Only if this is broken will a debtor be on the legal road to confronting what, in Scotland, are called Sheriff Officers (Money Advice Scotland 2014; StepChange 2014c).

15 Some data from the debt advice charity StepChange (formerly the Consumer Credit Counselling Service (CCCS)) is revealing in this respect. For instance, between 2003 and 2009, its clients owed on average between six and seven creditors (with a yet higher peak of 7.6 in 2008) (CCCS 2006, 2007, 2008, 2009, 2010). With specific reference to credit cards, data from 2012 showed that over half of its clients had two or more credit cards, while over one in 10 had five or more (StepChange 2013, p. 15).

16 Also, as a recent analysis of the top 383 collections companies in the UK shows, in 2008–2009, 26 per cent made a pre-tax loss (Plimsoll Analysis 2009, p. 3.2b). Some are clearly better at this work of 'captation' than others. More recent figures could not be obtained.

17 I share with Paul du Gay a hesitation about the epochalist assumptions that tend to be mobilised in the analysis of consumption practices (2004, p. 87).

18 The three companies that granted me entry did so, quite clearly, because of their confidence in their procedures and that they considered them to be highly 'compliant' with the regulatory guidelines. In addition, in those cases where I was sitting alongside a collections agent, listening in on their conversations, in a situation in which they were quite clear about my role as a researcher, in their mind perhaps with an eye for the sensational moment of exposure, are quite far from capturing collections 'in the wild', even if such a thing were possible. For example, it was made quite explicit to me while visiting Alpha, that I was initially sat with Juliet, because she was 'the best you can get in terms of compliance'. In other words, Alpha considered her a safe pair of hands to sit a curious researcher next to. However, I was able to compare these conversations to pre-recorded conversations in two of the agencies I visited, chosen at random, which provided some less obviously mediated insight into collection techniques. I was also able to sit and listen to a number of different collectors, with varying levels of experience, and sometimes different approaches, in the companies I visited, as well as being able to get a sense of the tone of the full range of conversations surrounding me.

19 It is possible for a contingency collection agency to access a defaulter's credit file, in the form of a search. This will show up on a debtor's credit file and, depending on the type of search, might impact negatively on their credit rating. The aim of such a search depends on the debtor's circumstance, however could include the need to view a debtor's wider payment history to other creditors prior to making or accepting a tailored individualised offer, or checking information that a debtor is providing (Experian 2009b). However, not only is such fine grained detail not of much use in the course of a routine collections conversation, as was made clear to me during my time at Beta, accessing credit files in this way incurs a cost and therefore is only used as required.

20 In fact, a number of these accounts had already been passed to other contingency agencies, which were in fact 'trading styles' of the original creditor; this practice will be examined in the following chapter.

21 This is not to say that it is excluded from consideration in its entirety; this is, however, principally framed around the twin issues of 'harassment' and 'mental health'. In relation to the former, debt collection takes place within a regulatory framework in which the collector must be able to demonstrate to the regulator that the conduct of their business is not 'oppressive or otherwise unfair or improper', with the Financial Conduct Authority having powers to potentially withdraw a company's credit license if they receive evidence that it is not acting accordingly. Practices considered improper or unfair include 'putting pressure on debtors or third parties' (third parties being those that might be nominated on a debtor's behalf); 'contacting debtors at unreasonable times and at unreasonable intervals'; 'making threatening statements

[...] or taking actions which suggest harm to debtors' (Office of Fair Trading 2012). Industry guidelines also require creditors and collectors to have processes and systems in place to deal with those with mental health issues; however, it is worth noting that the responsibility for diagnosing does not lie with the collector and that it thus only becomes an issue that needs to be considered 'from the point at which the creditor is made explicitly aware of (a) mental health problem(s)' (Money Advice Liaison Group 2009, p. 11).

22 This is not, of course, to claim that this field is homogeneous.

23 Such an approach might also, however, explore the role played by material devices or 'dispositifs', as outlined by Jäger and Maier (2009).

24 This bears comparison with Rafaeli and Sutton's (1991) conclusion that debt collectors employ what they call 'emotional contrast strategies' in their interactions with debtors.

25 Annemarie Mol and her colleagues have developed a renewed attention to care as having significant ethical and practical implications, while attending in particular its relational, socio-material articulations. In this endeavour, they build on formative feminist work on the ethics of care (see Gilligan 1982; Held 1993; 2006; Noddings 1984).

26 Collectors must not falsely or represent their authority and/or legal position at a particular moment in time (Office of Fair Trading 2012, p. 16).

27 For more information on the use and controversies surrounding the use of Charging Orders to achieve this, see Tutton (2009).

28 The better operations monitor conversations for both regulatory compliance and collections technique by listening to, and potentially scoring, random recorded calls. See *footnote 7* above.

29 This distinction refers to the fact that a collector might decide to effectively 'park' a debt that they are having little success with, rather than formally write it off. The former means choosing to temporarily halt collections activities, in the hope that the debtor's situation may improve over time, or that the collector might later find new information that might be of use (often tending to be more up-to-date contact details).

30 As Michael Guggenheim argues, we need to be cautious about naming sites as laboratories, because of the quite specific forms of socio-technical arrangement they perform. Given that these experiments depend on finding debtors in and through particular sites, this might be closer to what he calls not a laboratory but a 'locatory' (2012, pp. 111–112).

31 This argument is made with the caveat that this is a relatively new development in the world of debt collection (unlike its use in the lending decision; see Poon (2007)) and thus is, as Daniel, working at a major UK credit reference agency, suggested, not being uniformly used across the industry. Further, given that it privileged company information, it is not possible to provide a quantitative measure of how prevalent this is. However, Daniel listed a number of large UK creditors employing such techniques, including a number of major debt purchasers and high street lenders. It should also be noted that it may be the latter of these that are making the most sophisticated use of these techniques; these techniques are being undertaken, as he put it, by 'the bigger banks, who will do it properly'.

32 This depends on the data a company shares back – this principle of reciprocity underpins the credit referencing system in the UK (Steering Committee on Reciprocity 2011), as it does in many other countries (Experian 2014). This data, in turn, can be divided into 'negative' and 'positive'/'full' data (also sometimes referred to as 'black' versus 'white' data, respectively). Negative data refers to incidents of serious arrears or when an account is in default. Access to this type of data, which gives only partial insight into the debtor in question, is considered basic 'entry level' access (Experian 2014). It is positive data that is particularly valuable. This provides subscribers access to a range of information, including on credit limits and current balances, as well as

whether payments have been made on time or not. In the UK, this can be supplemented by so-called 'behavioural' data: for instance on the value of recent payments, how this compares to the minimum payment required, and whether a credit card borrower has used their card to withdraw cash (Gibbons 2013, p. 12).

33 Although their use of positive data before a portfolio is purchased is currently restricted (see Birkwood 2011, p. 41; Tessera 2010, p. 201).

34 UK debt purchasers have, since 2007, had access post-purchase to so-called 'white data' (see *footnote 32*, above). The industry is, however, lobbying to have access to this data pre-purchase, as reported by Tessera, a major UK debt purchaser (Tessera 2010).

35 As one industry figure writes, arguing for the value of such techniques:

> Of course, the biggest challenge facing collectors has not changed for decades – maybe even centuries! How do you tell the difference between the 'can't pays' and 'won't pays'? [...] Obviously there is little point chasing people who cannot pay. So the key is to identify those people that have the means to pay and then take steps to trace them.
>
> (Hamilton 2010)

36 This is the view from the collector's perspective. To otherwise use the language of reward here would not be only inappropriate, it would miss the multiple causal factors that lead (put simply) some debtors to be 'payers' and some not to be.

37 I was able to view a number of these while interviewing Daniel.

38 Not only has the chart been significantly simplified, the sequence of events, timings, number and types of letters used, the type of actions to which debtors can be subject to, as well as the number and type of teams at Beta, and their relation to one another, have been amended so as to avoid disclosing any privileged company information. Hence, this chart is indicative of some of the *principles* that can inform collections sequences, rather than a faithful representation of any one team or company's particular practices.

39 Other options available to the collector include requesting credit reports, used to assess the recent patterns of payments by the debtor on other credit accounts, or land registry searches, used to assess whether the debtor owns any property that might be relevant in assessing possible legal action that could be undertaken.

40 I build here on existing work that has examined how the encounter between collector and debtor is characterised by various forms of emotional management (Hill 1994; Poster 2013; Rafaeli and Sutton 1991; Sutton 1991).

41 On the relevance of experimentation as a method for market-making, see also Callon and Muniesa (2005), Lury (2004) and McFall (2009b).

42 This can be seen as an instance of what has been termed 'knowing capitalism' (see Savage and Burrows 2007; Thrift 2005) and mirrors the logic of various forms of algorithmic analysis and data mining that have come to characterise life under conditions of so-called 'big data'. This operates in a range of fields beyond markets, including security (Amoore 2011), government (Ruppert 2011; 2012), and popular culture (Beer and Burrows 2013). Also, Ossandón (2014, p. 440) has recently analysed similar processes in relation to consumer credit, examining some of the ways in which credit scores can be combined with other behavioural data across the credit cycle, in both lending and collections.

5 The amplification of calculative opacity

The creditor, the collector, the collections letter

Fair is foul and foul is fair ...

The three Witches, chanting together, *Macbeth*, Act I, Scene I

The business of extending credit has always also been the business of collecting debt. Their indelible connection is not, however, necessarily obvious. Take the monthly credit card statement as an example. As I outlined in the first chapter, part of the apparent function of this device is to (potentially) 'restore' some of the calculative apparatus that was absent at the point of transaction. By regulators in particular, it is idealised as a device that should enable the borrower to assess a specific slice of their past life in order to help them to manage and contain future uncertainty.

But the credit statement is also something else: part of its role is to act as a collections device. Even if it is not explicitly framed as such, its monthly arrival can nonetheless be seen as a routine deployment by the creditor, of a collections technology into the homes and everyday lives of debtors. After all, alongside its account of a borrower's past borrowing practices, it contains a quite explicit demand: that a minimum amount should be repaid to the creditor, by a given date.

Seen from within the debt collections industry, this indelible relationship between lending and collection can seem very self-evident; as Helen, a director at Alpha, the contingency collections agency that we visited in the previous chapter, put it to me: 'your credit card company every month sends you a statement, that's collecting their debt, you're paying them. Just because we tend to do it when it's gone into arrears or default, *[it] isn't any different*' (emphasis added). On one hand this is a conclusion that is self-serving: Helen tries to de-politicise consumer collections by including it under the umbrella of consumer lending more generally – an activity that is understood by many as routine and everyday. But, on the other, her assertion can simultaneously be read as (re-)politicising consumer lending. From the vantage point of the collections industry, therefore, the consumer lending business is also a collections business. Credit card statements from this perspective are not only mundane conveyors of account information, but also soft collections letters. This argument could be extended to include a range other apparently mundane devices: for instance, the direct debit – a technology for automatically taking repayment from a borrower's bank account on a monthly basis – or the text message from a creditor to a borrower informing him or her that a repayment is due.[1] Consumer lending, a financial technology often associated with the promise of pleasurable consumption, is thus never disconnected from the more unpleasant business of debt collection.

We should be cautious before accepting a redistribution of the politics of debt default that simply shifts the issue from one part of the credit industry to another – I will return to this question. However, for present purposes, it is at least important to recognise that the *work* of collections is distributed across both creditors (those legally owed a particular debt) and the self-defined 'debt collections industry'. As we have seen, this is an industry that has claimed to possess privileged knowledge about the art of collecting 'problem' debt (that is when more mundane collection technologies have failed to elicit a repayment). Consumer credit lending and collection should thus be considered as involving a set of very particular, very interconnected, practices within a larger consumer credit assemblage.

This chapter has two broad aims. The first is to explore this interrelationship further. Over and above how they are perceived from the outside, what, precisely, *are* the differences between the forms of collection respectively enacted by the consumer credit lending industry and the consumer collections industry? And how, and through what mechanisms, are differences produced and similarities obscured? In addressing these questions, much of the chapter focuses on a central component of the collections trajectory: the creditor's own *internal* collections process. In this internal collections trajectory and, in particular, in the branding work that has been practiced as part of it, we can begin to identify more clearly the generative capacity of the difference between creditor and collector. In order to do so, some scene-setting is necessary. The chapter, therefore, also highlights important recent changes in the relationship between creditors and collectors.

The chapter's second aim is to shed further light on the calculative effects of specific collections technologies. We have already seen how a defaulting debtor's calculative capacities are shaped by the arrival of collections devices, intersecting with the unfolding of their embodied daily lives, in a process that I have called the 'capture of affect'. The last chapter showed how these devices become harnessed together as part of strategically deployed collections trajectories. In the process, I examined the role played by one collections technology in particular: the collections telephone call.

This chapter tells much of the story of the relationship between the creditor and collector the collector through a second collections device: the collections letter.[2] This will enable a more precise analysis of the generic function of collections letters, which I argued in Chapter 2 can be seen as 'lures for feeling' to the debtor. With this in place, we can begin to focus on what role these lures play in shaping a debtor's calculative possibilities, as well as in *performing* the distinction between creditor and collector. It is in the space of intersection between these two organisational entities that the debtor is made most aware of the ontological shift that will be repeatedly returned to over the course of the collections process: between the debtor as customer – desired, entreated, and (put simply) 'good' – and the debtor as, simply, debtor – obliged, needed, and 'bad'. It is by looking here that some of the strangeness of the collections industry begins to reveal itself particularly clearly. It is a world, to return to Macbeth's witches at the beginning of this chapter, where fair at times becomes foul.

Before coming to this, it is important to be clear about how exactly the contemporary relationship between the creditor and the collector has come to be formatted. Chapter 3 looked at how the consumer debt collection industry has built up an increasingly self-confident identity over the course of the twentieth century. It is this that has allowed it to claim possession of the distinct forms of expertise required to collect defaulting debt. Creditors, meanwhile, have been largely happy for the collections industry to do so, given that it has tended to see the collection of defaulting debt as a somewhat peripheral concern. This is, however, often no longer the case.

The return of internal collections

Until relatively recently, if a consumer credit lender had to deal with a defaulting debt, there were only two principal options. Now, there are three.

The first option is to collect the debt in-house. For much of the twentieth century in the UK, this was the most common collections method (see Chapter 3). This involves collections work being conducted by the same organisation that lent funds to a borrower in the first place.

The second method, which arrived on British shores towards the latter half of the twentieth century, is to employ an external 'contingency' collections agency when and if whichever internal processes a creditor has in-house prove unsuccessful.[3] The last chapter looked in part at two such companies: Alpha and Delta. Companies like this are employed by creditors to collect on defaulting debts on commission, taking a percentage share of every debt recovered. A creditor using this method will tend to have a 'panel' of contingency agencies on its books, consisting of a number of different collections companies who effectively operate in competition with each other to collect on the same debt portfolio. At Alpha, for example, teams were often on a panel with three other collectors. Debts will get allocated to these agencies for a set period of time, during which they are assessed against the competition (often after six months, sometimes also at three months).[4] If it is more successful than other companies, it will be allocated greater shares of its client's debts. If it is less successful, this share will be reduced, or it may get taken off the client's books altogether.

For a long time this particular method of collections suited creditors. In the race to expand their share of the seemingly ever-expanding consumer lending market, the industry had not spent much time worrying about developing its collections operations to anywhere near the same degree of sophistication as its lending functions. Instead contingency agencies were left to skim whatever they could off the 'bad' debt that lenders had. The industry saw no real reason to overly concern itself with collections. As Richard, a contingency agency client relationships manager recalls,

> if you go back a few years, and certainly longer than when I joined [Alpha Agency] in 2000, [collections] was the back end of the process. The accounts had been 100 per cent provided for, and therefore they passed them out to the highest bidder, and if they got some cash back, hooray, bonus.

In other words, consumer credit lenders were able to maintain healthy balance sheets without the contribution of the debt collections industry, because of the profits being generated from their lending operations; the volume of 'bad' debt was by current standards, extremely low, meaning that it could be put down as just an unavoidable cost of being in the credit business ('100 per cent provided for'), without having a major impact on the overall profitability of the company.

However, in the late 1990s, a new, third model of collections arrived on British shores which began to change creditors' attitudes to defaulting debt: debt sale/debt purchase (the name depends on your perspective). This saw creditors selling entire portfolios of defaulting debt, potentially containing many hundreds or even thousands of individual credit accounts, to third parties. These third parties become the new creditor (for this reason I will sometimes draw a distinction between a debt purchaser and an 'original creditor').[5] Echoing the direction of travel of many collections technologies, this way of dealing with defaulting consumer credit debt originated in the US (see Roberts 2014a, pp. 11–13). Debt purchase is also at the heart of Beta's business model, one of the companies we encountered in the last chapter.

The first large volume debt purchase in the UK was in 1998 (Maynard 2008). The market initially occupied only a small part of the debt collections industry, with few sellers, and only relatively small portfolios changing hands. However, spurred to a significant degree by the sheer increase of so-called 'delinquent' consumer debt well before the arrival of the ongoing economic downturn, as detailed in the second chapter (see also Credit Management Research Centre 2008), the debt purchase market increased rapidly in size.[6] One industry survey at the end of 2008 went as far as to predict 'the demise of contingency models' (OC&C Strategy Consultants 2009, p. 4).[7] At that point, there was a sense that operating a purely contingent collections operation was backward-looking, leading many such companies to decide to also dip their toes into the water of debt purchase.[8]

One of the effects of the rise of the debt purchase industry was to highlight to creditors just how much economic value might still be hidden away in their defaulting credit accounts. As Daniel, an industry consultant at a major UK credit reference agency, told me, prior to the arrival of debt sale creditors might have been happy to use a combination of rudimentary (by contemporary standards) in-house collection practices and contingency agencies to collect on a fraction of their 'bad' debt. But then debt sale came along:

So, [you had] these companies going, yeah, we'll buy your debt off you. And the banks going, oh, we've taken provisions on that, [the bad debt has] been sitting there for the past few years, great, ok, we can get 10p in the pound for it, 15p, 8p, whatever it happened to be, brilliant. Let's do it, get it off our bottom line, we've actually made some money, fantastic.

The previous market model, in which a creditor was hoping at best for a small, fractional return on its defaulting debt, was changed by the arrival of debt sale. Old debts, which had almost nil value in accounting terms, were suddenly revived as assets with real value, able not only to be taken off a creditor's books altogether, but also to often generate, as Daniel suggests, upwards of an 8 per cent return.[9] International regulatory changes gave creditors further reasons to get 'bad' debt off the balance sheet.[10]

The unexpected arrival of the global economic crisis, however, put a major brake on what had previous seemed to be the debt purchase industry's unstoppable forward momentum. This might seem surprising: one of the almost inevitable effects of recessions is to bring with them higher levels of default (see Chapter 2, Figure 2.1). One might assume that this would be a boon for debt purchasers. However, while they may well have been interested in this new defaulting debt, the industry was faced with a particularly ironic problem: it sat ready and waiting to mop up some of the after-effects of the pre-crisis explosion of consumer lending, but couldn't. What only became clear once the crisis had unfolded was that the expansion of the debt purchase industry had *itself* been fuelled by the prodigious amount of credit that had previously been available. It was credit that had provided the capital that had fuelled the debt purchase industry, allowing it to invest in the debt portfolios it needed for its new way of working. With not only consumer lenders but also commercial lenders increasingly risk-averse, debt purchasers, like many others, found that the credit supply had run dry.

The recession brought with it a second problem: many debt purchasers were suddenly realising that they had paid significantly over the odds for debt portfolios before the crisis, whose predicted value was clearly now way off the mark. Looking back, an experienced industry figure, credited with having arranged the sale of one of the first debt portfolios in the UK, alluded to this period of overspending and to the loss of what he called 'pricing discipline'; as he put it, '[t]his is the sort of industry where, if you overpay for a portfolio, you can end up repenting for the next 10 years' (Willcox 2013). The result was to leave many collectors working and reworking old debt portfolios, with potentially diminishing returns. One industry figure described how Beta was well known within the industry to be 'trying to run down its book' and that 'their new purchases are miniscule'.[11] This was also noticed in Beta's call centre: after yet another unsuccessful collections call, one collector turned to me, frustrated. Since the crisis her commission levels had dropped significantly. This was partly, she said, because of the lack of 'fresh' accounts. This left collectors trying the same debtors again and again, with little realistic hope that their situation had changed.

The problem for collectors like this was not, however, just the absence of new accounts, for the crisis had another sting in the tail for collectors, one that had a major impact on both debt purchasers and contingency agencies. Each of the companies I visited was reporting significant decreases both in average levels of payments received and, in particular, in the number of debtors that would settle or 'settle in full' – in other words pay off either an agreed percentage of their debts, or even pay off their defaulting debts entirely.[12] Managers and call centre workers were near unanimous on the main reason for this: perhaps as significant as the growing levels of unemployment and generally declining economic conditions was the fact that debtors were experiencing the same problem as debt purchasers: an absence of readily available credit. In a further irony, the crisis revealed that, like so many businesses, debt collectors themselves had been benefitting from how easy it was for even defaulting consumer credit borrowers to borrow! Previously many debtors could be encouraged to consolidate their existing loans perhaps by taking out a new unsecured loan to pay off a series of creditors, or by releasing equity from their home, or by obtaining (probably borrowing) funds from another family member whose credit record was in a better state. In Beta's collections call centre, after a call that had ended with the debtor appearing to consider a settlement offer she was presented with, potentially by borrowing money from family members, the call operator turned to me and commented, 'that sort of call used to be normal. You know, she sounded like she was thinking about it. Often these days they are like "no, no, no"'. To be absolutely clear then, even the debt collections industry had been complicit in the expansion of consumer credit prior to the downturn. It was now struggling to profit from the consequences.

For (original) creditors this also presented a problem. Even if, from their point of view, defaults were never to be welcomed, they had become used to at least being able to pass these out to the debt purchase industry when necessary and to obtaining a much better level of return than they once had. Now, however, there were far fewer buyers and the prices these buyers would pay had dropped significantly. Further, as the crisis became a lengthy recession, the amount of defaulting debt they were holding was growing larger by the day.

Given how rudimentary creditors' own internal collections operations had long been, the result was somewhat unanticipated: creditors started to look once again at their own in-house collections departments. Whereas previously their almost total focus had been on the business of expanding their share of the consumer lending market, now it was important for creditors to become much better at undertaking collections work themselves. One major lender, for instance, shifted 250 people away from the lending arm of its business towards collections.[13] As one interviewee put it, 'the focus was always on lending. Now the focus is on collections and people are running very fast to do what they do better. But they've got 20 years to catch up, in a very short space of time'.[14] This shift is both practical and symbolic: consumer collections had firmly grabbed the attention of creditors.[15]

For this reason, many creditors are now undertaking work that is structurally identical to the wider collections industry. As with this industry, internal collections processes vary in sophistication and scope. They can range from the simple deployment of a small number of reminder and warning letters before a debt is passed out to an external agency, to full-scale debt collection practices that are as detailed and well thought through as those of some of the largest debt purchasers. Indeed, the fact that an original creditor has access to a debtor's entire history with that particular financial institution can provide it with far more data to be used in the kinds of econometric analysis that were explored in the last chapter.

Yet creditors seem to be somewhat shy about their renewed interest in this perhaps more murky work of collections. No original creditor is represented in the member's list of the UK debt collection industry's trade body, the Credit Services Association (CSA), for instance.[16] This is despite the fact that, in the UK at least, the regulator recognises that the regulation of debt collection applies to particular practices not particular types of companies.[17]

With this account of the return of internal, creditor-led collections now in place, our exploration of original creditors' collections activities can begin. To do so, I will present a dramatisation of a creditor's collections letter sequence, which puts into order some of the key stages through which an account might go through, when passing through a creditor's internal collections department.[18] This is a journey that tracks a particular moment in the recent history of the UK collections industry, providing a snapshot of practices as they were in 2009. Many collections techniques are the same now as they were then (any differences will be highlighted). In the first of the following two sections we will focus in part on a specific set of collections letters, sent by the internal collections department at the British retail bank Halifax. The principles that inform these letters remain, to the present day, largely unchanged and apply as much to internal collections operations as to the wider debt collections industry. In the second section, the historical context becomes far more relevant. Here we will examine a set of internal collections practices that have now become, in the UK at least, historical artefacts. This will, however, open up for view a logic that informs collection practices as much now as it did then, and in the UK as much as elsewhere. In the process, we will also learn more about that most material of collections lures: the collections letter.

Creditors as collectors

We begin with a Halifax credit card account that, at the point when we join it, is already quite far into the process of going 'bad'.[19] That is to say, the debtor, for whatever reason, is showing the creditor real signs that she or he is not willing or able to repay the full outstanding balance. The account is thus in arrears and is potentially heading towards default.[20] The result is that the account is passed to Halifax's internal 'Retail Bank Collections Team'. As shown in Figure 5.1, the letters this team sends out progress from an early stage collections letter (Letter

1), to a default notice (Letter 2), to a final 'last chance' letter (Letter 3). Each of these letters mark or draw attention towards a significant passage point in the journey into default. These are enacted by the deployment of a sequence of 'disentanglement' or detachment devices (Callon *et al.* 2002), serving both practical and symbolic functions. The first of these is designed to prevent the borrower building up any more credit. The key attachment device that mediated the customer-lender relationship up to this point – the credit card – is rendered inoperable, that is, 'cancelled'. At the same time, the creditor asserts its continuing claim over the device. It demands back redundant, effectively worthless pieces of plastic and electronics, cut into pieces. This seeks to effect a small, symbolic repossession (see Deville 2013b).

The second passage point is legal: the serving of a 'default notice'. An unsecured creditor will typically spend at least some time trying to collect on outstanding debts, however after between three and six months without payment having been received the borrower will be formally notified that a debt will go into 'default' (if repayment is not made within 28 days). This notification must be conveyed in written form before a creditor can take any action to recover all or part of a debt.[21] This letter is thus different from many associated with being subject to debt collection, in that it is filled with agency by a body outside of the collector: the legal framework within which the creditor is bound. It also marks a secondary passage point for the debtor, as the creditor must report the default to the credit reference agencies. This is, from the debtor's point of view, perhaps more serious than having a card cancelled. For, while missed payments will only have a temporary impact on a borrower's credit rating if repayments resume, a default stays on a credit file for six years. Having even one default on a credit file may severely impact the possibility of obtaining future credit through conventional routes for this period – as Daniel (see previous) put it 'when you have defaults on your credit file, you are instantly sub-prime, basically'.[22]

The final letter is less marking a passage point, as pointing towards one. It is framed as the last chance for the borrower to act, before the account is passed *away* from the creditor, towards a 'Debt Recovery Agent'. The message is clear: after this point, the debtor will have to deal with someone else.

It is important to recognise that in this journey from creditor towards collector, there are, to a greater extent than later in the collections cycle, *genuine* sanctions being threatened and enacted against the debtor. The debtor progressively loses their right to borrow from the creditor and, if they do not respond to Letter 3, their future right to other (non-sub-prime) credit. However, mixed in with these potential or actual sanctions is a range of other semiotic, often affectively oriented, devices that seek to shape the calculative space of the debtor. Based on an examination of hundreds of letters, from both internal and external collectors, variations of these are extremely common to collections practices. These include the deployment of explicit threats, including:[23]

- Threatening legal action: from highlighting – sometimes in bold – various possible legal outcomes, including action being taken in a 'county court',

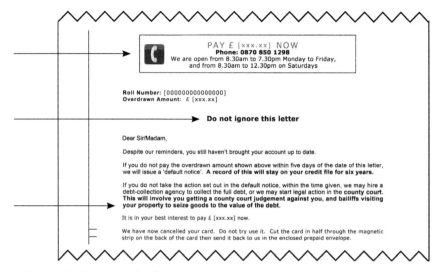

a Letter 1: Early stage collections.

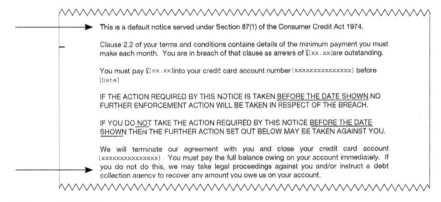

b Letter 2: Default notice.

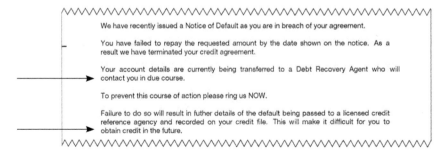

c Letter 3: Last chance.

Figure 5.1 Three internal collections letters.[24]

'bailiffs' and the particularly resonant promise of them 'visiting the property to seize goods to the value of the debt' (Letter 1), to the more nebulous threat of 'legal proceedings' (Letter 3).

• Threatening a debtor's credit file: although, it is worth noting that, by Letter 3, the threat has still not been carried out, despite being first raised in Letter 1. Notifying a credit reference agency of a default is an absolute passage point, not a continuum.

The letters also employ varied modes of address (see Chapter 4), including:

• Suggesting the borrower retains the (latent) capacity to self-govern: 'It is in your best interest …' (Letter 1); 'This will make it difficult for you to obtain credit in the future' (Letter 3); 'please' (Letter 3); …

• … as compared to seeing debtors as responding best to didactic orders: 'Do not ignore this letter' (Letter 1); 'Do not try to use it' (Letter 1); 'You must pay …' (Letter 2).

Finally, the letters employ use a range of mechanisms to attempt to be intensive, striking, and/or high impact, including:

• Strategically using colour, typographic and graphic design: Red to imply urgency (Letter 1; 'PAY£ … NOW' is in red), bold, centralised text (Letter 1); various other strategically HIGHLIGHTED SHOUTING throughout.

• Suggesting processes are being set in motion: the most resonant of these is in Letter 3, which speaks of 'Your account details […] *currently being transferred* to a Debt Recovery Agent' (Letter 3, emphasis added). The letter evokes action that is being taken in the present, to the extent that the reader is asked to imagine what is depicted as the physical labour of transferring account details to a third party, at the very point at which the letter is being read.

• Seeking to elicit immediate action: these are omnipresent in collections letters; here, they include: 'To prevent this course of action please ring us NOW'; 'PAY £ [xxx.xx] NOW' (in red); 'If you do not pay within five days of the date of this letter'; and so forth.

• Using capitalisation and syntax to imply or emphasise legal status: these include here a 'default notice' becoming a 'Notice of Default' between letters 2 and 3 and a 'debt collection agency' becoming a 'Debt Recovery Agent'.

These devices – ranging from the explicitly to the implicitly threatening, from attempts to elicit self governance, to attempts to impose a worldview on the debtor, to raising and lowering the affective intensity of the letter – can be seen as trying to successfully 'resonate' with the reader that picks it up (see Chapter 2).[25] That is to say, these letters do not operate in a vacuum: instead, they are affective 'lures', aimed at prompting calculative engagement by intersecting with both the readers' anxious anticipatory domestic landscapes and their emergent dispositional tendencies, with the latter including their very particular embodied history and expertise.

When grouped together, however, some of the weaknesses of the collector begin to seep through. What happens, for instance, to the very specific legal threats from Letters 1 to 3? A detailed range of consequences becomes a nebulous 'legal action', before disappearing altogether. Meanwhile, although the threat of potential damage to the debtor's credit file is raised first in Letter 1, by Letter 3 the credit reference agency has still not been notified. In fact, the only threat that is carried out over the course of this sequence is the serving of the default notice in Letter 2.

It is around these calculative challenges that some of the more obvious distinctions between the credit statement and the collections letter can be detected. I argued in Chapter 1 that the credit statement has at its heart the impossibility of providing a wholly stable calculative frame for the user that cannot pay off their full balance at the end of the month. For, even if this user were to sit down and attempt to construct a repayment plan, there will still at the heart of this calculation be the inevitable uncertainty that comes with having to depend on a future that is yet to pass (see Knight 1921).

The collections letter in this respect is not so different from the credit statement. But, rather than managing the opacity of future events, it seeks to *amplify* it. The very unknowability of the future provides an affordance to which it can connect a range of other potential opacities. Some of these cluster around the opacities that characterise many of our journeys through modern social life. These include the difficulty of understanding the language and functioning of legal and socio-economic processes – including the complexities of the credit scoring system, the role of the courts, bailiffs and so forth. But also, they attach to the broad lack of public understanding of how collections companies make their decisions.

The problem for the debtor is that unless she or he has the expertise to do the work of reading *against* the collections letter, such weaknesses are likely to remain hidden. Instead they are left wondering as to a range of potential future outcomes: Will a bailiff be sent round? Is it in my best interest to repay rather than damage my credit rating? Do I need access to consumer credit in the next six years? Do debt collectors really take people like me to court? The amplification of indeterminacy thus becomes a route into generating the kinds of anxious, affectively oriented forms of calculative and emotional intensity that the collector well knows is one of the prerequisites for prompting the debtor into contacting it and, potentially, repaying (at least something).

What this points to is what Michel Callon and John Law (2005) have termed the formatting not just of calculation but also 'non-calculation' (or, adapting Cochoy's (2002) term, 'non-qualculation'). These two aspects of calculation, they argue, go hand in hand. This may be true in the case of the credit statement, but it becomes particularly obvious, particularly exaggerated, in the case of the collections letter. As we have seen, one of its most significant moves is to interfere with calculative possibility. That is to say, part of its role is to prevent or impede certain forms of calculation. However, this is not to occlude the possibility of calculation altogether, but rather to shift the terrain *of* calculation. The debtor is quite specifically *not* invited to consider his or her state of indebtedness in the round, or which debt it makes sense to pay off first, when, and how, or whether it might be possible to renegotiate an outstanding debt (in due course, it often will be). The invitation is rather to consider the cost, to his or her near future, of not repaying *this* debt, *now*. Generating opacity in one calculative domain thus becomes a condition for generating calculative attention in another.

As we have seen, one of the key 'vectors' of opacity in collections letters is the deployment of threat (of some or other unwelcome action being taken). Brian Massumi writes that

> [a] threat is only a threat if it retains an indeterminacy. If it has a form, it is not a substantial form, but a time form: a futurity. The threat as such is nothing *yet* – just a looming. It is a form of futurity yet has the capacity to fill the present without presenting itself. Its future looming casts a present shadow, and that shadow is *fear*.
>
> (Massumi 2005, p. 35; original emphasis)

Massumi puts his finger on the very heart of the opacities that surround consumer debt collection. One the one hand, through threats (and perhaps attendant fear – although I would argue that this is only one possible affectively generated response), the present is made to live with that which *could* come to pass. As Philip Rose writes, drawing on the philosophy of Alfred North Whitehead, the present can be seen as 'a floating "now" [...] a continuous movement away from the Past and towards the Future' (2002, p. 33), in which the present becomes 'the active or actual condition for preserving the Past and for making the Future real' (p. 34). On the other, however, the efficacy of threat depends on the very impossibility of knowing what *will* come to pass. One of the effects of threat, therefore, is to fill the present with the indeterminacies of the future, making it vibrate with unknowability. It is this that is exploited by the collector, as a way to secure market attachment.

As undoubtedly central to collections work as threat is, looking at the letters above shows that they actually depend on a varied, potentially uneven 'patterning' of threat (see Pain 2009). This includes coupling threats to entreaties, and surrounding these with an array of semiotic prompts. Reading debt collections letters in these ways reveals not the articulation of a single unitary message or mode of ordering, but rather a range of not fully coherent messages, being articulated near simultaneously. The letters thus deploy a messy assemblage of 'lures for feeling', with the collector hoping that at least one will be grasped by the debtor.

As we have seen in the last two chapters, one way to make decisions about which affective lures to use, and when, might be to employ formalised experimental methods. But such approaches can also sit quite comfortably alongside and in interaction with other methods and forms of expertise. These range from circulating industry knowledge about debtors' likely responses to particular approaches, to the more formalised use of qualitative research methodologies. One of the managers at a collections agency where I was based, for example, described how their letters are circulated among key senior staff and minutely deconstructed before being sent out, with the language, the layout, all the potential subject of discussion. An example of a more structured examination of collections letters is provided by the results of a set of focus groups conducted by Experian. Its conclusions include the following:

Customers need to be threatened with the consequences of not paying.

Scare-tactics without the possibility of working out a solution are likely to result in a 'head in the sand mentality.'

Respondents expect a different approach and tone of voice depending on (a) the amount owed; (b) how overdue the debt is and (c) the type of company communicating to them.

Serious threats ([c]redit rating, legal action) tend to concern younger audience far more

Informal language is ineffective.

The prospect of home visits works for late payers.

The younger group favoured headlines in bold and red (since they were accustomed to waiting for 'red letters'). Older respondents were less influenced by red text. Respondents also suggested that using red to highlight more than one area of a letter is ineffective.

(Experian 2009c, p. 24)

Whether or not these insights reflect the reality of experiencing collections letters is not my interest here. What this survey stands for is the presence of routine debates within the industry about the precise layout of collections letters, mirroring similar debates about the content of phone calls and the usefulness/effectiveness of other collections methods (email, SMS, doorstep collections, for instance – all common topics in industry conferences and publications). In this case what is noteworthy is the absence of debates about economic calculation: presenting the raw financial implications of debt and coaxing debtors into cost–benefit calculations about their particular debt may be one part of collections, but here this is by and large replaced by the analysis of how exactly to generate moments of affective intensity, ranging from the use of colour, tone of voice, type of language used, the variable efficacy of specific threats, as well as – importantly – the possibility of relief, here coded as the need to offer at least the promise of a solution.

For reasons that will become clear, there is one specific threat that I would like to explore in more depth. It appears in the Halifax letters above: namely, the threat of an account being sent 'out' to what, in this instance, is called a 'Debt Recovery Agent'. We will thus rejoin this letter sequence at the point at which

Halifax apparently makes good on its threat to send the account out to an external agency. Specifically, the account is moved from being collected on by Halifax's internal collections team, to being collected on by 'Blair, Oliver and Scott'.

The generative potential of 'passing out' a debt

Blair, Oliver and Scott is, it seems, a debt collections company, with offices registered in Fife.[26] This, anyway, is what is suggested by the first letter shown in Figure 5.2, which was sent in 2009 and states that Blair, Oliver and Scott is 'a professional Debt Collection Agency'. The reality is, however, that now, as then, Blair, Oliver and Scott is a company with no permanent employees working for them directly.[27] Nor, as its annual accounts show, have they ever traded.[28] The reason for this may be contained in its name, the acronym for which mirrors that of its owners: Bank of Scotland (BOS). As public accounts show, Bank of Scotland plc is its parent company and has been since their earliest accounts were filed in 1994.[29] Bank of Scotland are however now part of the HBOS group (itself acquired by Lloyds TSB in 2008), which came into existence in 2001 when Bank of Scotland merged with Halifax. In this light, the reason for its letters being sent to Halifax debtors becomes clear: as Blair, Oliver and Scott's 2008 public accounts state: 'HBOS uses the Company's name in the collections administrative process' (Blair, Oliver and Scott Ltd 2009, p. 11).

'Blair, Oliver and Scott' is thus above all a brand, even if not one with a particularly high public profile. Until relatively recently, it is a brand that was used in HBOS' own internal collections operations. Including the apparently trade-marked hunting dog image, this brand was deployed in three principal ways: on letterheads; on a very basic two page website; and when the name was used in phone communications via its call centre. However, even if they answered to the Blair, Oliver and Scott brand name, this call centre was not populated by Blair, Oliver and Scott staff (it had none), but employees working for HBOS/Lloyds TSB. For the Fife address referred to a building in a business park branded with the Bank of Scotland logo. Yet the recipients of its letters and those that communicate with employees working under its name were not, it can be surmised, intended to realise this. The letters refer to their 'above named' 'client' Halifax, who has 'instructed' them to collect on their behalf (Figure 5.2). And yet the client is part of the group that owns the company.

I will come on shortly to the reasons both for the appeal to creditors of these apparently fake firms, or 'trading styles' as they are sometimes known, and for their recent demise. However, before doing so, it is important to appreciate how common this practice was. The table below shows a selection of the trading styles that have been deployed by many of the UK's largest retail banks and debt purchasers, at least up until 2009. It identifies two groups of trading styles. The first is the use of the conventional method of setting up trading styles – what can be termed 'trading styles proper'. This involves making the affiliation to the parent company/brand visible in small print somewhere in the letter (usually at

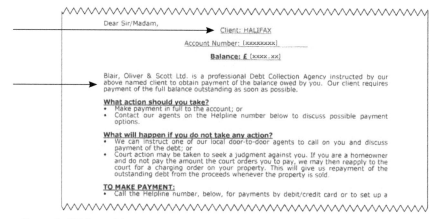

a Letter 1: 'Welcome' letter.

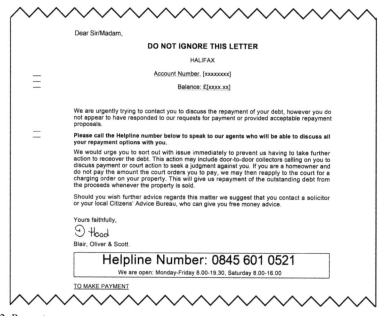

b Letter 2: Prompt.

Figure 5.2 Blair, Oliver and Scott collections letter cycle.[30]

the bottom).[31] This practice was extended to include not only companies branded as debt collection agencies, but also companies branded as solicitors. The second method is more complex and, in the case of Blair, Oliver and Scott, involved setting up subsidiary companies.[32] In this case, written communications with debtors did not have to make explicit the identity of the legal owner of the company. It was also possible to combine the two methods: thus, for example,

Table 5.1 Subsidiaries and collections trading styles of major UK creditors, 2009[33]

[DCA = Debt Collection Agency]	First level (parent company)	Second level (subsidiary [S] or trading style [TS] of parent company)	Third level (trading style of subsidiary company)
Major primary creditors	Barclays Plc (including Barclaycard)	Mercers Debt Collection Ltd (DCA [S])	Calder Financial (DCA)
	HBOS (now owned by Lloyds TSB)	Albion Collections (DCA [S])	
		Blair, Oliver and Scott (DCA [S])	
	HSBC	Metropolitan Collection Services Ltd (DCA [S])	Payment Services Bureau (DCA)
			Central Debt Recovery Unit (DCA)
		DG Solicitors (Solicitors [TS])	
	Lloyds TSB (see also separate entry for HBOS)	BLS Collections (DCA [TS])	
		MHA Collections (DCA [TS])	
	Royal Bank of Scotland Group (including NatWest)	Triton Credit Services Ltd (DCA [TS])	
Major debt purchasers	Cabot Financial	Fire (DCA [S])	
		Morgan Solicitors (Solicitors [TS])	
	capQuest	Telogram Limited (DCA [S])	
	Lowell Group	Red Debt Collection Service (DCA [TS])	
		Hamptons Legal (Solicitors [TS])	

both HSBC and Barclays Plc used companies branded as trading names of a subsidiary company. These were trading styles two levels removed from that of the first level parent company. In other words, the third level companies were effectively trading styles of trading styles.

Trading styles, in UK collections at least, are now a largely historical feature of the credit and collections industry.[34] While the generic practice using a different company name as a business style is perfectly permissible in virtually any industry in the UK, an exception is the consumer credit industry. The explicit use of trading styles as a collections tactic eventually came to the attention of the regulator.[35] As an industry guidance document puts it, the regulator sees 'no legitimate purpose in failing to be transparent' and that if the debt is 'escalated or transferred to a different department within the same company and/or to a different company within the same group of companies' the collection letters should make the relationship and the reason for the transfer clear (Credit Services Association & Office of Fair Trading 2013, p. 3).[36] In 2014 the practice (extremely) belatedly came to the attention of the wider public, with the regulator taking action against Wonga,[37] a high-profile online payday lender, found to have been sending collections letters to debtors from artificial law firm 'trading styles' (Financial Conduct Authority 2014), with the UK Student Loans Company also being accused of using similar tactics (Mason 2014).[38]

These collections devices still have much to teach us, however. They stand for fundamental features of the relationship between the original creditor and the external collections industry. Paul Rock noted the existence of very similar strategies being used in the UK in the 1960s. He concluded that trading styles enabled a creditor to '*embroider and enlarge* the threats he [*sic*] can offer' (1973, p. 68; emphasis added).[39] Or, to put this in the terms developed over the course of this book, the ability to mobilise multiple company identities not only allowed the creditor to amplify the threats used in its internal collections work, but also to deliver threat through different *modes* of captation. What the trading style gave the creditor was the ability to speak to the debtor in a different tone, to attempt a different mode of 'affective captation'. Why did the creditor did not simply use this tone in its standard internal debt collection procedures? The answer to this question relates to specific circulating public perceptions about both debt collections industry and the relationship between markets and morality.

In the focus groups mentioned above, conducted by Experian, one further question posed to participants concerned the relationship that exists between a (original) creditor and an external agency. The report concluded:

> Passing the debt to a third party debt recovery agency is a big motivator in repayment.

> Both groups shared the view that a third party's involvement is indication that the situation has seriously escalated, because:

> • The agency will only get paid if it recovers the debt

- An additional collection fee is a possibility
- A third party agency will not care about the long-term customer relationship: they have no need to tread carefully.

(Experian 2009c, p. 24)

Experian's focus groups put their finger on the resonant potential for the collector of the 'first move'. This is the move away from the creditor, to an external collections agency. In the space of this move is contained perhaps one of the most potent weapons for the creditor seeking to recoup their debt: the threat of an account being passed 'out'. Specifically, in asserting the belief that a third party will neither 'care about the long-term customer relationship' nor 'need to tread carefully', these focus group participants are invoking a very particular view of how the relationships between companies work. Theirs is an understanding of contemporary markets as spaces where the transfer of *legal* obligations is not always accompanied by the transfer of *moral* obligations.[40]

This is a phenomenon we are well aware of from other market domains. Periodically a clothing company that, in their dealings with customers, expresses a certain set of values, will be publicly exposed for exhibiting an apparently contradictory sets of values in their manufacturing processes – a reliance on child labour, say. The fact that the two companies may be legally related opens up an opportunity for activists: their charge is that just because one company employs another to conduct aspects of its business that it is either unwilling or unable to do itself does not change its responsibility for the subsidiary company's actions. Recognising the power of this charge an accused company will often invoke the need for better forms of audit practice, a popular mechanism for attempting to translate the values expressed in one organisational domain into another.[41] Either way, the conclusion many of us draw from such cases is that while we may feel that legal relationships between companies *should* correspond to moral relationships, we realise that, in practice, markets find it easier (and, often, more profitable) to focus on optimising the efficiency of the transfer of economic value between companies rather than moral value(s).[42]

What the focus group participants are suggesting in the case of debt collection is that this likely extends to the transfer of an account between a creditor and an external collector. Even if an agency is quite explicit about the legal responsibility not having left the original creditor (as in Blair, Oliver and Scott's reference to Halifax, the 'client'), a creditor's apparent decision to move an account externally is understood as a disavowal of their duty of (customer) *care*. The presumption is that being moved to an external agency means entering into a perhaps more mercenary and more brutal world, with the creditor largely washing its hands of whatever occurs within it.

The particular formatting of collections trading styles shows just how well creditors understood (and certainly still understand) this. For copyright reasons, the design of genuine trading styles cannot be shown here. However, Figure 5.3. illustrates the logic at play. Often, when a trading style is used, the brand is deliberately underworked. In the below two examples, both consist of a very

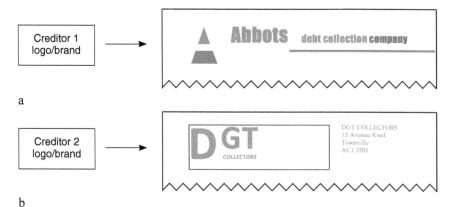

Figure 5.3 The logic of trading styles. [Fictitious trading style brand identities, drawing on principles used in genuine trading styles. In both cases, even though printed in monochrome, the text is intended to be bright red; in the case of 'Abbots', the shade of red is uneven].

simple, bold reddish, text-based logo, in which the branding is almost amateurish in its rough and ready appearance, extending in one case to a cheap-looking stencil effect in the letterhead, including faded shades of red.[43] Armed with this point of contrast, Blair, Oliver and Scott emerges as an exception: its brand identity is relatively worked through, incorporating a logo (the dog), and a muted, restrained look and feel as conveyed by a combination of blues in its letterhead. That being said, unlike the others, the company name, apparently incorporating three surnames, does echo the naming conventions of legal practices, which may be indicative of a deliberately different strategy. The combination of all these messages is clear: the debtor has moved from dealing with a major banking establishment, with decades of history and a reputation to consider, either to a small, perhaps amateurish operation that may have far fewer worries about pressing debtors harder for the money they owe, or to one more interested in pursuing a debtor through the courts.

Often the partialities of ties between market actors are assumed to be undesirable 'overflows' of markets (see Callon 1998a). Trading styles, however, reveal to what extent the creditor understands the public presumption that ties between companies are partial as an *opportunity*. The affordance that creditors sought to grasp with their deployment of trading styles is the existence of the collections industry as apparently external and separate from the lending industry and into which debtors presume a creditor's moral responsibilities do not flow. What the use of trading styles highlights is that, while the creditor has the *organisational* capacity to conduct collections itself, what it needs is the 'existence' of an external debt collections industry, understood as operating in a related but distinct market arena to the lending industry, composed of legally autonomous but interdependent companies.[44]

In the case of the use of collections trading styles, therefore, the creditor was attempting to itself *perform* a differentiated market space, in which, alongside their own collections operations, they 'manufactured' distinct collections agencies and solicitors. This can be seen as creditors' undertaking their own (economic) sociology of the market: they recognise it as a domain that is deeply 'social', embedded in cultural and moral relations and responsibilities, and draw on this to their advantage. They also recognise the calculative challenges faced by debtors in understanding the opacities of the debt collections industry and, with trading styles, sought to amplify them. By 'enacting' a move away from the creditor, the defaulter is forced to confront a new, unfamiliar entity, whose values are uncertain and whose actions are harder to predict. This also allowed the creditor to operate more freely in the lending market, by managing the risk of brand 'contamination'. It was by disentangling the work of lending and collections in this way that the creditor could (seek to) prevent the business of securing *voluntaristic* attachments – offering a lending 'service' – from becoming destabilised by the (more forceful) business of attempting to maintain and elicit value from attachments of *obligation*.

There are three broad lessons from the use of trading styles for our understanding of the contemporary work of debt collection. First, it provides further evidence that, whether carried out by an original creditor, an external debt collector, or a debt purchaser, this is an industry that relies on opacity (see Deville 2013a). Trading styles provided another way of attempting to amplify the opacities surrounding the relationships between different parts of the consumer credit industry. Collections work is not and *cannot* be primarily concerned with informational transparency. The very unknowability of whether or not a particular threat will be carried out is absolutely central to the success of debt collections work of all kinds.

Second, it highlights the potential for the creditor of moving an account between different organisations. This does not just have to be from original creditor to collector. If one particular contingency collector turns out to be unsuccessful in collecting a particular set of debts, after a set period of time, it is common practice to move the account to a different agency. A move may also be initiated by a debt being bought by a debt purchaser. Then, the sequence begins all over again – potentially from being worked internally, to being sent externally, to potentially (although relatively rarely in the UK) being sold once again. With each move, part of the hope is that a particular external company will simply be 'better' at collections than another. However, the move itself is an opportunity: each time the debtor is addressed by a different collector, the debt, the defaulting credit product, is 're-presented' to the debtor. This thus offers the opportunity to, once more, generate an intensive moment of calculative attention, perhaps as the debtor feels s/he has moved yet closer to legal action.

The third lesson concerns the particularly peculiar relationship between the creditor and the collector. The creditor *needs* the existence of a credit industry understood to be composed of two broad sets of ontologically distinct entities: one principally concerned with lending, one principally concerned with collecting.

Trading styles were an attempt to allow these two aspects of the business of consumer credit to work side-by-side, within the same organisation. That it ultimately failed, albeit after a very long run, perhaps indicates the degree to which we, and the regulators, would prefer to see them as separate.

The end of the trading style, while a likely inconvenience, does not pose a major threat to the creditor. It may have to use more external collectors in its collections process; or it may simply choose to sell more debts off wholesale to a debt purchaser. Either way, the collections industry remains ready, as it always did, to act as a vector through which the creditor can channel some of the unwanted associations that the vast expansion of consumer credit lending has generated.[45]

Conclusion

Compared to many other markets, the debt collections industry often seems peculiarly topsy-turvy: 'customers' are delivered to the industry already bound by obligation; calculation operates (in part) around the promise to be rid of a product, rather than to secure a new one; and collectors' language tends to operate more around threat than entreaty. However, looking at the role of collections letters and creditors' internal collections operations offers some revealing insights into why this might be, which have implications for considering the formatting of other market domains.

The careful design and deployment of collections letters points towards the complex interrelatedness of two central technologies of consumer credit: the credit statement and the collections letter. Both, it has been argued, can be seen as devices that manage future uncertainty. The statement seeks (sometimes in vain) to shut this uncertainty down. The collections letter makes use of this uncertainty to amplify the calculative challenges that a debtor is faced with, but only in order to generate calculative attention in another domain. It is not that calculation is irrelevant to collections practices. However calculative engagement is solicited far less by posing the problem of default around questions of economic optimisation – that is, what is or is not in a particular debtor's best financial interests – than by posing the question as being concerned with the immediate affective afterlife of a particular lived moment. What, exactly, will happen if I don't repay? What will my life be like? In order to generate such questions, opacity is strategically deployed as a way of shifting the terrain of calculative possibility.

The trading style is one particularly revealing example of such practices. It highlights the potential to the creditor of the first move away from 'lender', to an external agency. Without the existence of a collections industry, the creditor encountering a debtor apparently unwilling or unable to repay their debts would be faced with a stark binary choice: either it would have to imitate the full gamut of the practices developed by the collections industry, including absorbing all the bad will and controversy the latter generates, or it (eventually) writes the debt off. The promise of the external collections industry is to enable these two aspects of the business of consumer credit to be separated out, while enabling a single credit account to be subject to multiple moments of re-presentation. Trading styles were an attempt by the creditor to draw on some of this promise by 'performing' some the some of the features of the external collections industry itself. However, the very successful, very 'real' external collections industry stands and has always stood ready to take on this task if the creditor is not willing or able to do so.

Highlighting the interrelationships between the collections letter and the credit statement and the 'lender' and the 'collector' may also do some political work. It opens up the fiction of any easy separation between the lending and collections industry. Destabilising the separation between 'lender' and 'collector' does not mean that these two market entities should be pushed too quickly together. Bring them too close and the particular dynamics of collections practices are glossed as simply a necessary part of the business of consumer credit. Push them too far apart and the complicity of lenders in routine practice of collections is obscured. This begins to point to the ways in which the politics of consumer credit default is a resolutely distributed affair. Just how distributed will be examined in the conclusion that follows.

Notes

1 A practice used by some short term consumer credit lenders, or 'payday' lenders, as they are sometimes known. In the UK this practice is used by Wonga, perhaps the most controversial of the payday lenders (largely because of the high cost of its loans).
2 Specifically, the chapter draws on images of collections letters uploaded by users of the Consumer Action Group debt collection forum, a user generated debt advice resource. I am grateful to those participants who have put into public a mode of interaction that is framed as private.
3 Currently in the UK a period usually of at least 90 days.
4 Interview with Alpha company director.
5 For good overviews of the practices of debt purchase, see Braddock and Wordsworth (2006) and Berkley (2009).
6 Industry figures claimed an increase from around £2.5 billion worth of debt (this is the face value of the debt) purchased in 2004 (Maynard 2008), to a peak of perhaps around £8 billion in 2008 (Berkley 2009). Writing in early 2009, Berkley (2009) predicts a figure of between £8 billion and £10 billion for 2008. No published total for this year is available. However, as will be explored further later, the debt purchase market is held to have contracted significantly in 2009, in part due to the unavailability of refinancing options for debt purchasers as a result of the economic downturn. To put these figures in context, the CSA estimated towards the end of 2012 its members (including both debt purchasers and contingency agencies) were collecting on accounts owed around £28.2 billion worth of debt (Credit Services Association 2012c).
7 It is too early to tell whether this will come to pass or not. One of the effects of the downturn and the constriction on credit experienced by debt purchasers was for contingency agencies to find themselves suddenly in demand again, enjoying a so-called 'Indian summer' (OC&C Strategy Consultants 2009, p. 4).
8 In one 2008 survey, 46 per cent of agencies sampled offered a debt purchase service, an increase of 27 per cent since 2003; the number offering contingent ('trace and collect') work stayed broadly the same (Credit Management Research Centre 2008, pp. 156–157).

9 The prices Daniel refers to appear broadly accurate for the period. The Credit Management Research Centre concluded that in 2005/6, the average price paid for 'bad' debt was 8p in the pound. In 2007, when the debt purchase market was still booming, a sample of debt purchase prices again averaged out at 8p in the pound, with a range of between 5p and 18p (Credit Management Research Centre 2008, pp. 152, 170). This percentage is likely not dissimilar to that being paid for bad debt in the US: a recent government-led survey of the nine companies making up almost three quarters of the US debt purchase industry concluded that these companies paid on average four cents per dollar of the face value of the debt (although, of course, the price was significantly dependent on how old the debt was) (Federal Trade Commission 2013, p. ii).

10 The capital requirements stipulated in the Basel II agreement, which were implemented in the UK under the FSA at the end of 2007, became a major business opportunity for the debt purchase industry, in that it gave creditors an incentive to decrease the amount of 'bad' debt in their possession as a result of changes in how the amount of capital against which they could lend was calculated (Credit Management Research Centre 2008; Maynard 2004; Seib 2008).

11 A director of a commercial debt management company that I spoke to. These companies offer debtors a service: if they meet the qualifying criteria, debt management companies will try to negotiate with creditors on the debtors' behalf to reduce the overall outstanding balance, for a fee.

12 Daniel, the credit reference agency debt collection consultant, suggested that industry figures released by the CSA revealed a decrease of about one-third in one-off payments to its members, with average monthly payments dropping by £5 to about £23 a month. As these figures are not available to the public, they cannot be verified. See also: Maynard (2009).

13 Interview with Daniel.

14 Andrew, a credit reference agency sales director.

15 That said, debt collection in a downturn is not necessarily straightforward. One managing director noted that, '[w]hile more work is flooding into the industry, most debt collection operations are struggling to get settlement of debt in the same way as before' (Maynard 2009). An industry analysis of the top 383 companies in the UK debt collections industry, based on figures from the period soon after the downturn hit, showed that a large number of these companies are making sizeable pre-tax profits, over 40 of which made a margin of over 40 per cent. But beneath these big hitters, sits a large number of companies who are just about getting by: the second largest category (30 companies) includes those collection agencies making a margin of between 0 per cent and 5 per cent. Meanwhile, the third largest category (17 companies) includes those making a sizeable loss, with a loss margin of over 25 per cent (Plimsoll Analysis 2009, p. 3.2b; analysis of 2008–2009).

16 See the CSA's UK members list at www.csa-uk.com/uk-members-list [Accessed 14 February 2014].

17 Its guidance, it says, 'sets out the standards expected of ALL parties engaging in the recovery of consumer credit debts' (Office of Fair Trading 2012, p. 4; original emphasis, although in the original, the whole sentence is in bold, for the avoidance of all doubt). By contrast in the US, recent legislation (Frank 2010) designed to improve the protection offered to consumers dealing with collectors codified a separation between creditors and external collections, with much of the relevant regulatory apparatus applying solely to the latter (National Consumer Law Center 2012).

18 The sequence of letters depicted in this chapter has been reconstructed as faithfully as possible, however it is quite possible that it omits certain additional letters deployed by Halifax, or that the letters in this sequence are not always used together. Above all, it aims to represent principles that are common throughout the industry, while not making claims about the specificity of this one company's practices.

19 The choice of banking brand has been made primarily on the basis of the availability of letter evidence. As will be made clear later, similar strategies are not restricted to this one creditor. This section draws in part on work published in *Consumption Markets and Culture* (Deville 2014).

20 Default is often defined as having missed three consecutive payments (three months). As specified in recent industry guidance, unless there are particular circumstances which might warrant otherwise, the industry is expected *not* to routinely file accounts as being in default where payments have been missed for fewer than three months, but it is also expected *to* file default notices if payments have been missed for six consecutive months (Information Commissioners Office 2007, p. 6).

21 Which in accordance with amendments made in 2006, cannot commence until 14 days after being issued (Department for Business Information and Skills 2006, 14.36).

22 Default notices stay on a credit file for six years. Some lenders may choose to lend despite a default notice, however these tend to be sub-prime lenders, charging significantly higher interest rates.

23 See Rock's (1973, 51–106) analysis of the in many ways similar threats being deployed in the 1960s.

24 The image in 5.1a is traced from an original, lower resolution image.

25 See Massumi's use of resonance/resonation as a metaphor for the in-betweenness of the relations through which entities operating at different scalar registers intersect and interact with one another. Specifically Massumi is referring to intimate, corporeal forms of causality; as he puts it, resonation is the 'qualitative transformation of distance into an immediacy of self-relation' (Massumi 2002, p. 14). Also relevant is the analysis of the 'resonance machines' that have been argued to be characteristic of contemporary capitalism (Connolly 2005; drawing in part on Deleuze and Guattari 1987).

26 As we will see, they are not in fact a collections company themselves, but rather a brand. The company is still filing annual accounts, the most recent of which were on the 16 June 2014.

27 As their annual accounts state: '[t]he company employed no permanent staff directly. All staff and audit costs are borne by the parent undertaking' (Blair, Oliver and Scott Ltd 2009, p. 11).

28 As their annual accounts show, the only transactions on their accounts are the nominal £2 received annually from the parent company due as part of their conditions of ownership (Blair, Oliver and Scott Ltd 2009).

29 The company name was registered three year's earlier with Companies House in 1991.

30 The image in 5.2a is traced from an original, lower resolution image.

31 The tendency was to use a variety of legally required wordings including, for example, '... trading as ...', '... a trading style of ...', '... a registered business name of ...', '... is the practicing name of solicitors employed by ...'.

32 In the case of these subsidiary companies, phone numbers and addresses rarely matched the primary contact details of the parent and addresses could on occasion refer to solicitors' offices. As a result, the only definitive way of tracing these links involved finding, paying for (a nominal fee of £1 to Companies House) and then interpreting the specificities of a company's annual accounts.

33 This has been assembled by undertaking an analysis of scanned letters and by examining Companies House records.

34 This author was able to find suggestions that the following trading styles were still in active use in or later than 2013, even if just in ongoing communications with debtors (in the form of letters being sent from the organisation to debtors, as posted or discussed on the Consumer Action Group): Fire, DG Solicitors, Metropolitan Collection Services.

35 Now the Financial Conduct Authority.
36 In this respect, the UK's regulatory framework now broadly mirrors that of the US, where the current guidance accompanying the *Fair Debt Collection Practices Act* makes quite explicit that a collector may neither '[u]se any name other than the true name of the debt collector's business, company, or organization' nor '[f]alsely represent or imply that he or she is an attorney or that communications are from an attorney' (Federal Reserve Bank of the United States 2006, pp. 2–3). This relates to a section in the Act added in 1996 designed to prevent '[f]alse or misleading representations' on the part of the collector. See Federal Trade Commission (undated).
37 See *footnote 1*, this chapter
38 The government owned and funded not-for-profit company that provides subsidised loans for students in the UK.
39 Another advantage of using a trading style over sending out an account to a 'real' collections company was in part the ability to maintain control of the account by working it internally. There might also have been cost savings involved by not employing an external agency; creditors may also have used trading styles to benchmark ('Champion Challenge') the performance of its own collectors to genuinely external collections agencies (Credit Management Research Centre 2008, pp. 80–155).
40 For a detailed summary of the place of morality in markets, see Fourcade and Healy (2007).
41 Michael Power (1997) has documented accounts of the rise and efficacy of, and opacities within so-called 'audit culture'. See also: Strathern (2000); Dolan (2008).
42 This mirrors a division of labour within the social sciences, as explored by David Stark (2009), in which economics claims the study of the circulation of economic value with (in particular) sociologists left to study the circulation of social values. Beverly Skeggs (2014) meanwhile explores the ways in which economic value will always be 'haunted' by other forms of value.
43 This is apparently not a printing error, as it is consistent across a number of letters gathered from the Consumer Action Group.
44 In the original, on which the image is based, this is a conclusion shared by the Credit Management Research Centre. When it comes to Trading Styles, the authors suggest that, the '"separateness" from the bank is considered integral to the effectiveness of the debt recovery operation' (Credit Management Research Centre 2008, p. 110).
45 See Rock (1973, p. 55).

Conclusion

Bringing affect to markets

SALLY: Well there are a lot of people in debt, so they have been saying a lot on the telly lately. There are more in debt than out of it.

JOE: Does that make you feel a bit better about it in a way?

SALLY: Yeah, when they say there is a lot more people in debt yeah.

JOE: Why is that?

SALLY: [Because] there is somebody else going through the same experience. I'm not on my own with it.

* * *

JOE: Do you think there is any kind of, do you feel that there's a stigma attached to being in debt?

GARY: If you'd asked me a year ago I might have said yes. In this current climate I would probably say no.

JOE: So what changed, do you think?

GARY: Well it's become apparent, that everyone, sorry, not everyone, but a lot of people are living beyond their means.

There is at present a ubiquity to life in debt that can provide some minor comfort, despite the very real hurt that can result: at the very least, these borrowers say, we are not alone. As the unfolding global economic crisis continues to render clear, being unable to manage the uncertainties that come with borrowing is by no means a condition limited to individuals: a range of national governments and financial institutions have been shown to be just as vulnerable to the promises and pitfalls of indebtedness, irrespective of the diverse expertise at their disposal.

This apparently omnipresent entanglement between contemporary life and debt has led Maurizzio Lazzarato to identify debt as 'a universal power relation' given that 'everyone is included within it' (2012, p. 32). We may, for a variety of reasons, some of which I will return to below, want to hesitate before treating debt as the archetype for the varied and complex forms of exploitation and appropriation that characterise the routine encounters between people and economies.[1] At the same time, debt is undoubtedly an integral part of how the present is produced (see Berlant 2011, p. 4), finding its way into some of the most intimate corners of our daily existence. It is by attending to some of the particularities of the varied acts of production with which consumer credit becomes associated that this book has attempted to open up some of the problematics posed by debt and debt default: to debtors and collectors, as well as to our understanding of the relationship between societies and economies. In what follows, I will bring together some of the common threads that have emerged from this endeavour, as well as opening up some questions that remain to be answered.

The making of markets, the capture of affect

Markets are, as this book has sought to demonstrate throughout, composites of both human and non-human interaction. From the moment someone picks up a credit card, or takes out an unsecured loan, they are moving towards an engagement with a form of social and economic life that is saturated with multiple, variably enacted and enacting, socio-material devices. The credit card, the credit statement, the collections letter, the collections worker, the statistical analyst: each becomes a device involved in the 'calibration' of the conditions of market engagement, the conditions of calculative possibility, in other words (see Muniesa *et al.* 2007, p. 5).

Such devices, in turn, are actors that play a crucial role in the solicitation and elicitation of the attachment of people to markets. Describing markets in terms of attachment is a way to account for a generic feature of all market-oriented encounters: that they involve establishing and managing the relations between people and things. One of the more unusual features of consumer credit, like other forms of credit and indeed many other financial products, is that these market attachments become strung out over time. It is a product that depends on its ability to maintain the attachment of a debtor to a debt in diverse circumstances, in moments of both financial well-being and difficulty.

Following consumer credit, as it moves from a borrowing product to an apparently unavoidable financial obligation therefore allows an insight into the ways in which market attachments operate in a range of circumstances. One of the things that has become clear is that a feature of processes of market attachment is their ability to become tightly wound round people's dependence on, and relationship to, other attachments that operate across a diverse set of registers. When it comes to the life of default, many of these concern attachments that are highly personal, whether those that pertain to the body or to domestic life and its routines, sometimes lived alongside others.

It is partly this intimacy of attachment, in which boundaries between market and non-market blur and fragment, that makes tracing the circulation, intensification, and management of affect so crucial. There is, as I have sought to argue, real benefit to be had from bringing the intellectual architecture of affect theory to that work within or clustering around the economisation approach to economic sociology. Above all, it allows a closer focus on a domain of materiality that is curiously absent from many descriptions of market involvement within economic sociology: that of the bodies of market participants themselves and their embodied responses, drives and desires.

When it comes to following the work of debt collection the need to attend to this particular material domain becomes all the more self-evident. As we have seen, this is an industry that has long recognised that both its business and the unique forms of expertise it has accumulated are deeply concerned with what I would call affect. Collections organisations know full well that to get those unwilling or unable to repay to engage with them means establishing connections with people that operate in the crossing points of emotion and calculation. Over the course of its history, different resources have been brought to this task, including intuition, experience, the language of psychology and a variety of experimental methodologies. Throughout, it is clear that what is being attempted is to capture and profit from an aspect of human experience that concerns what is 'felt', often seemingly internally, despite these feelings coming to be so clearly wrapped up in a variety of social and economic processes.

This suggests a need at the very least to attend more symmetrically to the role played in economic settings by both 'devices' and 'dispositions', as called for by Franck Cochoy (2007). There is, as he suggests, much to be gained from examining in a more even-handed way both the formatting of market technique and how market devices orient themselves towards, stimulate and shape the embodied habits, moods, and reactions of those that they intersect with. Take the contemporary role of experimental and probabilistic testing within the collections process as an example: here it is minute, differentially embodied, dispositional tendencies that come to be targeted by the collections industry. This testing is put to work to identify those who are (marginally) more ready to be the target of a particular modality of market attachment than others. Or, as another, the strategic use within the collections industry of dispositional variations in its own staff: an embodied tendency to relate to others more one way rather than another becomes an object of managerial attention, with the aim being to maximise the chances that a particular telephone conversation will result in a debtor beginning to repay what he or she owes.

These examples also point to a proposition that I have sought to work through: that in tracing the role of affect in social and economic life, we need to be attentive to the ways in which the affective can become simultaneously involved with questions of emotion and (human) feeling and the generation of calculative attention. Given both debtors' constrained financial means and the competition within the collections industry, the collection organisation's task is to focus calculative attention on it, not a competitor. Generating an ongoing state of future oriented anxious anticipation is part of this. But by 'captating' or 'capturing' these emergent, affective affordances – 'lures for feeling', in Whitehead's terms – a collector hopes to achieve a debtor's calculative focus. Panic, fear, and relief are thus not simply by-products of collections practices, but registers through which to train a debtor's calculative attention on a particular debt.

This also brings to the fore what exactly is at stake in the (re)making of markets. It goes without saying that markets are being constantly remade. What is less obvious is that through the circulation of its devices and practices of attempted capture, the worlds of market participants are also being remade. Often this goes unnoticed: for instance, when a credit card inserts itself into the transaction between a buyer and a seller the difference, as compared to using cash, seems marginal. A different device, a different set of bodily movements, certainly. But the immediate result is the same: the transfer of an economic good from one party to another. Of course, it is where exactly one draws the boundary around the beginnings and ends of this encounter that matters. The use of consumer credit involves a commitment to living alongside and with a quite particular financial product. At the very least this requires dealing with the bureaucracy of repayment and mobilising the appropriate money management skills. But in the case of default, it can mean having the very routines and rhythms of life disrupted by the incursions of the collector and having to deal with and assess the range of threats and entreaties to which a debtor becomes subject. The shifts in the worlds of borrowers can thus range from the irritating and procedural to the almost overwhelming.

Attending to affect is thus not simply about attending more to just the embodied dimensions of life. It also demands considering life as emergent and constantly interrelated. This is the work done by thinking through 'feeling' as a quality not limited to the human. Things, people, entities of all kinds, are constantly feeling for one another, sometimes establishing closer connections, sometimes moving further apart. It is this that energises practices of capture and captation. Tracing emergence is not straightforward, however: these are processes that operate on the very limits of the empirical. It thus perhaps requires what Brian Massumi (2002, pp. 208–256) refers to as an 'expanded-empiricism'. This is an empiricism that is open to paying attention to the way things become – this rather than that, in this way rather than that way – rather than taking things as they apparently are. In this respect it shares much with the range of actor-network theory (ANT) inspired approaches that this book has drawn on. ANT has made its business to pay close empirical attention to the ways in which things come to formatted and enacted in the ways they are. But following practices and processes oriented around the affective requires an empiricism that is willing to look more explicitly to philosophy for resources. As Massumi writes, '[p]hilosophy is the activity dedicated to keeping wonder in the world' (p. 239), it is

> the movement of thought to the virtual fringe of things. It is the labor of making relation 'more' sensible, of making the 'more' of relation sensible, in a movement occurring purely in thought, logically prior to the point at which relation has actual terms.
>
> (pp. 241–242)

To put it a little more prosaically, philosophy, for the empiricist, becomes a device for sensitising attention – for becoming more open to the borderlines of existence, to the things, the processes, the forms of relation, and the forms of novelty ('the "more" of relation') that come to be gathered up in entities in their processes of becoming (whether something else, or something very similar). In this book, this is the work that has been done by affect and an attention to how it becomes subject to strategic acts of attempted capture, as well as, more specifically, by both Whitehead's lure, and Deleuze's fold. These are philosophical provocations that do not simply aim to describe better, but to prompt a reconsideration of fundamental assumptions about the 'problem' that is being addressed, both by the analyst and by those people and things within a particular empirical setting.

The distributed politics of consumer credit default

Bringing affect to markets also demands an attention to the politics of the relation and the in-between. This means, on the one hand, seeing the in-betweenness of life, its fringes, as spaces within which new and alternate modes of our coexistence with both people and things might be emerging. On the other, it also means recognising that it is in these very in-betweens that some of the most significant challenges to the recomposition of coexistence might lie.

When tracing this in-between, relational politics with respect to consumer credit default, we are immediately faced by the challenge of its particularly broad dispersal. This is a politics that is distributed across people, their bodies, the technologies they encounter, across the different spaces and times they inhabit, and across the specific sets of organisational and capitalist relations within and through which they operate.

Of this diverse assemblage, it is the last of these forces that is usually given prominence by those seeking to understand the political consequences of socioeconomic arrangements, including those that cluster around credit. This is quite understandable. Capitalism, and, more specifically, the destructive yet enduring neoliberal project(s) through which it is increasingly actualised (see Mirowski 2013), are forces that drive the debt economy and, within it, many of the dynamics of consumer credit lending and default. This includes the motivations of lenders and collectors as well as having much to do with the patterns of disadvantage that it both exploits and exacerbates. There is much more that can and should be told about how consumer credit default fits into this picture including, for instance, into the flows of global finance and the large scale patterning of social and economic inequality.

This book has, however, quite deliberately adopted a different starting point. Its interest has been in tracing the *quality* of relations within markets and between market actors. This means attending to the precise way in which things become connected and interrelated. It matters greatly how, exactly, the movement between market entities occurs and what the transformations are that they undergo within markets. This focus prevents categories including both capitalism and neoliberalism – inevitably abstractions within which are gathered a myriad of situated, diverse practices and process (see Gibson-Graham

2006) – obscuring and drawing attention away from what Berlant refers to as the 'messy dynamics of attachment, self-continuity, and the reproduction of life that are the material scenes of living on in the present' (2011, p. 15). It also opens up the manner in which relations we might identify as broadly capitalist come into being (see Halewood 2011, p. 149). In tracing the various processes of attachment that surround the work of both consumer lending and collection we come to see more clearly why a particular sometimes pernicious economic domain is formatted the way it is and how it continues to successfully reproduce itself. At the same time, it demands remaining open to how it bleeds into, depends on, and is sometimes resisted by, its encounter with other modes of living with one another. Capitalism, in these moments of encounter, exposes its 'rough edges', as Anna Tsing calls them, edges to which political and intellectual work can become attached (2013, p. 39).

One such edge is the encounter between the collector and the debtor as an embodied subject. On the one hand, what this encounter highlights is the degree to which market forces can intrude into aspects of experience that we tend to understand as personal and intimate. In the life of default, debt can come to form the variably actualised companion to potentially any act or form of social engagement. It sometimes exists as an unnoticed but not quite absent background to daily life, but at other moments, when it unfolds into consciousness or into an interaction with another person, it can begin to recompose a particular scene, in part according to its own dynamics. One moment of intensification is of course the intrusion of the collections device – this, after all, is a technology specifically designed to focus most if not all of a debtor's attention on their debt. But there are plenty of others – an unexpected question from another, for instance, or the threat of one's debt becoming a topic of an unexpectedly public conversation. On the other hand, it highlights the variable grip that markets can have on defaulting debtors. To be in default tends to require an acceptance of technologies of market attachment into the routines and habits of life, whether or not this is desired. However for some, this constant co-presence is particularly challenging. Take Jane, for instance, with whom we stayed with a while in the second chapter. She seemed painfully ill-equipped to deal with debt default. It is not simply that she lacks the calculative apparatus to respond to the prompts of the collector but because, in part as a result of her ME, in part as a result of her grief, she often found herself without the bodily authority to do so. The attachments between her and her debt become ingrained and 'sticky', as an issue that is articulated as a private, personal concern becomes intractably wrapped up with concerns that are, to her, equally private. The very ability for a defaulting debtor to operate successfully within this market domain and to be able to achieve any degree of detachment is therefore subject to a particularly embodied ontological politics.

The precise manner in which markets achieve this variable but often firm grip on people only comes into sharp focus, however, when we connect the domestic and embodied domain of default to the organisational processes around which the strategy of collections work is assembled. For, as much as individual calculative and bodily authority can make a difference in the life of default, the politics of default cannot be reduced to a matter of individual agency. This is in part because of the very distribution of calculative possibility across both people and devices. Calculative acts are not just a matter of cognitive or indeed bodily/emotional practice, they are also quite clearly socially and materially distributed. This should by now be a quite familiar claim. The point here, however, is that this is not just a matter of social (and economic) theory: it is something that organisations are well aware of. Their experiments, comparing the effects of sending out credit cards versus application forms, for instance, or formatting a collections letter this way rather than that way, render this quite transparent. The problem faced by individual borrowers, individual defaulters, is that their calculative acts, even if assisted by third parties (the debt advice industry, for instance, to which I will return further on), come head to head with organisations whose very ambition is to amplify calculative opacity, to shift calculation away from detached assessments of raw economic best interest, and towards responses that happen in and through intensive irruptions of affect.

Even here, however, we may want to hesitate before conclusively relocating the politics of default from the individual to the encounter between individual and organisation. This is the territory of regulation. While regulation and forms of consumer protection can do much to ameliorate some of these asymmetries of calculative possibility – the effective banning of trading styles in the UK as documented in the previous chapter would be a good example – there is much that escapes the regulatory gaze. This is in part because the collections industry, as with many other industries, operates in the borderlands of regulatory scrutiny. This means, for instance, developing practices that while not overtly misleading, are suggestive enough to be effective – the carefully worded implication of impending legal action or a visit from a bailiff, for instance. It also means, in a UK context, working particularly hard to solicit forms of engagement from the debtor without being able to mobilise an affordable and sympathetic legal system. But it is also because of the very inability of regulators to attend to the relational composition of markets. For many debtors the issue of consumer credit default is not necessarily located in the malpractice of one company but in the space of interaction between multiple companies. To be in default is usually to owe debts to many creditors simultaneously and, as a result, to be subject to many distinct attempts at collecting these debts. Regulatory scrutiny is, however, resolutely focused on the individual company. This 'organisational individualism', as we might call it, is at the very heart of market-oriented regulatory practice. Its aim is to ensure that market conduct falls as closely as possible into line with principles largely directed towards single organisations. Any interaction effects that might emerge from a user having to deal with multiple companies simultaneously are overflows that remain largely beyond its purview. In the case of consumer credit default, this raises the possibility that a user might deal with multiple, wholly regulatorily compliant companies, none of which could be found to be harassing or imposing undue pressure on an individual, but whose combined intrusions and solicitations might render daily life nearly unliveable. This is then truly a politics of the interstices.

Rough edges can also be detected in the organisational and everyday life of default: those moments when market logics either become exposed or distorted. An instance of the former concerns the very recognition by collectors of the partialities of market ties. The threat to 'pass out' a debt to an external agency makes strategic use of the widespread recognition that while markets may be good at transferring legal obligations, they are often poor at transferring moral obligations. In the attempt to turn this into a market opportunity, the weakness of markets is nonetheless laid bare. So too is the way in which the public politics of debt collection is distributed between the different organisational entities of the consumer credit industry: it suits lenders that there is a collections industry that is perceived as distinct, even if they are themselves routinely engaged in the more forceful work of debt collection. The binary that is established between lender and collector allows creditors to remain isolated from the difficult questions that arise from the inevitably opaque and seemingly more murky work of getting defaulting debtors to repay what is owed. As analysts and critics we should be wary of buying too quickly into such oppositions.

We should also not assume that markets always involve the invocation of particular models of subjectivity. It has been pointed out, often by drawing on Foucault's work on procedures of contemporary governmentality, that living a life in debt requires encountering an array of devices, practices, and discourses, clustering around a set of neoliberal ideals, that call on people to perform themselves as entrepreneurial, individually responsible, economic subjects (Langley 2008b; Marron 2009). This analysis can be seen to apply to many of the aspect of living the life of default. Responsibility for repayment is routinely individualised, while many of the appeals mobilised by debt collectors orient themselves quite explicitly towards a therapeutic mode of engagement. In these instances the debtor is seen as retaining the possibility for self-governance, even if this is a capacity that is seen as latent. However, this mode of engagement, this mode of attempted attachment, is by no means uniform. One alternate but highly consistent, sometimes indeed dominant, modality of attachments it that which mobilises appeals that operate through attempts to enact the debtor as an embodied subject of discipline, constituted by the legally binding obligations she or he is tied to. Here, the mode shifts towards the collector didactically seeking to impose its worldview over the debtor.

Foucault scholars may object – Foucault was quite explicit that the rise of a society dominated by techniques of governmentality did not mean the replacement of a society of discipline, or indeed a society of sovereignty, but rather their coexistence (Foucault 1991, p. 102; see also Foucault 2007, pp. 107–108). However, not only in the analysis of consumer credit but also in the far broader range of post-Foucauldian governmentality literature, this is a nuance to Foucault's argument that is not always brought to the fore. Actually, though, I would suggest that this is not a question of replacing a singular model of subjectivity with two, or even three, but being open to the messy coexistence of the multiple and not necessarily wholly compatible ways in which social and economic life becomes patterned. In our research practices we are always (co)participants in acts of 'cutting', 'reducing' and/or 'abstracting'.[2] The question thus becomes how to do so with care, while subjecting the specific contours of the phenomena being studied to the minimum of distortion as they are moved from a setting as situated and particular as lived experience to forms of research practice that are governed by a quite different set of procedures and expectations.

With respect to debt, and in a critical engagement with Lazzarato's work, Alberto Toscano (2014) argues that the search for a singular debt subjectivity has the effect of underestimating 'the opportunism of capital, its capacity to be relatively indifferent to our mentalities and desires'. Markets are resolutely, sometimes ruthlessly pragmatic (see McFall 2014), perhaps never more so when, as is the case in the deployment of econometric analysis, they start to act according to the logic of probability (see Lury 2004). Probabilistic logic ends up directing collections work towards those debtors who, through their actions and as detectable via a combination of variables, are shown to be more likely to respond positively to a particular set of prompts. The seemingly paradoxical effect is, to put it simply, that 'better' economic citizens are more likely to be targeted more intensively by the collector, with their more uncooperative counterparts being more likely to be ignored. As much as this is a loss for the debtor who believes that continuing to perform as a good, self-regulating economic subject will ultimately deliver some relief, it is a victory for recalcitrance (see Savransky 2014).

Coda: lines of flight?

There is one further potential rough edge to life in default that we should be attentive to: the possibility of an escape from capture, an escape from captation. Much of the focus of this book has been on the processes of attachment surrounding consumer credit default. We should not, however, neglect the possibility of detachment. From the perspective of most debtors, the only practical route to achieve this is by finding some way of uncoupling themselves from the debts that come to inhabit so much of their everyday life. However, is it possible that the life in default and the movements of attachment and detachment between debtor and collector might itself provide the conditions a more radical escape? Some novel entity that challenges the very terrain upon which processes of market attachment and detachment play out?

This is the question I will end with, in exploring emergent possibilities for what Deleuze might call 'lines of flight', while briefly highlighting the more conventional mechanisms for detachment available to the debtor. This includes some of the frustrations and new calculative opacities these may involve. I will then finish by examining whether it is possible to detect the emergence of novel social and material and relations that challenge the very assumptions upon which these mechanisms depend.

In the quest for market detachment, many debtors, including most of those that I met, turn to free, professional debt advice for support, often offered by not-for-profit or charitable organisations.[3] The general advice and resources such organisations offer can certainly help debtors to navigate some of the calculative complexities of default (see Orton 2010). Part of what third party debt advice brings is some form of commensurability to the imbalance of expert knowledge between debtor and collector. Many debtors I met drew a clear line between their experience of default pre- and post-debt advice. Part of what the advisor gives them is the ability to 'see through' the letters and phone calls they are receiving. Debt advice can expose the emptiness of many of the threats deployed by a collector, it can render far clearer the likelihood of a creditor taking immediate legal action, or not. Letters that might have been imagined as being tailored to an individual can come to be understood as an effect of a particular mass-mailing technology. Debtors can also learn to make certain demands of the collector in the course of their telephone conversations. This thus marks a curtailing of the potential for these collection technologies to generate the kind of anxious anticipation that they previously did.

Managing this process as an individual is a huge challenge, however. Given that most consumer credit debtors owe multiple creditors, this usually involves contacting each creditor separately and attempting to renegotiate a debt. What begins in these instances is, in effect, a negotiation over repayment. Each creditor will employ its own tactics in these negotiations including denying the very fact that renegotiation is a possibility. Even when this door is opened, knowing how far to push in the face of threats of impending legal action, even if assisted by resources from a third party, is extremely difficult for a debtor. Coupled with this are the significant bureaucratic challenges involved: writing multiple letters, ongoing justifications of income and expenditure: such activities involve very particular skills and capacities, which are by no means evenly distributed (see Chapter 2).

For many, this challenge will be excessively daunting. It is for this reason that in many countries in Europe and North America, a service industry has sprung up around the issue of credit default: the debt management industry (also referred to as the debt relief or credit counselling industry).[4] In the UK it includes both the not-for-profit organisations that also offer free advice to debtors and nakedly commercial entities. The specific service that such organisations offer is that they, rather than the debtor, will take on the responsibility for negotiating with the creditor as well as the bureaucratic labour of managing default and distributing monthly payments between the creditors.[5] Many of the debtors on such plans that I interviewed valued the particular ability of these plans to reduce the affective intensity of default – it was not that these organisations could make debt go away, but, by having the process of default managed by someone else, their involvement could substantially mitigate the degree to which debt inhabited their life.

The appeal of such services is therefore quite understandable. However, they are not open to all. Each provider will have a disposable income threshold, below which debtors will not qualify. This implies, in other words, a politics of entry. Further, for debtors that do quality, the fervent desire that they often have to rid themselves of the daily incursions of the debt collector can push them into making decisions that, in raw financial terms at least, make their position not better but worse. As a recent government review into the industry put it, 'debt management services are a "distress" purchase; consumers seeking debt management help tend to be over-indebted, vulnerable and desperate for help' (Business, Innovation and Skills Committee 2012, p. 4). The problem for debtors is that, in particular when they encounter commercial debt management companies,[6] they are encountering an industry that in the UK, as elsewhere, has been accused of malpractice.[7] This includes using misleading advertising, hosting websites designed to emulate not-for-profit providers, making inflated claims about the efficacy of their services, not complying with industry guidelines, and not making their fee structure transparent (ibid., pp. 28–29).[8]

The most long-standing route to market detachment is, of course, bankruptcy.[9] For those without significant assets for a creditor to reclaim, it offers a far more redemptive promise: to ultimately wipe the slate clean, to enable a debtor to begin their life anew, free from the attachments of debt. However, this too is a highly asymmetrically distributed promise. We saw in Chapter 2 how things like social routines and a lack of local infrastructure can become significant barriers for some debtors that might benefit from bankruptcy. Debtors applying for bankruptcy in the UK also have to find a £750 lump sum to pay associated fees before the process can commence. This amount is well out of the reach of many.[10] Further, as elsewhere,[11] bankruptcy in the UK is becoming less and not more readily available: currently, low-income debtors are exempt from around a quarter of the fees, but proposed government reforms mean that this provision may soon be removed.[12]

The result of these various and often major hurdles is to leave many defaulting debtors with little choice other than to continue to deal with creditors directly, perhaps with supplemental resources (e.g. standard letters, advice about how to respond in a given situation) provided by debt advisors, but with little hope that their situation will soon be stabilised, let alone resolved.

One of the major insights that theorists of affect have provided, however, is that nothing is ever fully captured. Something always escapes. Whether a singular moment of escape will coalesce into an entity that might problematise the world in any substantive way depends on whether the escaping entity encounters anything of 'relevance' to which to establish a connection.[13] For much of the history of consumer credit one of the many problems facing defaulting debtors was their isolation. Whether because of feelings of shame or because of the way debt is unevenly patterned amongst social groupings, the chance that one defaulting debtor might encounter another and be able to share their experiences was often low. The chance that two might become three, or four, or more, even lower. Writing on debt default in the early 1970s, in his underappreciated book *Making People Pay*, Paul Rock thus makes the following short observation: 'Debtors can be manipulated because they are kept apart and without significant support. In London at least [where his study was based], there does not appear to be a viable subculture of default' (1973: 8).

This situation has, however, changed. Many of the letters examined over the course of this study were drawn from an online discussion forum called the Consumer Action Group and, more specifically, its Debt Collection Industry Sub-forum. This is a space where debtors can visit and anonymously share their debt-oriented concerns and, more specifically, ask for advice about how to deal with particular collections prompts and which finds its counterpart in the US across a range of sites including the Credit Info Centre, ExpertLaw and myFICO discussion boards.[14] One rough indication of its success is the fact that, upon entering the name of pretty much any major UK debt collection agency into a search engine, followed by a term such as 'debt collection', the search will bring up a link to a Consumer Action Group forum post as one of its top five links. Another measure is to look at the sub-forum itself, which displays a total of around 34,000 separate threads dating from the present back to 2006, most of which are accompanied by multiple replies.[15]

These sites are places where defaulting debtors can be found to be engaged in the activity of 'talking back' (Lury 2004, p. 114).[16] A set of individualised attempts by defaulting debtors to detach themselves from their debts has, in part by virtue of the specific affordances made available by online platforms, succeeded in transforming a set of private concerns into a socio-materially mediated public issue (see Marres 2012). This marks the coming into being of something new: a distinct type of debtor public.

Moreover, the Consumer Action Group is a space where a nascent collective politics can, at crucial moments, be detected. As just one example to end with, take the following particularly forceful response, directed squarely at a collections industry, made by a user called OnMyWayOut.[17] This post encapsulates some of the implicit and explicit attacks made against the debt collection industry throughout the forum into one, manifesto-like statement:

> The reason most of us are here is because we have been harassed, lied to, intimidated, threatened, coerced and treated like dirt by companies who assume that because we aren't paying them it's because we won't pay. Our personal situations mean nothing to them, in fact our human rights mean nothing to them. If they had made a reasonable approach and taken circumstances into account they probably wouldn't have ended up with such a fight on their hands.
>
> Many people have found their way here because of their illegal, immoral and underhand tactics. Many people who were already in payment arrangements found this site when [Original Creditors] and DCAs [Debt Collection Agencies] started to demand increases in payments that the person could not meet. It is their own greedy fault that the worm has turned.
>
> [...] If and when they learn to treat people with debt problems as people, not rogues, delinquents or cash cows and they also learn to keep 100% within the laws of the land, not to pick and choose which bits they want to comply with, then they might get a better response from us.[18]

Not only does the post invoke a collective, it also captures many of the justifications frequently made elsewhere on the forum for an adversarial tone and for the site's very existence – although this attitude is not shared by all. Put simply, debt collectors do not deserve to be repaid because of the way they treat debtors and – contentiously – because of allegedly illegal practices. In particular, it reframes what debt collectors are and the obligations that are entailed in a relationship to a creditor.[19] This is an attempt to think outside of the binary of market attachment and detachment.

What the existence of these sites indicates is the emergence of a new social form that has grown out of the interstices of the issue of consumer credit default, one that is becoming engaged, at least in brief moments, in the (re)politicisation of the issue of consumer credit default. This is, then, a rough edge that does indeed, provide a line of flight. This is, however, less an escape from debt itself than from the previously isolated, individualised challenges of living life in default. There is work to be done to track how such instances of strident political articulation are complemented by more routine modes of engagement, given that the primary function of these sites remains the hosting of forms of collective, distributed calculation focused around specific prompts that they have received from collectors.[20] However in this very process, in the repeated encounter between defaulting debtors, we can observe the possibility of something emerging that is simultaneously different to and connected with what was there before.

As I hope this book does, these forums thus open up the politics of default through an encounter with its very devices. Focusing on the way devices pass through and become bound up in the intimacies of our lives reveals the highly mundane but utterly powerful processes through which creditors and collectors work to attach debtors to their debts. As I have shown, in their pursuit of this aim, often what matters is the manner in which they attempt to secure the capture of affect. So too can the manner of escape.

Notes

1 Alberto Toscano (2014), for instance, suggests that attention should not be on debt, but the asymmetries associated with exchange. Given that this book has not sought to develop a general theory of the economy, I prefer to leave this question open.

2 These terms each describe in many ways similar operations. See, on the ethics of the cut, Barad (2007, pp. 175–179) and Bell (2012, pp. 114–118), on reduction Bryant (2011), and on abstraction Halewood (2011, pp. 147–149). See also Deville *et al.* (forthcoming).

3 In the UK, this includes the Citizens Advice Bureau, National Debtline (run by the Money Advice Trust), Payplan and StepChange. For an overview of the role of debt advice in Europe see Eurofund (2012). In the US the largest industry body representing these organisations is the Association of Independent Consumer Credit Counseling Agencies.

4 Outside the UK, commercial debt management providers are found in countries including the US, Canada (Financial Consumer Agency of Canada 2013), Ireland (Debt Management Association of Ireland (undated), and Portugal (Eurofound 2012). In the US, formally not-for-profit firms may also sometimes operate, in effect, as commercial entities (see National Consumer Law Center 2004, 2006).

5 It should be noted that in managing to negotiate at least a partial repayment to each of the creditors, the debt counsellor also goes some way towards giving the creditors what they want: the promise of a borrower that will repay – even if repayment is only partial. Thus while these services have many undoubted benefits for the stressed out defaulting debtor, a creditor's decision to agree to a reduced settlement from the defaulter is a decision itself suffused with its own, precise calculative potency.

6 These are companies that charge a fee for their service, either upfront or spread over time. In the UK, the government is trying to encourage commercial debt management firms to sign up to a protocol which commits companies to not charging upfront fees (Hansard 2013).

7 While not-for-profit providers in the UK are more reputable than some of their more numerous US counterparts, their claim to offer a 'free' service has also been disputed. A director of a commercial debt management service asserted to me that some users of not-for-profit organisations can ultimately end up paying more than they would if using a service provided by a commercial rival. This claim is based on the differing ways in which not-for-profit debt management organisations derive their income as compared to commercial organisations. These receive a voluntary 'fair share' contribution from creditors for every account on which they negotiate a revised repayment schedule. The implicit (and contentious) suggestion is that not-for-profit organisations have a cosier relationship with creditors and will not push as hard to renegotiate a debt. A self-interested assertion, certainly, however, what is important here is that, even if this were true, it would be very hard for a debtor to ascertain this before signing up. Indeed, the very absence of these kinds of market decisions is one of the concerns of regulators, given that it seems very rare for debtors to 'shop around' different providers (Business, Innovation and Skills Committee 2012, p. 4).

8 In the UK the debt management industry has been the subject of a recent major review, which included inputs from a variety of consumer advocacy groups (Business, Innovation and Skills Committee 2012). Similar issues have been found in the US, as explored in particular by the National Consumer Law Center (2004, 2006). The Consumer Financial Protection Bureau (2014, p. 31) has also started to target companies accused of misleading customers and charging illegal fees.

9 In the UK, there is also the Debt Relief Order. This is designed to be an alternative to bankruptcy for those on low incomes. Currently it is for those with under £15,000 worth of debt and a disposable income of under £50 a month (Citizens Advice 2014). This has offered some debtors respite, although the £15,000 threshold was set in 2005 and has not increased since. The Citizens Advice service estimates, based on data from the first three quarters of 2011 to 2012 that this would have excluded almost 40 per cent of its clients (2012, p. 6).

10 The Consumer Credit Counselling Service, now StepChange, identified this as 'probably the single biggest issue preventing our clients from proceeding to bankruptcy' (2012, p. 2).

11 In the US, for instance, recent reforms have significantly swung the pendulum in the creditors favour in preventing numerous debtors from filing for bankruptcy. This is likely the outcome a combination of factors including increased costs, forced credit counselling, increased paperwork, and a range of other new procedural burdens (Lawless *et al.* 2008, pp. 380–381; Roberts 2014a, p. 10; 2014b, pp. 240–242).

12 The UK government is currently in the process of undertaking bankruptcy reform. It has proposed to remove the exemption that low-income debtors currently have from the court application fee, currently £175 (StepChange 2014d).

13 See p. 43, footnote 25, on questions of relevance.

14 The analysis that follows draws in part on a forthcoming article, in which the role of these online forums is explored in greater depth (Deville forthcoming).

15 Figures correct as of 30 June 2014; rounded to the nearest 10,000.

16 Indeed, the Consumer Action Group has itself become an object of controversy within the UK debt collections industry. This worry has also been revealed in public, in the form of an internal PowerPoint presentation that was leaked to the *Guardian* newspaper (Jones 2009). Industry figures also complained about the site in my interviews, with some calling for government regulation of the site or even going as far as to call for its outright ban.

17 In this instance, this is a response to a suggestion that the debt collections industry might be monitoring the forum (whether or not this was true, as we have seen, the industry's discomfort with the forum is genuine).

18 Available at: www.consumeractiongroup.co.uk/forum/showthread.php?158466-So-they-don-t-like-these-forums-!!&p=1701570&viewfull=1#post1701570 [Accessed 23 October 2014].

19 This is then a questioning of the very foundations of the credit economy, edging towards a justification of the kinds of 'strategic default' analysed by Melinda Cooper (forthcoming).

20 This is a project I am currently working on, in collaboration with Johnna Montgomerie and Liam Stanley.

References

Adams, V., Murphy, M. and Clarke, A.E., 2009. Anticipation: Technoscience, life, affect, temporality. *Subjectivity*, 28(1), pp. 246–265.

Ahmed, S., 1998. *Differences that Matter: Feminist Theory and Postmodernism*, Cambridge and New York: Cambridge University Press.

Ahmed, S., 2004. *The Cultural Politics of Emotion*, New York: Routledge.

Ahmed, S., 2010. Happy objects. In M. Gregg and G.J. Seigworth, eds., *The Affect Theory Reader*. North Carolina: Duke University Press, pp. 29–51.

Allon, F., 2010. Speculating on everyday life: The cultural economy of the quotidian. *Journal of Communication Inquiry*, 34(4), pp. 366–381.

Allon, F. 2013. No escape: Culture and economics in the present. *Communication and Critical/Cultural Studies*, 10(2–3), pp. 216–221.

Allon, F. and Redden, G., 2012. The global financial crisis and the culture of financial growth. *Journal of Cultural Economy*, 5(4), pp. 375–390.

American Collectors Association, 1956a. How to classify debtors in an interview. *The Collector*, November, pp. 7, 16.

American Collectors Association, 1956b. How to follow up when first demands fail. *The Collector*, October, pp. 8–9.

American Collectors Association, 1956c. You can resell the debtor. *The Collector*, December, pp. 11, 15–16.

American Collectors Association, 1974. Introducing the American Collectors Association. *The Collector*, 40(8), pp. S1–S5.

American Collectors Association, 1989. *ACA's First Fifty Years: The American Collectors Association: 1939-1959*, Edina, MI: American Collectors Association.

American Collectors Association, 1995a. Collected wisdom: Negotiating with debtors. *The Collector*, November, pp. 54–55.

American Collectors Association, 1995b. Collected wisdom: Using the sales approach to improve collections. *Collector*, August, p. 53.

American Collectors Association, 1996. Collected wisdom: Basic debtor appeals. *The Collector*, August, pp. 50–51.

American Collectors Association, 1997. Collected wisdom: Making the collection call. *Collector*, April, pp. 52–53.

Amoore, L., 2011. Data derivatives: On the emergence of a security risk calculus for our times. *Theory, Culture & Society*, 28(6), pp. 24–43.

Anderson, B., 2012. Affect and biopower: Towards a politics of life. *Transactions of the Institute of British Geographers*, 37(1), pp. 28–43.

Anderson, B., 2014. *Encountering Affect: Capacities, Apparatuses, Conditions*, Farnham: Ashgate.

Anderson, B. and McFarlane, C., 2011. Assemblage and geography. *Area*, 43(2), pp. 124–127.

Anon, 1948. Bill-collecting field uses new psychology methods. *The Collector*, December, p. 19.

Anon, 1949. Martin to preside at N.Y. parley of credit managers. *The Post Standard*, p. 9.

Anon, 1951a. Tested letters that collect. *The Collector*, February, pp. 13–14.

Anon, 1951b. Tested letters: Final notices. *The Collector*, May, p. 17.

Anon, 1962. EDP Seminar, 1962: 35 collectors from 14 states learned the role of data processing and how it can make business more profitable. *The Collector*, December, pp. 9–15.

Anon, 1966. Are banks taking over? *The Collector*, March, pp. 4–5.

Anon, 1976. Body attachment and body execution: Forgotten but not gone. *William and Mary Law Review*, 17(3), p. 543-570

Anon, 2003. Credit cards. *Daily Mail*, 2 May, p. 1.

Anon, 2007. 10.2m pay credit card penalties. *Daily Mail* [Online], 25 July. Available at: http://search.proquest.com/news/docview/320259266/A193057375974C41PQ/76?accountid=11149 [accessed 12 April 2014].

Ariztia, T., 2013. Unpacking insight: How consumers are qualified by advertising agencies. *Journal of Consumer Culture* [Advance Online Publication]. Available at http://joc.sagepub.com/content/early/2013/06/19/1469540513493204.abstract [accessed 16 December 2014].

Arthur, C., 2012. *Financial Literacy Education: Neoliberalism, the Consumer and the Citizen*, Rotterdam: Sense Publishers.

Arvidsson, A., 2005. Brands: A critical perspective. *Journal of Consumer Culture*, 5(2), pp. 235–258.

Aspers, P., 2005. *Markets in Fashion: A Phenomenological Approach*, London: Routledge.

Atwood, M., 2008. *Payback: Debt and the Shadow Side of Wealth*, London: Bloomsbury.

Austin, M.M. and Vidal-Naquet, P., 1977. *Economic and Social History of Ancient Greece: An Introduction*, Berkeley: University of California Press.

Back, L., 2007. *The Art of Listening*, London: Berg.

Bailey, M., 2010. Is it time to update your collections systems? *Credit Collections & Risk*, July, pp. 43–44, 46.

Bailey, T.L., 1968. Statement of Thomas L. Bailey on behalf of the American Bankers Association. In United States Senate Committee on Banking and Currency, ed., *Bank Credit-Card and Check-Credit Plans: Hearings Before the Subcommittee on Financial Institutions of the Committee on Banking and Currency, United States Senate, Ninetieth Congress, Second Session, on Credit Cards. October 9 and 10, 1968*. Washington: U.S. Government Printing Office, pp. 20–30.

Bailey, W.H., 1959. Collecting-credit reporting: Is it wise to do both? *The Collector*, December, p. 8.

Banasiak, D., 2009. *Accurate Collections in a Tough Economy: Statistical Scoring* [Online Webinar]. Available at: www.predictivemetrics.com/validationForm.asp?Source=webinar&Doc=/webinars/ProfitableCollectionsinToughEconomicTimes.wvx accessed 10 April 2010].

Bank of England, 2010. *Trends in Lending: Consumer credit* [Online]. Available at: www.bankofengland.co.uk/publications/other/monetary/ConsumerCreditOctober2010.xls [accessed 10 April 2010].

Bank of England, 2013a. *Lending to UK Businesses and Individuals: July 2013* [Online]. Available at: www.bankofengland.co.uk/publications/Documents/other/monetary/lendingtoukbusinessesandindividualsjuly2013.xls [accessed 29 March 2014].

Bank of England, 2013b. *Table A.5.6 Consumer Credit Excluding Student Loans* [Online]. Available at: www.bankofengland.co.uk/statistics/Documents/bankstats/2013/Jan13/TabA5.6.xls [accessed 22 October 2013].

Barad, K., 2007. *Meeting the Universe Halfway: Quantum Physics and the Entanglement of Matter and Meaning*, Durham, NC: Duke University Press.

Bar-Gill, O., 2006. Bundling and consumer misperception. *The University of Chicago Law Review*, 73(1), pp. 33–61.

Barnes, E.H., 1955. The relationship of biased test responses to psychopathology. *The Journal of Abnormal and Social Psychology*, 51(2), pp. 286–290.

Barnes, E.H., 1956a. Factors, response bias, and the MMPI. *Journal of Consulting Psychology*, 20(6), pp. 419–421.

Barnes, E.H., 1956b. Response bias and the MMPI. *Journal of Consulting Psychology*, 20(5), pp. 371–374.

Barnes, E.H., 1959. Anxiety motivates the debtor. *The Collector*, 26(4), pp. 6, 14.

Barry, A., 2001. *Political Machines: Governing a Technological Society*, London: The Athlone Press.

Bartle, A., 2011. The importance of accurate information. *Credit Collections & Risk*, June, p. 32.

Bartle, N.D., 1962. Punch-card collections. *The Collector*, March, pp. 9–11.

Bass, J., 1983. Dunners and defaulters: Collectors' work as a context for naming. *Journal of Contemporary Ethnography*, 12(1), pp. 49–73.

Baudrillard, J., 1998. *Consumer Society: Myths and Structures*, London: Sage.

Beckert, J., 2009. The social order of markets. *Theory and Society*, 38(3), pp. 245–269.

Beckert, J. and Harshav, B., 2002. *Beyond the Market: The Social Foundations of Economic Efficiency*, Princeton, NJ: Princeton University Press.

Beer, D. and Burrows, R., 2013. Popular culture, digital archives and the new social life of data. *Theory, Culture & Society*, 30(4), pp. 47–71.

Bell, V., 2007. *Culture and Performance*, Oxford and New York: Berg.

Bell, V., 2012. Declining performativity Butler, Whitehead and ecologies of concern. *Theory, Culture & Society*, 29(2), pp. 107–123.

Bennett, J., 2001. *The Enchantment of Modern Life: Attachments, Crossings and Ethics*, Princeton, NJ: Princeton University Press.

Bennett, R.J., 2012. Supporting trust: Credit assessment and debt recovery through Trade Protection Societies in Britain and Ireland, 1776–1992. *Journal of Historical Geography*, 38, pp. 123–142.

Berkley, L., 2009. Getting the facts straight. *Credit Management*, May, p. 24.

Berlant, L., 2006. Cruel optimism. *differences: A Journal of Feminist Cultural Studies*, 17(3), pp. 20–36.

Berlant, L.G., 2011. *Cruel Optimism*, Durham, NC: Duke University Press.

Beunza, D. and Stark, D., 2004. Tools of the trade: The socio-technology of arbitrage in a Wall Street trading room. *Industrial and Corporate Change*, 13(2), pp. 369–400.

Birkwood, A., 2011. What should be on a debt seller's checklist. *Credit Collections & Risk*, August, pp. 41–42.

Black, H., 1961. *Buy Now, Pay Later*, New York: Morrow.

Black, J., Hashimzade, N. and Myles, G., 2009. *A Dictionary of Economics, 3rd Edition*, Oxford: Oxford University Press.

Blair, Oliver and Scott, Ltd, 2009. *Directors Report and Financial Statements: Year Ended 31 December 2008*, London: Companies House.

Borch, C., 2007. Crowds and economic life: bringing an old figure back in. *Economy and Society*, 36(4), pp. 549–573.

Bowlby, J., 1969. *Attachment*, London: Hogarth Press.

Bowlby, J., 1973. *Separation: Anxiety and Anger*, London: Hogarth Press.

Braddock, N. and Wordsworth, P., 2006. Consumer debt sale. *Recovery* [Online], Spring. Available at: www.r3.org.uk/uploads/documents/spring2006.pdf [accessed 25 February 2010].

Brante, T., 1993. Reasons for studying scientific and science-based controversies. In T. Brante, S. Fuller and W. Lynch, eds., *Controversial Science: From Content to Contention*. Albany, NY: State University of New York Press, pp. 177–191.

Bremner, M.R., 2010. The Fair Debt Collection Practices Act: The need for reform in the age of financial chaos, *The Brooklyn Law Review*, 76, pp. 1553–1597.

Brennan, T., 2004. *The Transmission of Affect*, Ithaca, NY: Cornell University Press.

Bricker, J. *et al.*, 2012. Changes in U.S. family finances from 2007 to 2010: Evidence from the survey of consumer finances. *Federal Reserve Bulletin*, 98(2), pp. 1–80.

Bryant, L.R., Srnicek, N. and Harman, G., 2011. *The Speculative Turn: Continental Materialism and Realism*, Melbourne: re.press.

Buckmann, M., 2011. What does TCF mean to you? *Credit Collections & Risk*, March, p. 38.

Burchill, G., Gordon, C. and Miller, P. eds., 1991. *The Foucault Effect: Studies in Governmentality*, London: Harvester Wheatsheaf.

Burton, D., 2008. *Credit and Consumer Society*, London: Routledge.

Business, Innovation and Skills Committee, 2012. *Debt Management: Fourteenth Report of Session 2010-2012* [Online]. Available at: www.publications.parliament.uk/pa/cm201012/cmselect/cmbis/1649/1649.pdf [accessed 14 April 2014].

Butler, J., 1997. *The Psychic Life of Power: Theories in Subjection*, Stanford, CA: Stanford University Press.

Butler, J., 1999. *Gender Trouble*, New York and London: Routledge.

Butler, J., 2003. Violence, mourning, politics. *Studies in Gender and Sexuality*, 4(1), pp. 9–37.

Butler, J., 2004. *Undoing Gender*, New York and London: Routledge.

Byler, D.H., 1951. Collecting by telephone. *The Collector*, April, pp. 9–10.

Cairns, R. and Hotopf, M., 2005. A systematic review describing the prognosis of chronic fatigue syndrome. *Occupational Medicine*, 55(1), pp. 20–31.

Calder, L., 1999. *Financing the American Dream: A Cultural History of Consumer Credit*, Princeton, NJ: Princeton University Press.

Çalışkan, K. and Callon, M., 2009. Economization, part 1: Shifting attention from the economy towards processes of economization. *Economy and Society*, 38(3), pp. 369–398.

Çalışkan, K. and Callon, M., 2010. Economization, part 2: A research programme for the study of markets. *Economy and Society*, 39(1), pp. 1–32.

Callon, M., 1986a. Some elements of a sociology of translation: Domestication of the scallops and the fishermen of St. Brieuc Bay. In J. Law, ed., *Power, Action, and Belief: A New Sociology of Knowledge?* London: Routledge & Kegan Paul, pp. 196–233.

Callon, M., 1986b. The sociology of an actor-network: The case of the electric vehicle. In M. Callon, J. Law and A. Rip, eds., *Mapping the Dynamics of Science and Technology: Sociology of Science in the Real World*. London: Macmillan Press, pp. 19–34.

Callon, M., 1998a. An essay on framing and overflowing: Economic externalities revisited by sociology. In M. Callon, ed., *The Laws of the Markets*. Oxford: Blackwell, pp. 244–269.

Callon, M., 1998b. Introduction: The embeddedness of economic markets in economics. In M. Callon, ed., *The Laws of the Markets*. Oxford: Blackwell, pp. 1–57.

Callon, M., 2005. Why virtualism paves the way to political impotence. *Economic Sociology European Electronic Newsletter*, 6(2), pp. 3–20.

Callon, M., 2007. What does it mean to say that economics is performative? In D. MacKenzie, F. Muniesa and L. Siu, eds., *Do Economists Make Markets: On the Performativity of Economics*. Princeton, NJ and Oxford: Oxford University Press, pp. 311–357.

Callon, M., 2009. Civilizing markets: Carbon trading between in vitro and in vivo experiments. *Accounting, Organizations and Society*, 34(3–4), pp. 535–548.

Callon, M. and Law, J., 2005. On qualculation, agency and otherness. *Environment and Planning D: Society and Space*, 23(5), pp. 717–733.

Callon, M., Méadel, C. and Rabeharisoa, V., 2002. The economy of qualities. *Economy and Society*, 31(2), pp. 194–217.

Callon, M. and Muniesa, F., 2005. Peripheral vision: Economic markets as calculative collective devices. *Organization Studies*, 26(8), pp. 1229–1250.

Campbell, N.E., 1966. What is happening in the collections business. *The Collector*, June, pp. 6–8.

Campbell, V.L., 1948. Public relations: An address. *The Collector*, January, pp. 29, 32–24.

Caplovitz, D., 1968. Consumer credit in the affluent society. *Law and Contemporary Problems*, 33, p. 641.

Caplovitz, D., 1974. *Consumers in Trouble: A Study of Debtors in Default*, London: The Free Press.

Carder, R.H., 1961. A pre-collection letter series .<th>.<th>. using anxiety and inevitability themes. *The Collector*, 27(9), pp. 6–7, 11.

Carlson, K., 2011. Protecting your resources. *Collector*, October, pp. 38–39.

Carruthers, B. and Ariovich, L., 2010. *Money and Credit: A Sociological Approach*, Cambridge: Polity.

Carruthers, B.G. and Halliday, T.C., 2000. Professionals in systemic reform of bankruptcy law: The 1978 U.S. Bankruptcy Code and the English Insolvency Act of 1986. *American Bankruptcy Law Journal*, 74, p. 35.

CCR-2, 2012. Future opportunities for debt purchasers? *Credit Collections & Risk*, March, pp. 30–31.

Coelho, S. 2012. *The Use and Selection of Proper Remedial Tools: Maximising Your Collections Stage*. Presented at the CCR-interactive 2012, Guoman Tower Hotel, London, 28 September.

De Certeau, M., 1998. *The Practice of Everyday Life*, Berkeley, CA: University of California Press.

Channel 4, 2009. Undercover debt collector. *Dispatches* [Television Documentary Series], 20 July.

Chapman, J., 2003. Borrow on a credit card? Not me!: How the millionaire boss of Barclays bank stunned MPs yesterday with an astonishing admission. *Daily Mail*, 17 October, p. 1.

Citizens Advice, 2014. *Debt Relief Orders* [Online]. Available at: www.adviceguide.org.uk/england/debt_e/debt_help_with_debt_e/debt_relief_orders.htm [accessed 14 April 2014].

Citizens Advice, 2012. *Reform of the Process to Apply for Bankruptcy and Compulsory Winding Up: Response by Citizens Advice to the Insolvency Service* [Online]. Available at http://www.citizensadvice.org.uk/insolvency_service_consultation_on_reform_of_the_process_to_apply_for_bankruptcy_email_version_to_send.pdf [accessed 16 December 2014].

Cleary, A., 2010. Avoiding the old habits. *Credit Collections & Risk*, October, p. 35.

Clough, P.T., Goldberg, G., Schiff, R., Weeks, A. and Willse, C., 2007. Notes towards a theory of affect-itself. *ephemera: theory in politics & organization*, 7(1), pp. 60–77.

Clough, P.T., 2009. The new empiricism: Affect and sociological method. *European Journal of Social Theory*, 12(1), pp. 43–61.

Cobham, D., 2002. *The Making of Monetary Policy in the UK, 1975–2000*, Chichester: John Wiley & Sons.

Cochoy, F., 2002. *Une Sociologie du Packaging, ou l'Âne de Buridan Face au Marché*, Paris: Presses Universitaires de France.

Cochoy, F., 2007. A brief theory on the 'captation' of publics: Understanding the market with Little Red Riding Hood. *Theory, Culture & Society*, 24(7–8), pp. 203–223.

Cochoy, F., 2008. Calculation, qualculation, calqulation: Shopping cart arithmetic, equipped cognition and the clustered consumer. *Marketing Theory*, 8(1), pp. 15–44.

Cochoy, F., 2009. Driving a shopping cart from STS to business, and the other way round: On the introduction of shopping carts in American grocery stores (1936–1959). *Organization*, 16(1), pp. 31–55.

Cochoy, F., 2011. *De la Curiosité, l'Art de la Séduction Marchande*, Paris: Armand Colin.

Cochoy, F., 2012. La sociologie economique relationniste. In F. Cochoy, ed., *Du Lien Marchand: Comment le Marché Fait Société: Essai(s) de Sociologie Économique Relationniste*. Toulouse: Presses Universitaires du Mirail, pp. 19–54.

Cochoy, F. and Grandclément, C., 2005. Publicizing Goldilocks' choice at the supermarket: The political work of shopping packs, carts, and talk. In B. Latour & P. Weibel, eds., *Making Things Public: Atmospheres of Democracy*. Cambridge, MA: MIT Press, pp. 646–659.

Coe, N., 2013. The importance of TCF. *Credit Collections & Risk*, May, pp. 28–29.

Coleman, R., 2009. *The Becoming of Bodies: Girls, Images, Experience*, Manchester: Manchester University Press.

Collins, H., 1981. *Knowledge and Controversy: Studies Of Modern Natural Science*, London: Sage.

Collins, H., 2007. *Rethinking Expertise*, Chicago: University of Chicago Press.

Collins, H. and Evans, R., 2002. The third wave of Science Studies: Studies of expertise and experience. *Social Studies of Science*, 32(2), pp. 235–296.

Colorado Department of Regulatory Agencies Office of Policy and Research, 1999. *Regulation of Collection Agencies in Colorado: Collection Agency Board 1999 Sunset Review* [Online]. Available at: http://cdn.colorado.gov/cs/Satellite?blobcol=urldata&blobheadername1=Content-Disposition&blobheadername2=Content-Type&blobheadervalue1=inline%3B+filename%3D%22Collection+Agencies%2C+Regulation+of+-+1999+Sunset+Review.pdf%22&blobheadervalue2=application%2Fpdf&blobkey=id&blobtable=MungoBlobs&blobwhere=1251815543524&ssbinary=true [accessed 23 February 2014].

Coney, J., 2006. Holiday credit card bombshell: Millions are hit by soaring charges as the banks bite back. *Daily Mail*, p. 1.

Connolly, W.E., 2002. *Neuropolitics: Thinking, Culture, Speed*, Minneapolis, MN: University of Minnesota Press.

Connolly, W.E., 2005. The evangelical-capitalist resonance machine. *Political Theory*, 33(6), pp. 869–886.

Consumer Credit Counselling Service, 2006. *CCCS Statistical Yearbook 2005* [Online]. Available at: www.cccs.co.uk/Portals/0/Documents/media/reports/statisticsyearbooks/ stats-yearbook-2005.pdf [accessed 10 April 2010].

Consumer Credit Counselling Service, 2007. *CCCS Statistical Yearbook 2006* [Online]. Available at: www.cccs.co.uk/Portals/0/Documents/media/reports/statisticsyearbooks/ stats-yearbook-2006.pdf [accessed 10 April 2010].

Consumer Credit Counselling Service, 2008. *CCCS Statistical Yearbook 2007* [Online]. Available at: www.cccs.co.uk/Portals/0/Documents/media/reports/statisticsyearbooks/ stats-yearbook-2007.pdf [accessed 10 April 2010].

Consumer Credit Counselling Service, 2009. *CCCS Statistical Yearbook 2008* [Online]. Available at: www.cccs.co.uk/Portals/0/Documents/media/reports/statisticsyearbooks/ stats-yearbook-2008.pdf [accessed 10 April 2010].

Consumer Credit Counselling Service, 2010. *CCCS Statistical Yearbook 2009: Appendices* [Online]. Available at: www.cccs.co.uk/Portals/0/Documents/media/reports/statisticsyearbooks/stats-yearbook-appendices-2009.pdf [accessed 10 April 2010].

Consumer Credit Counselling Service, 2012. *Response to the Insolvency Service Consultation on Reform of the Process to Apply for Bankruptcy and Compulsory Winding Up* [Online]. Available at: www.stepchange.org/Portals/0/Documents/media/reports/additionalreports/CCCS_response_IS_Reform_of_bankruptcy_and_winding_up.pdf [accessed 14 April 2014].

Consumer Financial Protection Bureau, 2013a. *Fair Debt Collection Practices Act: CFPB Annual Report 2013* [Online]. Available at: http://files.consumerfinance.gov/f/201303_ cfpb_March_FDCPA_Report1.pdf [accessed 30 October 2014].

Consumer Financial Protection Bureau, 2013b. *Protecting You* [Online]. Available at: www.consumerfinance.gov/protecting-you/ [accessed 12 October 2013].

Consumer Financial Protection Bureau, 2014. *Strategic Plan, Budget, and Performance Plan and Report* [Online]. Available at: http://files.consumerfinance.gov/f/strategic-plan-budget-and-performance-plan-and-report-FY2013-15.pdf [accessed 14 April 2014].

Cooper, M., forthcoming. The strategy of default: Liquid foundations in the house of finance. *Polygraph: An International Journal of Culture and Politics*.

Countryman, V., 1976. A History of American Bankruptcy Law. *Commercial Law Journal*, 81, pp. 226–232.

Court, M., 2011. Embracing the future of collections. *Credit Collections & Risk*, June, p. 36.

Credit Management Research Centre, 2008. *Credit and Debt Management Survey 2008* [Online]. Available at: www.cmrc.co.uk/wp-content/uploads/CreditandDebtSurvey2008.pdf [accessed 15 April 2014].

Credit Services Association, 2011. *CSA DBSG Annual Exhibition and Conference Programme: Building a Stronger Future* [Online]. Available at: www.csa-uk.com/media/ editor/file/CSA%20Conference%20Delegate%20Prog.pdf [accessed 27 November 2012].

Credit Services Association, 2012a. *Credit Services Association: Code of Practice* [Online]. Available at: www.csa-uk.com/media/editor/file/CSA%20Code%20of%20 Practice%281%29.pdf [accessed 27 November 2012].

Credit Services Association, 2012b. *CSA Revises Code in Advance of New Regulatory Regime* [Online]. Available at: www.csa-uk.com/csa-news/73/csa-revises-code-in-advance-of-new-regulatory-regime [accessed 27 November 2012].

Credit Services Association, 2012c. *Data Gathering Initiative: Q2 2012 Results Announced* [Online]. Available at: www.csa-uk.com/csa-news/72/data-gathering-initiative-q2-2012-results-announced [accessed 14 February 2014].

Credit Services Association and Office of Fair Trading, 2013. *Guidance Document: Use, Format and Content of Standard Debt Collection Letters* [Online]. Available at http://www.csa-uk.com/assets/documents/factsheets/format_and_content_of_standard_debt_collection_communication.pdf [accessed 16 December 2014].

Crowther, G., 1971. *Consumer Credit: Report of the Committee*, London: Her Majesty's Stationery Office.

Dányi, E., 2011. *Parliament Politics: A Material Semiotic Analysis of Liberal Democracy,* Unpublished PhD, Lancaster: Lancaster University.

Danziger, K., 1997. *Naming the Mind: How Psychology Found Its Language*, London; Thousand Oaks, CA: Sage.

Debt Management Association of Ireland, (undated). *Debt Management Explained* [Online]. Available at: www.dmai.ie/debt_management.html [accessed 14 April 2014].

Deleuze, G., 1988a. *Bergsonism*, New York: Zone Books.

Deleuze, G., 1988b. *Spinoza, Practical Philosophy*, San Francisco: City Lights Books.

Deleuze, G., 1999. *Foucault*, London: Continuum.

Deleuze, G., 2001. *The Fold: Leibniz and the Baroque*, London: Athlone Press.

Deleuze, G. and Guattari, F., 1987. *A Thousand Plateaus: Capitalism and Schizophrenia*, Minneapolis: University of Minnesota Press.

Deloitte, 2009. *Achieving Excellence in Default Management* [Online]. Available at: www.deloitte.com/assets/Dcom-UnitedStates/Local%20Assets/Documents/us_fsi_BS_Default%20management_sept08.pdf [accessed 10 October 2014].

Department for Business Information and Skills, 2006. *Amendments to Consumer Credit Act* [Online]. Available at: www.opsi.gov.uk/acts/acts2006/en/06en14-a.htm [accessed 10 April 2010].

Department for Business Innovation and Skills. 2011. *Consumer Credit and Personal Insolvency Review: Formal Response on Consumer Credit* [Online]. Available at: www.gov.uk/government/uploads/system/uploads/attachment_data/file/31841/11-1341-consumer-credit-and-insolvency-response-on-credit.pdf [accessed 10 October 2014].

Department of Trade and Industry, 2003. *Fair, Clear and Competitive: The Consumer Credit Market in the 21st Century* [Online]. Available at: http://webarchive.nationalarchives.gov.uk/20090609003228/www.berr.gov.uk/files/file23663.pdf [accessed 10 October 2014].

Deville, J., 2012. Regenerating market attachments: Consumer credit debt collection and the capture of affect. *Journal of Cultural Economy*, 5(4), pp. 423–439.

Deville, J., 2013a. Are we all sociologists now? *Credit Collections & Risk*, February, pp. 17–18.

Deville, J., 2013b. Paying with plastic: The enduring presence of the credit card. In J. Gabrys, G. Hawkins and M. Michael, eds., *Accumulation: The Material Politics of Plastic*. London: Routledge, pp. 87–104.

Deville, J., 2014. Consumer credit default and collections: The shifting ontologies of market attachment. *Consumption Markets & Culture*, 17(5), pp. 468-490.

Deville, J., forthcoming. Debtor publics: Tracking the participatory politics of consumer credit. *Consumption Markets & Culture*.

Deville, J., Guggenheim, M. and Hrdličková, Z., forthcoming. Introduction. In *Practising Comparison: Logics, Relations, Collaborations*. Manchester: Mattering Press.

Devlin, J.F. and Wright, M., 1995. The changing environment of financial services. In M. Wright, T. Watkins and C. Ennew, eds., *Marketing Financial Services*. London: Routledge, pp. 1–32.

DiMaggio, P., 1994. Culture and economy. In N. Smelser and R. Swedberg, eds., *The Handbook of Economic Sociology*. New York and Princeton, NJ: Russell Sage Foundation and Princeton University Press, pp. 22–57.

Dobbin, F., 1994. *Forging Industrial Policy: The United States, Britain and France in the Railway Age*, Princeton, NJ: Princeton University Press.

Dodd, N., 1994. *The Sociology of Money: Economics, Reason and Contemporary Society*, Cambridge: Polity Press.

Dolan, C.S., 2008. Arbitraging risk through moral values: The case of Kenyan fairtrade. In G. De Neeve, P. Luetchford, J. Pratt and D.C. Wood, eds., *Research in Economic Anthropology*. Bingley: JAI Press, pp. 271–296.

Dowling, E., 2012. The waitress: On affect, method and (re)presentation. *Cultural Studies ↔ Critical Methodologies*, 12(2), pp. 109–117.

Dowling, E., Nunes, R. and Trott, B., 2007. Immaterial and affective labour: Explored. *ephemera: theory in politics & organization*, 7(1), pp. 1–7.

Dressen, T., 2013. Spring forum. *Collector*, May, pp. 48–52.

Duffy, I.P.H., 1985. *Bankruptcy and Insolvency in London During the Industrial Revolution*, New York: Garland.

Duncan, A.J., 1995. From dismemberment to discharge: The origins of modern American bankruptcy law. *Commercial Law Journal*, 100, pp. 191–220.

Dunn, S., 2007. Credit card firms face new charges probe. *The Independent on Sunday*, p. 1.

Duschinsky, R., 2014. Interpreting a grimace of fear in the context of play: Between Bowlby and Deleuze. In *Unit of Play Seminar Series*, 11 February, London: Goldsmiths, University of London.

Elder, G., 1942. Desirable attributes of collectors' personnel. *The Collector*, March, p. 6.

Engelhardt, T.H. and Caplan, A.L., 1987. *Scientific Controversies: Case Studies in the Resolution and Closure of Disputes in Science and Technology*, Cambridge: Cambridge University Press.

Entwistle, J. and Slater, D., 2014. Reassembling the cultural. *Journal of Cultural Economy*, 7(2), pp. 161–177.

Eurofound, 2012. *Household Debt Advisory Services in the European Union* [Online]. Available at: www.eurofound.europa.eu/pubdocs/2011/89/en/1/EF1189EN.pdf [accessed 14 April 2014].

European Parliament & Council of the European Union, 2008. Directive 2008/48/ec of the European Parliament and of the Council of 23 April 2008 on credit agreements for consumers and repealing Council Directive 87/102/Eec. *Official Journal of the European Union*, L133, pp. 66–92.

Experian, 2009a. *Experian Collections Landscape Report: An Experian White Paper*, Nottingham: Experian.

Experian, 2009b. *Guidance on the Use of Experian Credit Bureau Data to Aid Collections Activity: A Briefing Paper from Experian* [Online]. Available at: http://www.experian.co.uk/assets/decision-analytics/briefing-papers-global/ExperianDA_BP_CreditBureauData.pdf [accessed 10 October 2014].

Experian, 2009c. The impact of the effective use of tone of voice in collection letters [Online]. *Credit Management in Australia*, July, pp. 22–24.

Experian, 2014. *Data Sharing and Credit Referencing* [Online]. Available at: www.experian.co.uk/responsibilities/compliance/data-share-cred-ref.html [accessed 23 March 2014].

Experian Data Analytics, 2009. *In Collections, It's Not What You Say, It's How You Say It. Boost Your Returns By Improving Relationships* [Twitter post]. Available at: http://twitter.com/Experian_DA/status/2739961491 [accessed 10 October 2014].

Experian Decision Analytics, 2008. *Identifying the Optimum Collections Strategy Through the Use of Champion Challenger Analytical Tools* [Online]. Available at: www.experian.ie/assets/decision-analytics/white-papers/experian_champion_challenger.pdf [accessed 27 November 2012].

Fagin, B., 1985. A successful technique for contacting debtors. *Collector*, January, p. 7.

Fearey, J.L., 1944. The evolution of the collections business. *The Collector*, January, p. 20.

Federal Reserve Bank of the United States, 2014. *Charge-Off and Delinquency Rates on Loans and Leases at Commercial Banks* [Online]. Available at: www.federalreserve.gov/releases/chargeoff/chgallnsa.htm [accessed 29 March 2014].

Federal Reserve Bank of the United States, 2006. *Consumer Compliance Handbook: Fair Debt Collection Practices Act* [Online]. Available at: www.federalreserve.gov/board-docs/supmanual/cch/fairdebt.pdf [accessed 26 March 2014].

Federal Reserve Bank of the United States, 2013a. *Consumer Credit. G.19. Consumer Credit Outstanding (Levels) (Millions of Dollars; Not Seasonally Adjusted). Nonrevolving* [Online]. Available at: www.federalreserve.gov/releases/g19/HIST/cc_hist_nr_levels.html [accessed 22 October 2013].

Federal Reserve Bank of the United States, 2013b. *Consumer Credit. G.19. Consumer Credit Outstanding (Levels) (Millions of Dollars; Not Seasonally Adjusted). Revolving* [Online]. Available at: www.federalreserve.gov/releases/g19/HIST/cc_hist_r_levels.html [accessed 22 October 2013].

Federal Trade Commission, undated. *Fair Debt Collection Practices Act. As amended by Public Law 104–208, 110 Stat. 3009 (30 September 1996)* [Online]. Available at: www.ftc.gov/enforcement/rules/rulemaking-regulatory-reform-proceedings/fair-debt-collection-practices-act-text [accessed 26 March 2014].

Federal Trade Commission, 2013. *The Structure and Practices of the Debt Buying Industry* [Online]. Available at http://www.ftc.gov/sites/default/files/documents/reports/structure-and-practices-debt-buying-industry/debtbuyingreport.pdf [accessed 16 December 2014].

Federation of European National Collection Associations, 2010. *Newsletter 60* [Online]. Available at: www.fenca.org/files/download/e0401c54e9210f8 [accessed 14 February 2014].

Feinberg, R.A., 1986. Credit cards as spending facilitating stimuli: a conditioning interpretation. *Journal of Consumer Research*, 13(3), pp. 348–356.

Financial Conduct Authority, 2014. *Wonga to Pay Redress for Unfair Debt Collection Practices* [Online]. Available at: www.fca.org.uk/news/wonga-redress-unfair-debt-collection-practices [accessed 2 July 2014].

Financial Consumer Agency of Canada, 2013. *Debt Reduction Companies: Beware of 'Too Good to Be True' Offers* [Online]. Available at: www.fcac-acfc.gc.ca/eng/about/news/pages/ConsAlert-ConsAvis-0.aspx?itemid=170 [accessed 14 April 2014].

Financial Services Authority, 2007. *Treating Customers Fairly – Guide to Management Information* [Online]. Available at: http://www.fca.org.uk/your-fca/documents/fca--treating-customers-fairly--guide-to-management-information [accessed 10 October 2014].

Finley, M.I., 1964. Between slavery and freedom. *Comparative Studies in Society and History*, 6(3), pp. 233–249.

Finn, M.C., 2003. *The Character of Credit: Personal Debt in English Culture, 1740–1914*, Cambridge and New York: Cambridge University Press.

Fitch, C., Hamilton S., Bassett, P. and Davey, R. 2011. The relationship between personal debt and mental health: A systematic review. *Mental Health Review Journal*, 16(4), pp. 153–166.

Fleming, B., 2010. Which method is best for you? *Credit Collections & Risk*, September, pp. 21–22.

Fligstein, N., 2001. *The Architecture of Markets: An Economic Sociology of Twenty-First-Century Capitalist Societies*, Princeton, NJ: Princeton University Press.

Ford, J., 1988. *The Indebted Society: Credit and Default in the 1980s*, London: Routledge.

Foucault, M., 1975. *Discipline and Punish: The Birth of the Prison*, Harmondsworth: Penguin.

Foucault, M., 1991. Governmentality. In G. Burchill, C. Gordon, and P. Miller, eds., *The Foucault Effect: Studies in Governmentality*. London: Harvester Wheatsheaf, pp. 87–104.

Foucault, M., 2007. *Security, Territory, Population: Lectures at the Collège De France, 1977–78*, Basingstoke: Palgrave Macmillan.

Foucault, M., 2008. *The Birth of Biopolitics: Lectures at the College de France, 1978–1979*, Basingstoke: Palgrave Macmillan.

Fourcade, M. and Healy, K., 2007. Moral views of market society. *Annual Review of Sociology*, 33, pp. 285–311.

Fox, J.L., 2012. Do we have a debt collection crisis? Some cautionary tales of debt collection in Indiana. *Loyola Consumer Law Review*, 24(3), pp. 355–388.

Frank, B., 2010. *Dodd–Frank Wall Street Reform and Consumer Protection Act*. H.R. 4173. United States House of Representatives, Washington DC [Online]. Available at: www.sec.gov/about/laws/wallstreetreform-cpa.pdf [accessed 24 October 2014].

Fredriksen, A. and Sullivan, S., 2014. Agencement/assemblage. In A. Fredriksen, S. Bracking, E. Greco, J.J. Igoe, R. Morgan and S. Sullivan, eds., A Conceptual Map for the Study of Value: An Initial Mapping of Concepts for the Project 'Human, Non-Human and Environmental Value Systems: An Impossible Frontier?', *LCSV Working Paper Series* [Online]. Manchester: Leverhulme Centre for the Study of Value, pp. 10–13. Available at: http://thestudyofvalue.org/wp-content/uploads/2013/11/WP2-A-conceptual-map.pdf [accessed 30 March 2014].

Freeman, G.E. and Salvin, F.H., 1859. *Falconry: Its Claims, History, and Practice*, London: Longman, Green, Longman, and Roberts.

Furness, B., 1968. Statement of Miss Betty Furness, Special Assistant to the President for Consumer Affairs, accompanied by Leslie V. Dix, Director for Legislative Affairs. In United States Senate Committee on Banking and Currency, ed., *Bank Credit-Card and Check-Credit Plans: Hearings Before the Subcommittee on Financial Institutions of the Committee on Banking and Currency, United States Senate, Ninetieth Congress, Second Session, on Credit Cards. October 9 and 10, 1968*. Washington: U.S. Government Printing Office, pp. 63–71.

Galis, V., 2011. Enacting disability: How can science and technology studies inform disability studies? *Disability & Society*, 26(7), pp. 825–838.

Gardiner, M.E., 2000. *Critiques of Everyday Life*, London: Routledge.

Du Gay, P., 2004. Self-service: Retail, shopping and personhood. *Consumption Markets & Culture*, 7(2), pp. 149–163.

Gibbons, D., 2013. *Does Increased Credit Data Sharing Really Benefit Low Income*

Consumers? [Online]. Available at: www.responsible-credit.org.uk/uimages/File/Does%20Increased%20Credit%20Data%20Sharing%20Benefit%20Low%20Income%20Consumers%20final.pdf [accessed 3 May 2013].

Gibbs, A., 2010. After affect. In M. Gregg and G.J. Seigworth, eds., *The Affect Theory Reader*. North Carolina: Duke University Press, pp. 196–205.

Gibbs, A.L., 1942. The use of the telephone in effecting collections. *The Collector*, March, pp. 9, 16.

Gibson, F.P. and Fichman, M., 2006. When threats and encouragements are effective in bargaining: The case of credit collectors. *Cognition & Emotion*, 20(8), pp. 1108–1131.

Gibson, J.J., 1977. The theory of affordances. In R. Shaw and J. Bransford, eds., *Perceiving, Acting, and Knowing. Toward an Ecological Psychology*. Hillsdale, NJ: Lawrence Erlbaum Associates, pp. 67–82.

Gibson-Graham, J.K., 2006. *'The' End of Capitalism (as We Knew It): A Feminist Critique of Political Economy*, Minneapolis: University of Minnesota Press.

Gilbert, E., 2005. Common cents: Situating money in time and place. *Economy and Society*, 34(3), pp. 357–388.

Gilligan, C., 1982. *In a Different Voice: Psychological Theory and Women's Development*, Cambridge, MA: Harvard University Press.

Goffman, E., 1959. *The Presentation of Self in Everyday Life*, Garden City, NY: Doubleday.

Gomart, E. and Hennion, A., 1999. A sociology of attachment: Music amateurs, drug users. In J. Law and J. Hassard, eds., *Actor Network Theory and After*. Oxford: Sociological Review and Blackwell, pp. 220–247.

Goodyear, G., 1986. Motivating responses may help overcome debtors' objections. *Collector*, December, p. 12.

Graeber, D., 2011. *Debt: The First 5,000 years*, Brooklyn, NY: Melville House.

Grossberg, L., 2010. Affects future: Rediscovering the virtual in the actual. In M. Gregg and G.J. Seigworth, eds., *The Affect Theory Reader*. North Carolina: Duke University Press, pp. 309–338.

Guggenheim, M., 2012. Laboratizing and de-laboratizing the world changing sociological concepts for places of knowledge production. *History of the Human Sciences*, 25(1), pp. 99–118.

Guseva, A., 2008. *Into the Red: The Birth of the Credit Card Market in Postcommunist Russia*, Stanford, CA: Stanford University Press.

H.L. Steiner Organization, 1966. A tribute. *The Collector*, July, p. 1.

Halewood, M., 2011. *A.N. Whitehead and Social Theory: Tracing a Culture of Thought*, London: Anthem Press.

Hamilton, L., 2010. Credit (information) where it is due. *Credit Collections & Risk*, September, pp. 37–38.

Han, C., 2012. *Life in Debt: Times of Care and Violence in Neoliberal Chile*, Berkeley, CA: University of California Press.

Hansard, 2013. *House of Commons Hansard Ministerial Statements for 05 Nov 2013* [Online]. Available at: www.publications.parliament.uk/pa/cm201314/cmhansrd/cm131105/wmstext/131105m0001.htm [accessed 14 April 2014].

Haraway, D., 1997. *Modest_Witness@Second_Millennium. FemaleMan©_Meets_ OncoMouse: Feminism and Technoscience*, New York and London: Routledge.

Harbers, H., Mol, A. and Stollmeyer, A., 2002. Food matters: arguments for an ethnography of daily care. *Theory, Culture & Society*, 19(5–6), pp. 207–226.

Hari, J., 2009. Cruel and out of control: The new face of debt collecting. *Independent*, 14 August, p. 26.

Hart, K., 2000. *The Memory Bank: Money in an Unequal World*, London: Profile Books.

Hartmann, J., 2003. Examining healthcare. *Collector*, November, pp. 24–26.

Hatch, P.D., 1950. *Don't Shoot the Bill Collector*, New York: Thomas Y. Crowell Company.

Held, V., 1993. *Feminist Morality: Transforming Culture, Society, and Politics*, Chicago: University of Chicago Press.

Held, V., 2006. *The Ethics of Care: Personal, Political, and Global*, Oxford and New York: Oxford University Press.

Hennion, A., 2007. Those things that hold us together: Taste and sociology. *Cultural Sociology*, 1(1), pp. 97–114.

Hennion, A., 2013. D'une sociologie de la médiation à une pragmatique des attachements. *SociologieS* [Online]. Available at: http://sociologies.revues.org/4353 [accessed 10 July 2013].

Henry S. Fulks, Publisher, 1945. The inseparable trio. *The Collector*, March, p. 18.

Hill, R.P., 1994. Bill collectors and consumers: A troublesome exchange relationship. *Journal of Public Policy & Marketing*, 13(1), pp. 20–35.

Hochschild, A.R., 1983. *The Managed Heart: Commercialization of Human Feeling*, Berkeley: University of California Press.

Holland, P., 2011. The one hundred billion dollar problem in small claims court: Robo-signing and lack of proof in debt buyer cases. *Journal of Business and Technology Law*, 6(2), pp. 101–129.

Hudson, K., 1982. *Pawnbroking: An Aspect of British Social History*, London: Bodley Head.

Hyman, L., 2011. *Debtor Nation: The History of America in Red Ink*, Princeton, NJ: Princeton University Press.

Information Commissioners Office, 2007. *Data Protection Technical Guidance: Filing Defaults with Credit Reference Agencies* [Online]. Available at: www.ico.gov.uk/upload/documents/library/data_protection/detailed_specialist_guides/default_tgn_version_v3%20%20doc.pdf [accessed 10 October 2014].

Ingham, G., 2004. *The Nature of Money*, Cambridge: Polity Press.

Insight, 2009. Lloyds bank staff 'put frighteners' on debtors: Debt collectors are harassing customers with talk of home repossessions and blacklists. *Sunday Times*, 12 April, p. 7.

International Labour Office, 2012. *ILO Global Estimate of Forced Labour: Results and Methodology, Geneva: International Labour Office* [Online]. Available at: www.ungift.org/doc/knowledgehub/resource-centre/ILO_Global_Estimate_of_Forced_Labour_2012.pdf [accessed 18 March 2014].

Irwin, A. and Michael, M., 2003. *Science, Social Theory and Public Knowledge*, Maidenhead: Open University Press/McGraw-Hill.

Jackson, R.E., 1968. Statement of Royal E. Jackson, Chief of the Bankruptcy Division, Administrative Office, US courts. In United States Senate Committee on Banking and Currency, ed., *Bank Credit-Card and Check-Credit Plans: Hearings Before the Subcommittee on Financial Institutions of the Committee on Banking and Currency, United States Senate, Ninetieth Congress, Second Session, on Credit Cards. October 9 and 10, 1968*. Washington: U.S. Government Printing Office, pp. 30–61.

Jäger, S. and Maier, F., 2009. Theoretical and methodological aspects of Foucauldian critical discourse analysis and dispositive analysis. In R. Wodak and M. Meyer, eds., *Methods of Critical Discourse Analysis*. London: Sage, pp. 34–61.

Jarman, N., 2011. Capital letters: Implementing a comprehensive letter strategy can help streamline your expenses. *Collector*, November, pp. 40–42.

Jasanoff, S., 2003. Breaking the waves in Science Studies: Comment on H.M. Collins and Robert Evans, 'The third wave of Science Studies'. *Social Studies of Science*, 33(3), pp. 389–400.

Al-Jassem, D., 2013. 60,000 Saudis unable to repay their debts. *Arab News* [Online]. Available at: www.arabnews.com/60000-saudis-unable-repay-their-debts [accessed 17 February 2014].

Johnson, J.W., 1966. From 5011: The scientific approach. *The Collector*, August, p. 23.

Jones, R., 2009. Debt collectors hit out at advice websites. *Guardian* [Online], 2 December. Available at http://www.theguardian.com/money/2009/dec/02/credit-services-association-debt-websites [accessed 16 December 2014].

Jordan, D.D., 1967. Curbs on credit cards issued by banks being sought by Patman in House bill. *Wall Street Journal*, 29 August, p. 28.

Joseph, M., 2010. Doing time: Subjectivities of credit and debt. In *Quorum Seminar Series*, 24 March, London: Queen Mary, University of London.

Joseph, M. 2014. *Debt to Society: Accounting for Life Under Capitalism*. Minneapolis: University of Minnesota Press.

Jurgens, R. and Hobbs, R.J., 2010. *The Debt Machine: How the Collection Industry Hounds Consumers and Overwhelms Courts* [Online]. Available at: www.nclc.org/images/pdf/debt_collection/debt-machine.pdf [accessed 30 March 2013].

Kahn, J., 2011. *Cash or Card: Consumer Perceptions of Payment Modes*. Auckland: Auckland University of Technology.

Kane, W.R., 1947. The telephone in connection with collections work. *The Collector*, January, p. 28.

Kean, B.B., 1947. Effecting collections through the honor system. *The Collector*, January, pp. 23, 27.

Kelly, A.H., 2012. The experimental hut: Hosting vectors. *Journal of the Royal Anthropological Institute*, 18, pp. S145–S160.

Kiely, S., 2011. New guidance no excuse for debtors not paying. *Credit Collections & Risk*, October, p. 7.

Kirton, T., 2010. Meaning business: The need for litigation. *Credit Collections & Risk*, January, p. 25.

Klein, L., 1999. *It's in the Cards: Consumer Credit and the American Experience*, Westport, CT: Praeger.

Klein, N., 2000. *No Logo*, London: Flamingo.

Knight, F., 1921. *Risk, Uncertainty and Profit*, New York: AM Kelley.

Knight, H.J., 2010. *An Empirical Investigation of Pricing and Competition in the UK Credit Card Market*. Unpublished PhD. Nottingham: University of Nottingham. Available at: http://etheses.nottingham.ac.uk/2243/1/523699.pdf [accessed 22 February 2014].

Knox, H., O'Doherty, D., Vurdubakis, T. and Westrup, C., 2010. The devil and customer relationship management: Informational capitalism and the performativity of the sign. *Journal of Cultural Economy*, 3(3), pp. 339–359.

Lane, J.H., 1941. Collection psychology. *The Collector*, December, pp. 5, 7.

Langley, P., 2008a. Financialization and the Consumer Credit Boom. *Competition and Change*, 12(2), pp. 133–147.

Langley, P., 2008b. *The Everyday Life of Global Finance: Saving and Borrowing in America*, Oxford: Oxford University Press.

Langley, P., 2014. Equipping entrepreneurs: Consuming credit and credit scores. *Consumption Markets & Culture*, 17(5), pp. 448–467.

Lapuz, J. and Griffiths, M.D., 2010. The role of chips in poker gambling: An empirical pilot study. *Gambling Research: Journal of the National Association for Gambling Studies (Australia)*, 22(1), p. 34.

Latour, B., 1987. *Science in Action: How to Follow Scientists and Engineers Through Society*, Cambridge, MA: Harvard University Press.

Latour, B., 1988. A relativistic account of Einstein's relativity. *Social Studies of Science*, 18(1), p. 44.

Latour, B., 1993. *We Have Never Been Modern*, London: Harvester Wheatsheaf.

Latour, B., 1996. Do scientific objects have a history? Pasteur and Whitehead in a bath of lactic acid. *Common Knowledge*, 5, pp. 76–91.

Latour, B., 2005. *Reassembling the Social: An Introduction to Actor-Network-Theory*, Oxford: Oxford University Press.

Latour, B., 2010. Coming out as a philosopher. *Social Studies of Science*, 40(4), pp. 599–608.

Latour, B. and Lépinay, V.A., 2009. *The Science of Passionate Interests: An Introduction to Gabriel Tarde's Economic Anthropology*, Chicago: Prickly Paradigm Press/University of Chicago Press.

Law, J., 1994. *Organizing Modernity*, Oxford: Blackwell.

Law, J., 2008. On sociology and STS. *Sociological Review*, 56(4), pp. 623–649.

Law, J. and Ruppert, E., 2013. The social life of methods: Devices. *Journal of Cultural Economy*, 6(3), pp. 229–240.

Law, J. and Smullen, J. eds., 2008. *A Dictionary of Finance and Banking. 4th Revised Edition*, Oxford: Oxford University Press.

Lawless, R.M., Littwin A.K., Porter K.M., Pottow J.A.E., Thorne D. and Warren E., 2008. Did bankruptcy reform fail? An empirical study of consumer debtors. *American Bankruptcy Law Journal*, 82, pp. 349–406.

Lazarus, J., 2013a. De l'aide à la responsabilisation. L'espace social de l'éducation financière en France. *Genèses*, pp. 76–97.

Lazarus, J., 2013b. *L'Épreuve de l'Argent. Banques, Banquiers, Clients*, Paris: Calmann-Lévy.

Lazarus, J., forthcoming (a). A la recherche des normes contemporaines de l'argent: elements pour une analyse de la promotion de l'education financiere. *Terrain-Théories*.

Lazarus, J., forthcoming (b). Gouverner les conduites économiques par l'éducation financière: L'ascension de la financial literacy. In S. Dubuisson-Quellier, ed., *Gouverner les Conduites*.

Lazzarato, M., 1996. Immaterial labor. In P. Virno and M. Hardt, eds., *Radical Thought in Italy: A Potential Politics*. Minneapolis: University of Minnesota Press, pp. 133–147.

Lazzarato, M., 2012. *The Making of the Indebted Man: An Essay on the Neoliberal Condition*, Cambridge MA: MIT Press.

LeBaron, G. and Roberts, A., 2012. Confining social insecurity: Neoliberalism and the rise of the 21st century debtors' prison. *Politics & Gender*, 8(1), pp. 25–49.

Lee, O.W., 1949. Public relations: A cure-all. *The Collector*, June, p. 11.

Lefebvre, H., 1991. *Critique of Everyday Life*, London: Verso.

Leonard, E., 1990. *Get Shorty*, New York: Delacorte Press.

Lesman, M., 1946. Psychology and its use in the collection office. *The Collector*, November, pp. 26, 34.

Leyshon, A. and Thrift, N., 1999. Lists come alive: Electronic systems of knowledge and the rise of credit-scoring in retail banking. *Economy and Society*, 28(3), pp. 434–466.

Linam, O.A., 1956. Color is important on collection notices. *The Collector*, October, p. 15.

Lockman, R.H., 1948. Psychology as a collection tool. *The Collector*, April, pp. 33–34.

Lopes, D.S., 2013. Metamorphoses of credit: Pastiche production and the ordering of mass payment behaviour. *Economy and Society*, 42(1), pp. 26–50.

Lury, C., 2004. *Brands: The logos of the global economy*, London: Routledge.

Lury, C., 2009. Brand as assemblage. *Journal of Cultural Economy*, 2(1), pp. 67–82.

Lusk, G.M., 1946. Psychology: Its use in the collection business. *The Collector*, June, p. 32.

MacKenzie, D., 2006. *An Engine, Not a Camera: How Financial Models Shape Markets*, Cambridge, MA: MIT Press.

MacKenzie, D., 2007. Is economics performative? Option theory and the construction of derivative markets. In D. MacKenzie, F. Muniesa and L. Siu, eds., *Do Economists Make Markets: On the Performativity of Economics*. Princeton, NJ and Oxford: Oxford University Press, pp. 311–357.

MacKenzie, D., 2009. *Material Markets: How Economic Agents Are Constructed*, Oxford and New York: Oxford University Press.

Maestro, 2007. *Benefits of Maestro* [Online]. Available at: www.maestrocard.com/uk/about/benefits.html [accessed 5 June 2007].

Magri, S., Pico, R. and Rampazzi, C., 2011. *Which Households Use Consumer Credit in Europe* [Online], Banca D'Italia. Available at: www.bancaditalia.it/pubblicazioni/econo/quest_ecofin_2/QF_100/QEF_100.pdf [accessed 21 February 2014].

Manchester, A.H., 1980. *A Modern Legal History of England and Wales 1750–1950*, London: Butterworths.

Mann, B.H., 2002. *Republic of Debtors: Bankruptcy in the Age of American Independence*, Cambridge, MA: Harvard University Press.

Manning, R., 2000. *Credit Card Nation: The Consequences of America's Addiction to Credit*, New York: Basic Books.

Marcus, A., 1985. Real property and society in the premodern Middle East: A case study. In A.E. Mayer, ed., *Property, Social Structure, and Law in the Modern Middle East*. Albany, NY: State University of New York Press, pp. 109–129.

Marres, N., 2007. The issues deserve more credit: Pragmatist contributions to the study of public involvement in controversy. *Social Studies of Science*, 37(5), pp. 759–780.

Marres, N., 2009. Testing powers of engagement: Green living experiments, the ontological turn and the undoability of involvement. *European Journal of Social Theory*, 12(1), pp. 117–133.

Marres, N., 2012. *Material Participation: Technology, the Environment and Everyday Publics*, Basingstoke: Palgrave Macmillan.

Marron, D., 2009. *Consumer Credit in the United States: A Sociological Perspective from the 19th Century to the Present*, New York: Palgrave.

Marron, D., 2012. Producing over-indebtedness. *Journal of Cultural Economy*, 5(4), pp. 407–421.

Mason, R., 2014. Student Loans Company debt collection letters lead to calls for compensation. *Guardian* [Online], 3 July. Available at: www.theguardian.com/money/2014/jul/03/student-loans-company-debt-collection-letters-compensation-wonga [accessed 18 August 2014].

Martin, I., 2010. *Centring the Computer in the Business of Banking: Barclays Bank and Technological Change, 1954–1974*. Unpublished PhD. Manchester: University of Manchester.

Martin, R., 2002. *Financialization of Daily Life*, Philadelphia: Temple University Press.

Di Martino, P., 2005. Approaching disaster: Personal bankruptcy legislation in Italy and England, c.1880–1939. *Business History*, 47(1), pp. 23–43.

Massumi, B., 2002. *Parables for the Virtual: Movement, Affect, Sensation*, Durham, NC and London: Duke University Press.

Massumi, B., 2005. Fear (the spectrum said). *positions: east asia cultures critique*, 13(1), pp. 31–48.

Maurer, B., 2006. The anthropology of money. *Annual Review of Anthropology*, 35, pp. 15–63.

Maurer, B., 2012a. Late to the party: Debt and data. *Social Anthropology*, 20(4), pp. 474–481.

Maurer, B., 2012b. Payment: Forms and functions of value transfer in contemporary society. *Cambridge Anthropology*, 30(2), pp. 15–35.

Maynard, K., 2004. The debt sale market: Help to shape its future. *Credit Management*, October, p. 34.

Maynard, K., 2008. *The Spread of Debt Sale* [Online]. Available at: www.cabotfinancial. com/download/97 [accessed 10 October 2014].

Maynard, K., 2009. What's in store for debt buyers? *Credit Management*, January, p. 21.

McFall, L., 2009a. Devices and desires: How useful is the 'new' new economic sociology for understanding market attachment? *Sociology Compass*, 3(2), pp. 267–282.

McFall, L., 2009b. The agencement of industrial branch life assurance. *Journal of Cultural Economy*, 2(1), pp. 49–65.

McFall, L., 2011. A 'good, average man': Calculation and the limits of statistics in enrolling insurance customers. *The Sociological Review*, 59(4), pp. 661–684.

McFall, L., 2014. *Devising Consumption: Cultural Economies of Insurance, Credit and Spending*, London: Routledge.

McFall, L. and Ossandón, J., 2014. What's new in the 'new, new economic sociology' and should Organisation Studies care? In P. Adler, P. du Gay, G. Morgan and M. Reed, eds., *Oxford Handbook of Sociology, Social Theory and Organization Studies: Contemporary Currents*. Oxford: Oxford University Press, pp. 510–533.

McGinnis, C.L., 1953. Pre-collection service. *The Collector*, March, p. 6.

Meltzer, H., Bebbington, P., Brugha, T., Jenkins, R., McManus, S. and Dennis, M.S., 2011. Personal debt and suicidal ideation. *Psychological Medicine*, 41(4), pp. 771–778.

Meltzer, H., Bebbington, P., Brugha, T., Farrell, M. and Jenkins, R., 2013. The relationship between personal debt and specific common mental disorders. *The European Journal of Public Health*, 23(1), pp. 108–113.

Merriam-Webster, 1996. *Merriam-Webster's Dictionary of Law*, Springfield, MA: Merriam-Webster.

Meyer, M., 2009. From 'cold' science to 'hot' research: The texture of controversy [Online]. Available at: www.csi.ensmp.fr/Items/WorkingPapers/Download/DLWP. php?wp=WP_CSI_016.pdf [accessed 10 October 2014].

Michael, M., 2006. *Technoscience and Everyday Life: The Complex Simplicities of the Mundane*, Maidenhead: Open University Press.

Miller, D., 1998. *A Theory of Shopping*, Ithaca, NY: Cornell University Press.

Miller, D., 2002. Turning Callon the right way up. *Economy and Society*, 31(2), pp. 218–233.

Milman, D., 2005. *Personal Insolvency Law, Regulation and Policy*, Aldershot: Ashgate Publishing.

Mind, 2007. *In the Red: Debt and Mental Health* [Online]. Available at: www.mind.org. uk/assets/0000/0102/In_the_red.pdf [accessed 28 January 2014].

Mind, 2011. *Still in the Red: Update on Debt and Mental Health* [Online]. Available at: www.mind.org.uk/media/273468/still-in-the-red.pdf [accessed 28 January 2014].

Miracle, F.E., 1941. Psychology in Collection Letters. *The Collector*, August, pp. 3, 9.

Mirowski, P., 2013. *Never Let a Serious Crisis Go to Waste: How Neoliberalism Survived the Financial Meltdown*, London and New York: Verso.

Mol, A., 2002. *The Body Multiple: Ontology in Medical Practice*, Durham, NC and London: Duke University Press.

Mol, A., 2008. *The Logic of Care: Health and the Problem of Patient Choice*, London and New York: Routledge.

Moles, P. and Terry, N., 2005. *The Handbook of International Financial Terms*, Oxford: Oxford University Press.

Money Advice Liaison Group, 2009. *Good Practice Awareness Guidelines: For Consumers with Mental Health Problems and Debt. Second Edition* [Online]. Available at: www.malg.org.uk/dmhdocuments/Mental%20Health%20Guidelines%20Ed%202%20 Final%202009.pdf [accessed 22 March 2014].

Money Advice Scotland, 2014. *Resources* [Online]. Available at: www.moneyadvice scotland.org.uk/content/resources [accessed 13 February 2014].

Montgomerie, J., 2006. The financialization of the American credit card industry. *Competition and Change*, 10(3), pp. 301–319.

Montgomerie, J., 2007. The logic of neo-liberalism and the political economy of consumer debt-led growth. In S. Lee and S. McBride, eds., *Neo-Liberalism, State Power and Global Governance*. Dordrecht: Springer, pp. 157–172.

Montgomerie, J., 2009. The pursuit of (past) happiness? Middle-class indebtedness and American financialisation. *New Political Economy*, 14(1), pp. 1–24.

Moor, L., 2012. Beyond cultural intermediaries? A socio-technical perspective on the market for social interventions. *European Journal of Cultural Studies*, 15(5), pp. 563–580.

Morgan, J., 2004. Banks make millions from 'unfair' credit card charges. *The Times*, 27 October, p. 1.

Morris, N. and Rothman, D.J. eds., 1998. *The Oxford History of the Prison: The Practice of Punishment in Western Society*, Oxford: Oxford University Press.

Moser, I., 2006. Disability and the promises of technology: Technology, subjectivity and embodiment within an order of the normal. *Information, Communication & Society*, 9(3), pp. 373–395.

Moser, I., 2009. A body that matters? The role of embodiment in the recomposition of life after a road traffic accident. *Scandinavian Journal of Disability Research*, 11(2), pp. 83–99.

Moser, I. and Law, J., 1999. Good passages, bad passages. In J. Law and J. Hassard, eds. *Actor Network Theory and After*. Oxford: Sociological Review and Blackwell, pp. 196–219.

Mullineux, A., 2012. *UK Banking After Deregulation*, Oxford: Routledge.

Muniesa, F., 2009. Attachment and detachment in the economy. In P. Redman, ed., *Attachment: Sociology and Social Worlds*. Manchester: Manchester University Press, pp. 111–141.

Muniesa, F., Millo, Y. and Callon, M., 2007. An introduction to market devices. *Sociological Review*, 55(s2), pp. 1–12.

Nadelmann, K.H., 1957. On the origin of the bankruptcy clause. *The American Journal of Legal History*, 1(3), pp. 215–228.

National Consumer Law Center, 2004. *Credit Counseling in Crisis Update: Poor Compliance and Weak Enforcement Undermine Laws Governing Credit Counseling Agencies* [Online]. Available at: www.nclc.org/images/pdf/credit_counseling/report_cc_enforcement.pdf [accessed 14 April 2014].

National Consumer Law Center, 2006. *The Life and Debt Cycle: Part Two: Finding Help for Older Consumers with Credit Card Debt* [Online]. Available at: https://getoutofdebt.org/wp-content/uploads/2012/06/rising_debt_part2.pdf [accessed 14 April 2014].

National Consumer Law Center, 2012. *Comments of National Consumer Law Center on Behalf of its Low Income Clients On Defining Larger Participants in Certain Consumer Financial Product and Service Markets (Debt Collection and Consumer Reporting)* [Online]. Available at: https://www.nclc.org/images/pdf/rulemaking/nclc_larger_participant_debt_collector_april2012.pdf [accessed 14 February 2014].

Negri, A., 1999. Value and affect. *Boundary 2*, 26(2), pp. 77–88.

Nichols, R.E., 1967. B of A's Peterson cautions banks on 'credit-card race'. *Los Angeles Times*, 17 March, p. C14.

Nocera, J., 1994. *A Piece of the Action: How the Middle Class Joined the Money Class*, New York: Simon & Schuster.

Noddings, N., 1984. *Caring: A Feminine Approach to Ethics & Moral Education*, Berkeley: University of California Press.

O'Brien, P.H., 1941. The new psychological system of collections. *The Collector*, July, p. 14.

O'Neil, P., 1970. A little gift from your friendly banker. *Life*, March, pp. 48–58.

Obermaier, K., 2009. Debt collection: Adopting the right attitude. *The Times*, 10 February, p. 12.

OC&C Strategy Consultants, 2009. The CMDC index. *Credit Today*, October, Special Supplement.

Odih, P., 2007. *Advertising in Modern and Postmodern Times*, London: Sage.

Office for National Statistics, 2010. *Household Income: Top to Bottom Income Ratio Four-To-One* [Online]. Available at: www.statistics.gov.uk/cci/nugget.asp?id=334 [accessed 10 April 2014].

Office of Fair Trading, 2012. *Debt Collection: OFT Guidance for Businesses Engaged in the Recovery of Consumer Credit Debts* [Online]. Available at: www.oft.gov.uk/shared_oft/consultations/OFT664Rev_Debt_collection_g1.pdf [accessed 10 October 2014].

Orton, M., 2010. *The Long-Term Impact of Debt Advice on Low Income Households* [Online], Warwick Institute for Employment Research and Friends Provident Foundation. Available at: http://www2.warwick.ac.uk/fac/soc/ier/research/debt/year_3_report.pdf [accessed 10 October 2014].

Osborne, T.R., 1941. Does the collector give the debtor a square deal? *The Collector*, July, p. 8.

Osborne, T.R., 1964. The changing credit scene. *The Collector*, September, pp. 9–10.

Ossandón, J., 2014. Sowing consumers in the garden of mass retailing in Chile. *Consumption Markets & Culture*, 17(5), pp. 429–447.

Pain, R., 2009. Globalized fear? Towards an emotional geopolitics. *Progress in Human Geography*, 33(4), pp. 466–486.

Payne, C., 2012. *The Consumer, Credit and Neoliberalism: Governing the Modern Economy*, Oxford: Routledge.

Peebles, G., 2013. Washing away the sins of debt: The nineteenth-century eradication of the debtors' prison. *Comparative Studies in Society and History*, 55(3), pp. 701–724.

Peterson, A.P., 1943. Use of the telephone in handling collections. *The Collector*, September, pp. 10, 16, 18.

Phillips, J., 2006. Agencement/assemblage. *Theory, Culture & Society*, 23(2–3), pp. 108–109.

Pia Pozzato, M., 2001. Au supermarché: Libertés et contraintes dans le temple de la consommation. *Protée*, Printemps, pp. 57–63.

Pinch, T.J. and Bijker, W.E., 1984. The social construction of facts and artefacts: Or how the sociology of science and the sociology of technology might benefit each other. *Social Studies of Science*, 14(3), pp. 399–441.

Plimsoll Analysis, 2009. *UK Debt Collection Industries: An Overview*, Stockton: Plimsoll Publishing Limited.

Poon, M., 2007. Scorecards as devices for consumer credit: The case of Fair, Isaac & Company Incorporated. In M. Callon, Y. Millo and F. Muniesa, eds., *Market Devices*. Oxford: Blackwell, pp. 284–306.

Poon, M., 2009. From new deal institutions to capital markets: Commercial consumer risk scores and the making of subprime mortgage finance. *Accounting, Organizations and Society*, 34, pp. 654–674.

Poster, W.R., 2013. Hidden sides of the credit economy: Emotions, outsourcing, and Indian call centers. *International Journal of Comparative Sociology*, 54(3), pp. 205–227.

Poswa, H.J., 1941. There is a human being at the other end of the line! *The Collector*, August, p. 14.

Poulter, S., 2004. Credit card meltdown; spend now, pay later binge may force interest rate rise. *Daily Mail*, 5 May, p. 1.

Poulter, S. and Wilkes, D., 2004. Credit 'kills' a family man; Ministers to be told how father-of-two committed suicide over £70,000 debt from 19 credit cards, *Daily Mail*, 11 March, p. 1.

Power, M., 1997. *The Audit Society: Rituals of Verification*, Oxford: Oxford University Press.

Probyn, E., 2010. Writing shame. In M. Gregg and G.J. Seigworth, eds., *The Affect Theory Reader*. North Carolina: Duke University Press, pp. 70–90.

Purvis, M., 2010. Strategic solution, not a tactical fix. *Credit Collections & Risk*, June, p. 30.

Rafaeli, A. and Sutton, R.I., 1991. Emotional contrast strategies as means of social influence: Lessons from criminal interrogators and bill collectors. *Academy of Management Journal*, 34(4), pp. 749–775.

Raghubir, P. and Srivastava, J., 2008. Monopoly money: The effect of payment coupling and form on spending behavior. *Journal of Experimental Psychology: Applied*, 14(3), pp. 213–225.

Ranjith, G., 2005. Epidemiology of chronic fatigue syndrome. *Occupational Medicine*, 55(1), pp. 13–19.

Rasher, A., 1970. The growth of chains and conglomerates in the collection industry, *The Collector*, September, pp. 13, 26.

Reiter, J.J., 1947. Tracing and collecting by post card. *The Collector*, June, pp. 32–34.

Remley, R., 2006. Keeping the customer. *Collector*, March, pp. 60–62.

Richardson, T., Elliott, P. and Roberts, R., 2013. The relationship between personal unsecured debt and mental and physical health: A systematic review and meta-analysis. *Clinical Psychology Review*, 33(8), pp. 1148–1162.

Ritzer, G., 1995. *Expressing America: A Critique of the Global Credit Card Society*, Thousand Oaks, CA: Pine Forge Press.

Ritzer, G., 2005. *Enchanting a Disenchanted World: Revolutionizing the Means of Consumption*, Newbury Park, CA: Pine Forge Press.

Roberts, A., 2014a. Doing borrowed time: The state, the law and the coercive governance of 'undeserving' debtors. *Critical Sociology*, 40(5), pp. 669–687.

Roberts, A., 2014b. New constitutionalism, disciplinary neoliberalism and the locking-in of indebtedness in America. In S. Gill and A.C. Cutler, eds., *New Constitutionalism and World Order*. Cambridge: Cambridge University Press, pp. 233–246.

Rock, P., 1973. *Making People Pay*, London: Routledge & Kegan Paul.

Rojas, P., 2014. *The Uses of Attachment: Some Reflections on Robbie Duschinsky's 'A Grimace of Fear or Anger in the Context of Contended Play: Filming Disorganised Attachment'* [Online]. Available at: www.gold.ac.uk/media/Rojas,%20Patricio%20-%20The%20Uses%20of%20Attachment.pdf [accessed 10 October 2014].

Rona-Tas, A. and Hiss, S., 2010. The role of ratings in the subprime mortgage crisis: The art of corporate and the science of consumer credit rating. *Research in the Sociology of Organizations*, 30(Part A), pp. 115–155.

Rose, N., 1996a. Governing 'advanced' liberal democracies. In A. Barry, T. Osborne and N. Rose, eds., *Foucault and Political Reason: Liberalism, Neo-Liberalism and Rationalities of Government*. London: UCL Press, pp. 37–64.

Rose, N., 1996b. *Inventing Our Selves: Psychology, Power, and Personhood*, Cambridge and New York: Cambridge University Press.

Rose, P., 2002. *On Whitehead*, Belmont, CA: Wadsworth and Thompson Learning.

Rosso, A., 2008. The software evolution: The past present and future of collection software. *Collector*, June, pp. 24–30.

Rosso, A., 2012. Collections in a mobile world. *Collector*, December, pp. 16–19.

Rosso, A., 2013. Building a better health care collector. *Collector*, August, pp. 20–23.

Ruppert, E., 2011. Population objects: Interpassive subjects. *Sociology*, 45(2), pp. 218–233.

Ruppert, E., 2012. The governmental topologies of database devices. *Theory, Culture & Society*, 29(4–5), pp. 116–136.

Savage, M. and Burrows, R., 2007. The coming crisis of empirical sociology. *Sociology*, 41(5), pp. 885–899.

Savransky, M., 2012. Capturing the social sciences: An experiment in political epistemology. *Critical Legal Thinking: Law & the Political* [Online]. Available at: http://criticallegal thinking.com/2012/08/01/capturing-the-social-sciences-an-experiment-in-political-epistemology/ [accessed 15 April 2014].

Savransky, M., 2014. Of recalcitrant subjects. *Culture, Theory and Critique*, 55(1), pp. 96–113.

Schillmeier, M., 2010. *Rethinking Disability: Bodies, Senses, and Things*, Oxford: Taylor & Francis.

Schmidt, L., 1949. Twenty years as a Kansas Collector. *The Collector*, July, p. 8.

Schoeing, T.R., 1965. In defence of the large agency. *The Collector*, February, pp. 5–6.

Schüll, N.D., 2012. *Addiction by Design: Machine Gambling in Las Vegas*, Princeton, NJ: Princeton University Press.

Schwarzkopf, S., 2009a. Discovering the consumer: Market research, product innovation, and the creation of brand loyalty in Britain and the United States in the interwar years. *Journal of Macromarketing*, 29(1), pp. 8–20.

Schwarzkopf, S., 2009b. What was advertising? The invention, rise, demise, and disappearance of advertising concepts in nineteenth- and twentieth-century Europe and America. *Business and Economic History Online*, 7, pp. 1–27.

Scott, S.P., 2001. *The Civil Law: Including the Twelve Tables, the Institutes of Gaius, the Rules of Ulipan, the Opinions of Paulus, the Enactments of Justinian, and the Constitutions of Leo*, Union, NJ: The Lawbook Exchange, Ltd.

Scully, M.J., 1983. Debt collection in the United Kingdom. *Collector*, March, p. 14.

Sease, J.L., 1947. The evolution of the collection agency. *The Collector*, February, p. 18.

Sebald, W.G., 2002. *The Rings of Saturn*, London: Vintage.

Seib, C., 2008. Market for offloading bad debt balloons as banks free up capital, *The Times* [Online], 10 May. Available at: http://business.timesonline.co.uk/tol/business/industry_sectors/banking_and_finance/article3904501.ece [accessed 10 October 2014].

Seigworth, G.J. and Gregg, M., 2010. An inventory of shimmers. In M. Gregg and G.J. Seigworth, eds., *The Affect Theory Reader*. North Carolina: Duke University Press, pp. 1–25.

Skeggs, B., 2014. Values beyond value? Is anything beyond the logic of capital? *The British Journal of Sociology*, 65(1), pp. 1–20.

Soman, D., 2003. The effect of payment transparency on consumption: Quasi-experiments from the field. *Marketing Letters*, 14(3), pp. 173–183.

Stalder, F., 2001. *Making Money: Notes on Technology as Environment*. Unpublished PhD. Toronto: University of Toronto.

Star, S.L., 1999. The ethnography of infrastructure. *American Behavioral Scientist*, 43(3), pp. 377–391.

Stark, D., 2009. *The Sense of Dissonance: Accounts of Worth in Economic Life*, Princeton, NJ: Princeton University Press.

Stearns, D.L., 2011. *Electronic Value Exchange: Origins of the VISA electronic payment system*, London and New York: Springer.

Steering Committee on Reciprocity, 2011. *Information Sharing: Principles of Reciprocity* [Online]. Available at: www.scoronline.co.uk/files/scor/por_version_33_final_september_2011.pdf [accessed 10 October 2014].

Stengers, I., 2003. *Cosmopolitiques*, Paris: La Découverte.

Stengers, I., 2005. Whitehead's account of the sixth day. *Configurations*, 2005(13), pp. 35–55.

Stengers, I., 2008. Experimenting with refrains: Subjectivity and the challenge of escaping modern dualism. *Subjectivity*, 22(1), pp. 38–59.

Stengers, I., 2011. *Thinking with Whitehead: A Free and Wild Creation of Concepts*, Cambridge, MA and London: Harvard University Press.

StepChange, 2013. *StepChange Debt Charity: Statistical Yearbook 2012* [Online]. Available at http://www.stepchange.org/Portals/0/Documents/media/reports/statisticsyearbooks/Statistical_Yearbook_2012.pdf [accessed 16 December 2014].

StepChange, 2014a. *England Wales Court Action* [Online]. Available at: www.stepchange.org/Debtinformationandadvice/Whatyourcreditorscando/Courtaction/EnglandWalescourtaction.aspx [accessed 13 February 2014].

StepChange, 2014b. *Northern Ireland Court Action* [Online]. Available at: www.stepchange.org/Debtinformationandadvice/Whatyourcreditorscando/Courtaction/NorthernIrelandcourtaction.aspx [accessed 13 February 2014].

StepChange, 2014c. *Scotland Court Action* [Online]. Available at: www.stepchange.org/Debtinformationandadvice/Whatyourcreditorscando/Courtaction/Scotlandcourtaction.aspx [accessed 13 February 2014].

StepChange, 2014d. *UK Bankruptcy Costs* [Online]. Available at: www.stepchange.org/

Debtinformationandadvice/Debtsolutions/Bankruptcy/BankruptcycostsUK.aspx [accessed 14 April 2014].

Stephens, H., 2011. A quicker link. *Collector*, December, pp. 24–26.

Stewart, K., 2007. *Ordinary Affects*, Durham, NC: Duke University Press.

Still, K., 2010. Working together to get a fair 'share of wallet'. *Credit Collections & Risk*, p. 40.

Stran, G., 2008. A different view. *Credit Management*, September, p. 29.

Strathern, M., 2000. *Audit Cultures: Anthropological Studies in Accountability, Ethics and the Academy*, London: Routledge.

Sullivan, T.A., Warren, E. and Westbrook, J., 1999. *As We Forgive Our Debtors: Bankruptcy and Consumer Credit in America*, Washington, DC: Beard Books.

Sullivan, T.A., Warren, E. and Westbrook, J., 2000. *The Fragile Middle Class: Americans in Debt*, New Haven, CT: Yale University Press.

Sutton, R.I., 1991. Maintaining norms about expressed emotions: The case of bill collectors. *Administrative Science Quarterly*, 36(2), pp. 245–268.

Syron, J., 2012. Use data to understand your debtor. *Credit Collections & Risk*, June, p. 46.

Tebbutt, M., 1983. *Making Ends Meet: Pawnbroking and Working-Class Credit*, Leicester and New York: Leicester University Press and St. Martin's Press.

Tessera, 2010. *SCOR Decision to Help Industry* [Online]. Available at: www.tessera.co.uk/Archive/2010/November/news-04.php [accessed 17 February 2011].

The ME Association, 2010. *The Symptoms and Diagnosis of ME/CFS: Typical Features of ME/CFS* [Online]. Available at: www.meassociation.org.uk/index.php?option=com_content&view=article&id=90%3Asymptoms-and-diagnosis&catid=38%3Aabout-me&Itemid=173&limitstart=1 [accessed 17 February 2011].

The Prime Minister's Office, 2010. *CCR Petition* [Online]. Available at: http://petitions.number10.gov.uk/CCRpetition/ [accessed 17 February 2011].

The Sheriffs Office, 2014. *Guide to Judgement Enforcement* [Online]. Available at: http://thesheriffsoffice.com/ebook/Sheriffs_Office_Guide.pdf [accessed 8 April 2014].

The UK Cards Association, 2013. *Annual Report 2013* [Online]. Available at: www.theukcardsassociation.org.uk/wm_documents/Final%20AR_2012_interactive_sml.pdf [accessed 22 February 2014].

Thrift, N., 2005. *Knowing Capitalism*, London: Sage.

Thrift, N., 2007. *Non-Representational Theory: Space, Politics, Affect*, London: Routledge.

Toscano, A., 2014. Alien mediations: Critical remarks on The Making of the Indebted Man. *The New Reader* [Online], 1. Available at: http://thenewreader.org/Issues/1/AlienMediations [accessed 10 October 2014].

Toynbee, P., 2008. Don't expect to find a banker down at bankruptcy court: It's boom time for debt and repossessions, as my old neighbour can testify. So what is the point of us owning banks? *Guardian*, 25 October, p. 33.

Trezza, M., 1998. Fighting the deadly virus. *Collector*, October, pp. 20–23.

Tsing, A., 2013. Sorting out commodities: How capitalist value is made through gifts. *HAU: Journal of Ethnographic Theory*, 3(1), pp. 21–43.

Turner, E.H., 1943. Art of collecting. *The Collector*, March, p. 8.

De Tute, S., 2012. TCF – Actions speak louder than words. *Credit Collections & Risk*, July, p. 42.

Tutton, P., 2009. *Out of Order: CAB Evidence on the Use of Charging Orders and Orders for Sale in Debt Collection* [Online]. Available at: www.infohub.moneyadvicetrust.org/

content_files/files/citizens_advice_evidence_briefing_out_of_order_final.pdf [accessed 27 November 2012].

Tze-wei, N., 2009. Pay off cards or go to jail: Beijing. *South China Morning Post* [Online]. Available at: www.scmp.com/article/701423/pay-cards-or-go-jail-beijing [accessed 17 February 2014].

U.S. Code, 2012. *Title 11. Bankruptcy* [Online]. Available at: www.law.cornell.edu/uscode/pdf/uscode11/lii_usc_TI_11_CH_7_SC_II_SE_727.pdf [accessed 10 October 2014].

Vargha, Z., 2011. From long-term savings to instant mortgages: Financial demonstration and the role of interaction in markets. *Organization*, 18(2), pp. 215–235.

Vickers, A., 2004. Credit card madness; Spend, spend Britons run up 75% of Europe's entire debts on plastic. *Daily Express*, 17 March, p. 1.

Vogt, B.A., 2001. State v. Allison: Imprisonment for debt in South Dakota. *South Dakota Law Review*, 46, pp. 334–368.

Wadsworth, J.E., 2013. *The Banks and the Monetary System in the UK, 1959–1971*, London: Routledge.

Wainwright, T., 2011. Elite knowledges: Framing risk and the geographies of credit. *Environment and Planning A*, 43(3), pp. 650–665.

Walsh, G.R., 1966. Inroads in the collections business. *The Collector*, November, p. 7.

Watts, W.H., 1953. Collect 'em by telegraph. *Collector*, January, pp. 6–7.

Weistart, J., 1971. Consumer protection in the credit card industry: Federal legislative controls. *Michigan Law Review*, 70, pp. 1475–1544.

Which?, 2013. *Cost Of PPI Scandal Now More Than Double the Cost of the Olympics* [Online]. Available at: https://press.which.co.uk/whichstatements/cost-of-ppi-scandal-now-more-than-double-the-cost-of-the-olympics/ [accessed 23 March 2014].

Whitehead, A.N., 1978. *Process and Reality*, New York: The Free Press.

Whitehead, A.N., 2004. *The Concept of Nature*, New York: Prometheus Books.

Wilkis, A., 2013. *Las Sospechas del Dinero: Moral y Economía en la Vida Popular*. Buenos Aires: Paidos.

Willcox, I., 2012. Understanding credit risk with psychology. *Credit Collections & Risk*, July, p. 19.

Willcox, I., 2013. Experience and flexibility are essential to survival. *Credit Collections & Risk*, July, pp. 12–13.

Williams, R., 1977. *Marxism and Literature*, Oxford: Oxford University Press.

Wodak, R. and Meyer, M., 2009. *Methods of Critical Discourse Analysis*, London: Sage.

Woodfine, P., 2006. Debtors, prisons, and petitions in eighteenth-century England. *Eighteenth-Century Life*, 30(2), pp. 1–31.

Woolgar, S. and Lezaun, J., 2013. The wrong bin bag: A turn to ontology in science and technology studies? *Social Studies of Science*, 43(3), pp. 321–340.

Woolgar, S. and Neyland, D., 2013. *Mundane Governance: Ontology and Accountability*, Oxford: Oxford University Press.

Worthington, S., 2001. Introduction: Affinity credit cards: a critical review. *International Journal of Retail & Distribution Management*, 29(11), pp. 485–508.

Wynne, B., 2003. Seasick on the third wave? Subverting the hegemony of propositionalism: Response to Collins and Evans (2002). *Social Studies of Science*, 33(3), pp. 401–417.

Zelizer, V., 1985. *Pricing the Priceless Child: The Changing Social Value of Children*, New York: Basic Books.

Zelizer, V., 1994. *The Social Meaning of Money: Pin Money, Paychecks, Poor Relief, and Other Currencies*, Princeton, NJ: Princeton University Press.

Zelizer, V., 2002a. Enter culture. In M.F. Guillén, R. Collins, P. England and M. Meyer, eds., *The new economic sociology: Developments in an emerging field.* New York: Russell Sage Foundation Publications, pp. 101–125.

Zelizer, V., 2002b. Intimate transactions. In M.F. Guillén, R. Collins, P. England and M. Meyer, eds., *The New Economic Sociology: Developments in an Emerging Field.* New York: Russell Sage Foundation Publications, pp. 274–300.

Zelizer, V., 2005. *The Purchase of Intimacy*, Princeton, NJ and Oxford: Princeton University Press.

Zimmerman, D.H., 1966. Reminiscences of a thirty year man. *The Collector*, March, pp. 6–7.

Zwick, D. and Denegri Knott, J., 2009. Manufacturing customers: The database as new means of production. *Journal of Consumer Culture*, 9(2), pp. 221–247.

Index

Page numbers in *italics* denote tables, those in **bold** denote figures.

For Product Safety Concerns and Information please contact our EU
representative GPSR@taylorandfrancis.com
Taylor & Francis Verlag GmbH, Kaufingerstraße 24, 80331 München, Germany

www.ingramcontent.com/pod-product-compliance
Ingram Content Group UK Ltd.
Pitfield, Milton Keynes, MK11 3LW, UK
UKHW020958180425
457613UK00019B/737